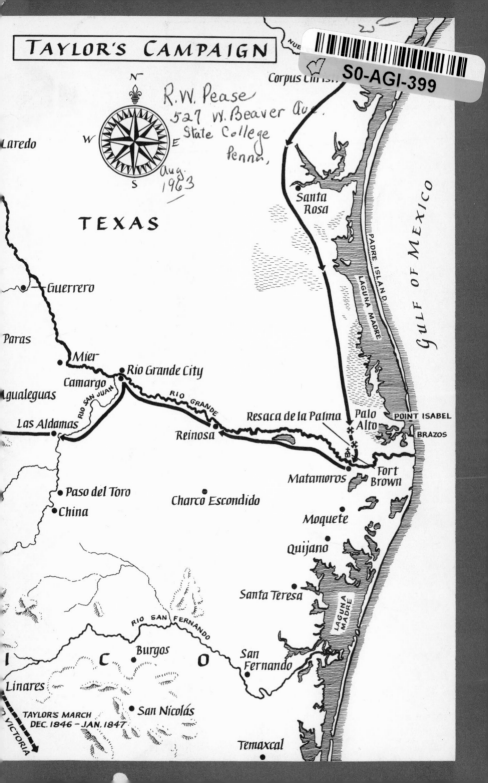

TAYLOR'S CAMPAIGN

TEXAS

GULF OF MEXICO

R.W. Pease
527 W. Beaver Ave.
State College
Penna,
Aug. 1963

Laredo
Guerrero
Paras
Mier
Camargo
Igualeguas
Las Aldamas
Reinosa
Paso del Toro
China
Charco Escondido
Rio Grande City
Rio San Juan
RIO GRANDE
Resaca de la Palma
Reinosa
Matamoros
Fort Brown
Moquete
Quijano
Santa Teresa
LAGUNA MADRE
RIO SAN FERNANDO
Burgos
San Fernando
Linares
San Nicolás
Temaxcal

Corpus Christi
Santa Rosa
PADRE ISLAND
LAGUNA MADRE
Palo Alto
POINT ISABEL
BRAZOS

MEXICO

TAYLOR'S MARCH
DEC. 1846 – JAN. 1847

TO VICTORIA

SO-AGI-399

ZACH TAYLOR'S
LITTLE ARMY

Books by Edward J. Nichols

ZACH TAYLOR'S LITTLE ARMY
TOWARD GETTYSBURG: A BIOGRAPHY OF GENERAL
JOHN F. REYNOLDS
HUNKY JOHNNY, *a novel*
DANGER! KEEP OUT, *a novel*

ZACH TAYLOR'S
LITTLE ARMY

EDWARD J. NICHOLS

Maps by Rafael Palacios

DOUBLEDAY & COMPANY, INC.
GARDEN CITY, NEW YORK
1963

Note

When armies cross borders—or when they try to create them—varying spellings of surname and place are among the consequences. For example, "Monterey" sometimes appears with a double r, derived from the Spanish. The San Juan River at Monterey has been called the Santa Catarina in some texts. In the interests of consistency, the more or less standard versions are used.

LIBRARY OF CONGRESS CATALOG CARD NUMBER 63–7728
COPYRIGHT © 1963 BY E. J. NICHOLS
ALL RIGHTS RESERVED
PRINTED IN THE UNITED STATES OF AMERICA
FIRST EDITION

TABLE OF CONTENTS

LIST OF ILLUSTRATIONS

Portrait of Zachary Taylor
Captain Samuel Ringgold
Ringgold's Battery in Action
Tents at Corpus Christi, Texas
President James K. Polk
General William J. Worth
General John E. Wool
The Battle of Palo Alto
General Taylor's Headquarters at Walnut Springs
General Antonio Lopez de Santa Anna
General Winfield Scott
Action at Buena Vista

MAPS

CHAPTER I

INSTRUMENT OF POLICY

Six Presidents of the United States took turns in the dealings with Mexico that finally sent Zachary Taylor down to the southern border of Texas in 1845.

Mexico—in the first years of the nineteenth century a poor country populated 60 per cent by pure-blooded Indians, 22 per cent by a mixture of Indian and European, and 18 per cent by Europeans. Countless local armies kept bleeding each other out, and their leaders jockeyed to gain brief stays of shaky control in what passed for government in the capital city.

A frontier of nearly 2500 miles divided the two countries when Mexico won its revolution against Spain in 1821. The combined Mexican state of Coahuila and Texas absorbed a great stretch of boundary immediately southwest of the line. The Texas province in itself included about 250,000 square miles. It was a land of big sky and it seemed to have everything. On the debit side rolled wastes of canebrake, sagebrush, and desert; but there also were vast sweeps of hardwood and pine, prairies deep in black loam for growing cotton, and lighter

1

soils for grains. Buffalo and mustang close-cropped the grass on the cold high plains of the north. Rivers worming south to the warm Gulf—Sabine, Trinity, Brazos, San Antonio—promised food, harbors, and commerce.

Mexico, still heady over winning its independence, had no idea of losing Texas. Yet Texas was a long, long way from the new country's capital. Texas looked huge, tempting—and vulnerable. Mexico's hold on it was slim and she faced bad luck in having an equally heady young nation above her Texas boundary.

1

The Texas boundary made trouble early. President Thomas Jefferson caught the heat first in a parade of American statesmen who would be hounded by this and other problems boiling up from the border to the south. In 1803 Napoleon sold the United States 828,000 square miles of land at three cents a mile. The Louisiana Purchase proved a famous bargain, adding up in the end to 14 states or parts of states in the Union.

But did the purchase include Texas? Had that immense and almost empty territory come over from Spain to France in the first place? Did Napoleon have it to sell? Never look a gift horse in the mouth, or something to that effect, was the French answer to American doubts. As an agent for President Jefferson, James Monroe spent three futile years trying to get a boundary fixed, either from France or from Spain. How much of Texas did we buy, if we bought any of Texas at all?

Shortly after James Madison followed Jefferson in the presidency in 1809, troubles with Britain built up to the War of 1812. Mexico moved offstage. But in 1819 Monroe was party once more to a great purchase, this time as President. For

2

$5,000,000 Spain gave up the Floridas, along with any claims it held to the northwest, running all the way to the Pacific. As Secretary of State, John Quincy Adams fought Monroe's battle to give the United States a fixed western boundary. For months Adams had badgered the Spanish minister, haggling and niggling over every inch of ground. He was proud of the result, with some reason. As he wrote: "The acknowledgment of a definite line of boundary to the South Sea [Pacific] forms a great epocha in our history."

But not an inch of the new ground included Texas, though Adams might have brought that in, too. The Spanish minister carried secret instructions to yield if pressed about the southern territory. Of course the American Secretary of State had no knowledge of the instructions then. Critics soon jumped on both him and Monroe for letting themselves be duped out of a vital chunk of the old Louisiana Purchase. Monroe knew this argument by rote. It all went back to 1803 and that fuzzy western boundary. Fuzzy or not, the western boundary had originally included Texas. Or so Henry Clay was insisting, as well as Andrew Jackson and others. And now, in the Transcontinental Treaty of 1819 the President and his Secretary of State had thrown Texas away.

Adams' glow in winning his country a first foothold on the Pacific damped out in the fuss over Texas. So as President, following Monroe in 1825, he tried to buy the province. He tried twice, but Mexico was not interested.

Next came Andrew Jackson, who succeeded Adams in 1829. "Old Hickory" tried too, in his first year as President. "I have full confidence," Jackson wrote his personal agent in Mexico, "you will effect the purchase of Texas, so important to the perpetuation of that harmony and peace between us and the Republic of Mexico." Again *no* for an answer. Like Adams, Jackson would not give up. In the meantime Texas had been slipping away from peoples who could not colonize—Latins and Indians—to a people who did it only too well—the Anglo-Saxons.

For a short while Texans wrestled the question of whether to work out their problems within the Mexican Republic or whether to break away. Their answer soon came in the person of Antonio López de Santa Anna. The Mexican president rode north early in 1836 and took command of 6000 troops around Béxar (now San Antonio) with the aim of breaking up any gestures of independence on the part of American colonists in Texas. His men occupied the town on February 23, and on March 6 some 2000 of them attacked and slaughtered the 188 defenders of a nearby mission called the Alamo.

"In this war there are no prisoners," Santa Anna had written one of his generals a week before. Between March 20 and 27 his order was carried out again when odds of 4 to 1 forced Colonel James W. Fannin to surrender 500 men near Goliad. The Mexicans killed 357 prisoners, the wounded colonel included.

These atrocities left no doubt of the Texans' answer now. Santa Anna's first skirmishes had already led to a convention which severed connections with Mexico on March 2. Then on April 21 the newly confirmed commander-in-chief, Sam Houston, avenged the Alamo and Goliad in the battle of San Jacinto. An embarrassed and accommodating prisoner turned up in Santa Anna himself. Indeed, he admitted, all hostilities should cease, Mexican troops should evacuate Texas, and Texan independence should be acknowledged. As it happened, Santa Anna was buying his freedom by signing agreements that his government at home refused to honor, except for withdrawing her army. Mexico would not give up so easily, not even when the Congress of the United States, on July 4, 1836, recognized Texas as an independent republic.

4

By now, of course, events had made academic any American offers to buy Texas. No matter how Mexico felt, her old province was actually no longer hers to sell.

At least recognition had that meaning for the United States, and obviously to most Texans. But when the old owner showed signs of resisting the amputation, Jackson changed to threats. The huge debts Mexico owed us, he said in 1837, along with other indignities imposed on our citizens in that country, were enough to justify war.

A financial panic during the same year sidetracked Texas as an issue, both for the incoming President, Martin Van Buren, and for the Congress. Although the starry hope of annexing the new Republic was already in the air, Van Buren cooled it off for his single term in office.

In 1840 the Democrats wrote a platform without saying a word about Texas. Whigs went to the hustings without a platform. It was the year of "Tippecanoe and Tyler, too." And Tyler it was when old warrior William Henry Harrison died in April 1841, a month after his inaugural. As President, John Tyler quickly got Texas back into the news. As a Southerner he preached annexation. Let Texas *become* a slave state, or four slave states, and the Abolitionists be damned. But Daniel Webster was Tyler's first Secretary of State, and he gave annexation his hung-browed, cold New England stare.

Within two years Tyler had a new secretary, a more accommodating man from his own South. Abel P. Upshur was soon talking with money again, and with good reason. Just suggest annexing Texas and a Mexico already riled would erupt. Besides, Great Britain was showing too much interest in the new Republic. Buying Mexico off would clear the way for absorbing Texas peacefully. Once tucked safely into the Union, she would no longer tempt meddlers from overseas.

The Mexican minister in Washington listened politely

5

enough to Upshur. But Juan Almonte still dreamed of reconquest—of his country's winning back the Lone Star State. At this point history turned ironic. On February 28, 1844, Upshur went aboard the USS *Princeton* for a Potomac cruise. Her captain had invited important people in Washington to inspect the world's first naval ship driven by screw propeller. In a salute to the occasion one of the *Princeton's* equally modern guns (called the "Peacemaker") blew up. The accident killed both Upshur and Secretary of the Navy Thomas W. Gilmer.

Upshur's death eventually brought in John C. Calhoun. The new secretary's urge to add Texas to the slave state economy matched Tyler's own sectional bias about as well as Upshur's had. Together they swung back toward annexation as a better bet than purchase. And now the seventh President to get involved with Texas moved onstage in 1845. President James K. Polk would be a willing actor, and quite a cast was waiting in the wings: James Buchanan as Secretary of State; Zachary Taylor, Ulysses S. Grant, and Franklin Pierce as soldiers; young congressman Abraham Lincoln[1]; and others.

There they were. Starting with President Jefferson, twelve men who had held or were going to hold highest office all felt the mark of Mexico and her Texas province. In addition, the mark touched three statesmen who fell short of the presidency: Henry Clay, Daniel Webster, and John C. Calhoun. All three played heavy supporting roles in the southwest drama. Even

---

[1] In point of time Lincoln barely edged into the list, but Texas figured in his future. As a freshman representative in the National House near the close of 1847, he offered resolutions and two weeks later (in 1848) spoke out against the Mexican War. For his remarks the pro-war voters of his Illinois district helped to seal off his national career for a decade. An aside in the speech itself, defending the right of Texas to "secede" from Mexico, hung on in cold type to haunt Lincoln when he was President.

the president of a more restricted area made the cast: Jefferson Davis would fight under Taylor.

2

But in 1845 it was Polk's turn to worry the problems churning up along his country's southwest border—and below. With Polk in the White House, America's flexible Mexican policy stiffened. Early in May the War Department had flushed Brevet Brigadier General Zachary Taylor out of the cozy security of Fort Jesup, Louisiana. Orders began to pour in, spaced apart but still orders. "Put your forces into a position where they may most promptly and efficiently act in defense of Texas. . . . Move forward to the north of the Sabine River or any other point on the Gulf of Mexico as in your judgment may be most convenient for an embarkation to the western frontier of Texas. . . . If there is no forage in the country, the dragoons must leave their horses and serve as infantry."[2]

"Your ultimate destination is on or near the Rio Grande."

Boundary trouble again. In going on its own, Texas had pushed its border farther south against Mexico than any agreed on before. Mexico howled. The War Department kept feeding orders to Taylor: "The Rio Grande is claimed [by Texas] as the boundary line between the two countries. You will approach the line as prudence dictates. . . . Avoid acts of aggression. . . . The President desires at least part of your troops west of the Nueces."

This order to occupy land that Mexico called its own showed where Polk stood on the boundary question. As the next in-

---

[2] Dragoons, unlike cavalry, were trained and equipped to fight either mounted or on foot. They existed as a matter of economy.

7

structions made clear, he was pressing hard: "Find out the number of Mexican troops at Matamoros. . . . Find out what Texas can furnish. . . . What do you need?"

What did Taylor need? Mostly he needed more heart for a war that Polk seemed set on bringing about. As of summer 1845, Taylor went along with Tom Benton of Missouri. When a Tyler treaty to annex Texas lost out in the Senate, Benton had charged that the treaty would force war with Mexico "unconstitutionally, perfidiously, clandestinely, and piratically." Old Zachary Taylor may have been hard put to spell all the words, but he liked their resonant bellow.

The new commander was an odd soldier anyhow, in many ways a "made" one. Not that Taylor's record looked bad. He had won the United States Army's first brevet for his defense of Fort Harrison (Indiana) against the Indians in 1812. The feat made him a hero throughout the Ohio Valley. But in 1815 he quit the service when he was passed over for promotion to major.

Captain Taylor went back to the family holdings near Louisville, more than 10,000 acres. He would take up farming in the gentlemanly tradition of his transplanted Virginia forebears. "I do not regreat the change in calling, or the course I have pursued," he wrote one of his relatives. Zach could be pulled both ways. He liked soldiering, and he liked farming. But ambition took him back into the Army within a year when a vacancy at the rank of major fell open. Even so, the farmer in him would never wear off. In 1823 he bought a Louisiana plantation, and more land later in Mississippi.

Next followed the wearing years of frontier duty, "sleeping forty years in the woods, and cultivating moss on the calves of his legs." A political foe said this about Old Zach later, and it was as unfair as it was colorful. But military posts on the raw edges of the West did put a strain on morale. Seconds lagged into minutes, minutes into hours, and hours finally into days. Taylor lightened the numbing routine, whenever he could, by having his family with him. The good china and the mahogany pieces would be hauled to each new post to set up housekeeping. Meanwhile he took care of his men and kept them properly busy. Taylor was a conscientious soldier.

One fighting talent he lacked was hate. No frontier officer in his day saw more Indian warfare. Indians had killed one of his brothers; once they brutally hacked up the body of one of his men. In the Black Hawk War they scalped over a hundred more. Still Taylor could not hate Indians. He took their part against white trespassers and squatters. He sat through endless Indian councils, listened to their complaints, and tried to protect their rights.

In 1837, the Seminoles in Florida began to wear Taylor down with two and a half years of maddening war. Hit and run, hide out, strike at night war. Small bands suddenly appeared, as suddenly vanished over a territory of 52,000 square miles. If a man could ever learn hate, campaigning like this should teach him. But Taylor rode it out, knee deep in mud along with his men. In the Battle of Okeechobee they named him Old Rough and Ready, and the best of them fought well because he led them well. At the war's end, all the general felt was age, and a "sigh for peace, quiet, and retirement on a snug little farm."

So in picking Zach Taylor, the Polk Administration had found a leader both incapable of hating an enemy and apparently slow in warming up to his new assignment. But on July 4, 1845, Texas declared in favor of annexation to the United States. To Mexico it meant war. To Taylor, now sixty-one years old, it meant heading an invasion on foreign soil. He wrote the Adjutant General in Washington on July 20: ". . . the War Department may rest assured I will take no step to interrupt friendly relations between the United States and Mexico."

What a saber-swinging warrior! If President Polk wanted to keep his tough policy from spilling over too far, how could he have picked a better man?

3

Polk was moving Taylor south for more than the defense of Texas—a lot more. His mind was set on adding to the country no less than Upper California and what would become the states of New Mexico, Arizona, Nevada, Utah, the western slope of Colorado, and the southwest corner of Wyoming. If possible, Polk preferred to get all of this Mexican territory without fighting. This showed judgment on his part since he had done nothing to prepare for war. The plan for putting Taylor and some 4000 troops on Mexico's border was at best a menacing gesture against 8,000,000 people. But if it encouraged some kind of serious negotiating, it would serve the purpose.

Let Mexico sell what she had never held by right of proper colonization. Money would pay off her heavy foreign debts, including over $8,000,000 owed the United States—or at least the fourth of it awarded by a claims commission. With her economy straightened out, Mexico might finally stabilize her government.

Like Tyler, Polk hungered for expansion. If anything, the new phrase "Manifest Destiny" understated his reach. The Southwest was only part of what he wanted. Another slogan rang equally sweet in his ears: "Fifty-four Forty or Fight." Not that Polk expected to get all the Northwest Territory of Oregon. People had been shouting the slogan before he came into office, so getting a line as far up as fifty-four, forty in latitude was no boast of his. Still, it made a good first card to play in dealing with Britain.

James K. Polk was shrewd. He was also, a historian wrote, plodding, laborious, methodical, precise, calculating, secretive, intense, ambitious, conscientious, honest, limited, cold, formal, humorless, pedestrian. A man either guilty or worthy of all these adjectives might just make a good bargain. Join *limited* and *plodding* to *calculating, ambitious,* and *intense,* and the result is single-minded focus on an objective. The objective: expansion in two parts, (1) a 900-mile coastline with the immense depth of country behind it (Oregon territory); and (2) the whole southwest reach to the Pacific (northern Mexico).

Polk, with his tidy, narrowed view, isolated from so much warmth in the world about him, sat alone at night with his diary and its sum of the day's callers, bills, resolutions, orders, memos, letters, decisions, doubts, suspicions. But if as President he lacked full stature, he could be counted on at least to press both Britain and Mexico in his urge to see a bigger United States.

Press he did, to the point that a two-front war looked possible. Holding out for all of Oregon north to 54° 40′ was a gamble. Polk insisted that "The only way to treat John Bull is to look him straight in the eye." Brave talk, but at one stage John Bull seemed to react by staring right back. Sir Robert Peel, for example: "We too have rights respecting this territory of Oregon. We are resolved—and we are prepared—to maintain them." Another voice in the House of Commons was already calling on the "All-powerful God of battles" and "the thundering broadsides" of Her Majesty's ships.

If trouble did come, it had better break in Taylor's sector. The War Department had begun stripping America's frontier posts and coastlines to give him an army in the Southwest. General-in-Chief Winfield Scott would soon be complaining that Taylor had more than enough troops for any "defensive exigency." On the administration's word, that was their only mission; so Scott was viewing with proper alarm. In the whole Northeast hardly a company of soldiers was left. One lone regiment thinned out from Lake Champlain to the west in a line of more than 1300 miles.

Not all the skinning to build Taylor an army killed some of the doubts about what he could do. In May of 1845 the *National Intelligencer* in Washington was warning the country against overconfidence. "The Mexican troops are much better calculated for campaigns in those hot dry plains than any troops we can raise." Also there was the matter of provisioning. Our army could never live off the country—not that country. The light and hardy Mexican horses would carry their men into battle while our animals were starving. Let the government be warned, the story ended, that Mexico already might have 15,000 cavalry and flying artillery on the border of the Rio Grande.

By early fall another paper, *Niles' National Register*, was guessing that Polk did not expect war with Mexico. Otherwise he would be doing something about it. Editor Jeremiah Hughes guessed right on the first count. Polk had confided to his diary on August 30, 1845, that Mexico would not make war. As to doing something about it, the President was all action— all politics.

The silky iron of diplomacy kept probing for positions between Washington and the City of Mexico. A resident American dentist served as secret agent for Polk in the Mexican capital. Throughout the fall of 1845 Dr. William S. Parrott fed reassuring words to his President in long, illegible letters that reached Washington in only three weeks' time, "for such were the improvements in methods of transportation." Mexico, he said, would negotiate at least her Texas claims.

That sounded like a good start. Polk soon had a special minister poised to move down with authority to bargain. If Mexico would only grant a Texas boundary along the Rio Grande from mouth to source—yes, and throw in Upper California, New Mexico, and maybe a bit more, even $40,000,000 would not be too much "if it could not be had for less."

The President's airy optimism bothered his Secretary of State. A worrier to begin with, James Buchanan saw only resistance from Britain on Oregon and from Mexico on Texas. When Polk said, "We should stand on our rights against them and leave the rest to God and country," Buchanan wondered. Take Britain alone—how far would God support America in a war for Oregon above the 49th? And yet he played Polk's game. To the British minister in Washington, Buchanan regretted that he must say *no* to any arbitration which assumed that country's title to one acre of Oregon. The *no* came only "after having bestowed on it that respectful consideration so eminently due to any proposition emanating from the British Government." It was *no* in a glove, but still *no*.

Britain on its side of course restated its rights, which were "incompatible with the exclusive claim advanced by the United States."

Let's not argue, was Buchanan's answer. Then he went on to argue that the United States had the best claim to the whole territory. Anyhow, of what use could Oregon be to Great Britain—at the most, a remote colonial possession.

And to the country south of Texas more of same, only tougher. Mexico, after all, was not Great Britain. Buchanan again: "He [Polk] is anxious to preserve peace, although prepared for war." *Prepared* was a strong word for Zach Taylor's little force, but correspondence between Washington and the

City of Mexico ground on into winter. Meanwhile Polk's special minister, John Slidell, the man who hoped to buy off Mexico's threats and buy in her northern provinces, was knocking on closed doors. Wrong credentials, said the Mexican foreign minister. Nobody would talk to Slidell.

At home everybody seemed to be talking. Polk, in his annual message to Congress in December, beamed his pride in bringing Texas into the Union: ". . . the history of the world may be challenged to furnish a parallel." He approved his own patience with Mexico in the face of her unpaid debts and other claims. He liked his liberal concession to Britain in agreeing to discuss compromise on Oregon. Following any failure to settle, "this government will be relieved of all responsibility."

Oregon? John C. Calhoun wanted a policy of "Masterly Inactivity." Why not? Oregon would never be slave territory. To Senator Lewis Cass of Michigan it was too late for inactivity. War with Great Britain was almost inevitable. Senator Ambrose H. Sevier of Arkansas said it would come because only force impressed Britain. But Webster thought the country was safe, at least for the present.

In the House, failing John Quincy Adams had been talking all along. He already had damned the joint resolution to annex Texas. Texas in the United States was a victory for the slave aristocracy. But on the Northwest, Adams stood by the President, complete with verses from the first chapter of Genesis— emphasis on replenishing the earth (Oregon), and subduing it. And without the labor of slaves! Adams would even take Oregon all the way up to 54° 40′. There would be no war, he insisted. If Great Britain refused to give in, Polk would.

Two issues, slavery and expansion, called the tune in both Congress and the country. They colored or blurred or highlighted nearly every speech and vote. They broke across party lines and got in the way of nice, clear-cut differences on the tariff, banking or internal improvements. The plantation South stood for Texas and the growth of slave territory. The Northeast fought that but liked expansion in Oregon. The Ohio and Mississippi Valleys split both ways on slavery; not at all on the drive for new land, anywhere.

For Polk there was only one issue. The bickering over slavery annoyed him, Southerner though he was. It clouded his dream of an America filled in from coast to coast, and on the Pacific reaching north from below San Francisco as far into Oregon as he could bluff Great Britain. The single issue worth fighting for was expansion. Polk still thought he could keep out of war, but if his all-out policy of pushing west called for it— well, it was "a mere continuation of policy by other means."

Should the Clausewitz maxim have to be applied in the end, it was sure to involve Brigadier General Taylor and the little army now about to assemble at New Orleans and points below.

4

At Fort Jesup, Louisiana, in August 1845, Band Instructor Cioffi had his men rehearsing "Annexation March and Quick Step." But he was well behind the push south. Most of Taylor's new troops had already channeled into New Orleans, while a few had moved even farther down. In New Orleans they jammed barracks and spilled over into cotton presses renting at $100 a day. Lieutenant Braxton Bragg landed his Company E of the 3rd Artillery. Where were the horses the War Department promised him? Now he would have to ship out as infantry. This went hard with Bragg, who had a temper to match his pride.

Infantry companies came sweating into this Crescent City

from as far away as Mackinaw, Sault St. Marie, and western posts, Crawford, Hutchison, and Snelling; from Rhode Island, New York, and Key West on the east coast. Mostly they came down the rivers, through canals, or by sea. Not a mile of railroad lay west of Galena, Illinois, in the north or of Memphis farther south. No north–south tracks ran anywhere inland away from the east coast, and of course none at all beyond the Mississippi. Waterways did the main work even though the "steam boats" kept blowing up. Papers carried steamboat disaster columns as a regular feature. One paper editorialized on the future of this new power: "That steamers are destined to rival, if not supersede sailing ships of the Navy, seems to be adopted as a 'fixed' fact. Results so far do not inspire confidence."

Taylor's army was growing. By now its destination was Corpus Christi, a trading post inside Aransas Bay on the west bank of the Nueces. The leave-taking from New Orleans impressed Captain William Seaton Henry: "The moon was just rising as we marched out, gilding the domes and the house-tops, and caused our bayonets to glisten in the mellow light. The deep shadows on one side of the street, the bright moonlight on the other, the solemn quiet of the sleeping city disturbed so harshly by the martial music of the column. . . ."

Captain Henry was a West Pointer, sensitive to the mood and shape of war. Here they came, the men from the Military Academy—those "novelists and magazine writers," effete, arrogant dabblers in art, French, and drawing. Or so they were dubbed by a military committee of the House in 1837. The Point had found the going rough ever since its start in 1802. Seven years later a Secretary of War actually stopped appointing cadets to West Point. Only 71 graduates were available for the War in 1812. A year after the war began, Congress failed to vote funds to operate the academy. In 1819 a devoted instructor gave it three more years at best. A representative from Tennessee tried to push through a resolution cutting off rations and pay for cadets.

So far Sylvanus Thayer had saved West Point. He took over a foundering school in 1817 and left it a solid four-year institution in 1833. But by then how many graduates could find berths in an army of 4000 men? Over a hundred young officers left the service in the single year of 1836—among them, Jefferson Davis, Albert S. Johnston, Joseph E. Johnston, and George Gordon Meade. Only now, with the promise of fighting ahead, were they coming back in.

Thanks to Thayer, the military academy could staff the Army's lower and middle levels of command. In uniform once more, Lieutenant Meade hurried south, asking his wife to send on his *Maps of the Stars*, published by the Society for the Diffusion of Useful Knowledge. Lieutenant Ulysses S. Grant already in New Orleans, pulled out, fretting about the yellow fever, about citizens who fought duels at twenty paces, and about a senile colonel who had not led a drill for years and dropped dead in the first evolutions.

Lieutenant Samuel G. French, shipping out from Baltimore, had the good luck to bypass New Orleans. His bad luck was turtle steak at every meal from Key West all the way down to Aransas Bay. But at least French was going to Texas. The rest of his company had missed out, including Lieutenant William Tecumseh Sherman. Young Sherman wanted to fight. In 1840 he left the Point itching for one of Sam Colt's patent rifles, which fired "ten times in succession as fast as you can cock the trigger." Three years later he was hoping the government "would invent a new Florida war," and now in 1845 he was hot for Texas. But instead of following French, he was being shipped out to the quiet of California.

West Pointers were no new experience for Taylor. One of

them married his second daughter—over the old man's protest. No Army life for a girl of his, not if he could prevent it. But Jefferson Davis got his Sarah, only to lose her a few weeks later to malaria fever. As for another marriage, if Zach gave his daughters the run of the post, what could he expect? And all these elegant West Pointers around? Adjutant William Wallace S. Bliss, for example, with a warm eye on seventeen-year-old Betty.

Another West Pointer went on board with the general at New Orleans. Colonel Ethan Allen Hitchcock was an old friend, dating from 1819, when he did a turn as Taylor's adjutant. Yes, and lent him Hume's *History of England*, then wrote in his journal that it was about the only book his commander ever read.

On the way down from the Crescent City he could make new entries. Taylor's insistence on crossing the sand spits of Aransas from St. Joseph's Island into Corpus Christi Bay was insane. Why, Colonel Hitchcock sputtered in ink, did the old man have to get them stuck on a bar? Two days and two nights cramped aboard a lighter, with every native fisherman around as audience. More humbling yet, Taylor hired them for transport. "He [Taylor] was quite beside himself with anxiety, fatigue, and passion," but he would not take advice—notably Hitchcock's. "All comments agree that our safe arrival was little short of a miracle."

For a friend, Hitchcock was downright carping. Next, according to him, the general made a poor choice for a gun position, then wanted to make a move from camp that might cut them off from supplies. Finally, and worst of all, neither Taylor nor Colonel William Whistler could form a brigade into line! Colonel David E. Twiggs could manage it only by cheating. "As for maneuvering, not one of them can move a step in it. Egotism or no egotism, I am the only field officer

18

on the ground who can change a single position of the troops according to any but a militia code."

This was the strongest contempt Hitchcock could register. West Point arrogance? Probably. Taylor, Whistler, and Twiggs had not studied at the academy. But how many of its graduates could have led 800 troops through infested, waist-high swamp to drive Indians who had the pick of the ground? Old Rough and Ready had done it at Okeechobee. Yet he welcomed the West Pointers without prejudice, full of theory and empty of experience as they were.

Well, all right, one prejudice. Taylor did not like artillery officers. Drones, he called them. Look for the red-stripers to pick soft billets close to their homes whenever they could. The officers in charge of his guns had better stand up to their work.

The army just forming was to match West Pointers against the old line officers on a wider scale than ever before. Here was the first full product of Thayer's miracle. It would be judged by a generation of soldiers who never saw the Point as cadets, but who held most of the rank and gave most of the orders. How much would they take from men fired up by Dennis Hart Mahan? Like Thayer before him, Professor Mahan had come back from Europe rich in the new methodology of war— of Vauban, Jomini, Napoleon, and the School of Engineering and Artillery at Metz. Until Mahan could write his own texts, he talked and talked and filled blackboards with theories of fluid offensives, the science of logistics, the influence of terrain on strategy and tactics, and the value of interior lines. "Mahan's the man" was already a glowing slogan to cadets by the end of the 1830s.

Wisely, the new lieutenants and captains kept their store of raw knowledge to themselves. They let alumnus Hitchcock pick the old-timers apart. Later, possibly, they might make some observations of their own.

Meanwhile, in the process of moving Taylor's force from the islands outside, the inevitable happened. On September 13 the steamer *Dayton* exploded, killing seven men and injuring seventeen. The disaster ended two West Point careers. The lieutenants had won an assignment that "Cump" Sherman missed, but their luck ran out on the shoals of Corpus Christi Bay. Noncombat losses began long before this army came into being, and in this army they continued to mount. Attrition always set in ahead of the battles.

The general finally got his men over the bars and the sand spits. He did it without help from marine charts or coastal surveys of any kind, of which none existed. But new worries followed. One turned up in Major General Edmund P. Gaines, commanding the Western Department of the United States Army, headquarters New Orleans. He was Taylor's senior both in rank and years; when sick he "cured himself without the use of drugs"; he never carried an umbrella; and he still had a sharp, clear eye. Why should he be left out of events brewing to the south?

Rumors—another nuisance for Taylor. Rumors plus Gaines already had Zach attacked, whipped, his army prostrate without guns, his infantry without ammunition except what remained in its cartridge boxes. In 1845, in the year of Sam Morse and his "Magnetic Telegraph" and chess games played between Baltimore and Washington, the fresh marvel of communication was far from linking a continent in the matter of minutes. Rumors moved slowly but they outran truth—anywhere from ten or twelve days to three weeks. Along their paths they sucked up distortion and color, then dumped it in full whirl over a city like New Orleans.

New Orleans had a rumor of its own to match those rolling

in from below. The way a local paper had it, General Gaines was threatening to lead 40,000 troops into Mexico—no less than a second campaign of Austerlitz. He went around the city making ridiculous speeches to the greatest crowd of loafers and rowdies ever lined up for free food and clothes, "regular Falstaff's men—well calculated to fill a ditch."

Like rumors generally, this one had some root in fact. Gaines had been after the War Department for just such a command. Admitting to his sixty-eight years, he said he was the only United States soldier who ever won a battle at the head of a division against the British Army. "Under these circumstances, I *claim, as a right*, the command of the proposed expedition." Proposed, that is, by Gaines himself.

General Gaines actually did call on Louisiana for 12,000 volunteers. A thousand of them got as far as New Orleans, and several small companies even reached Taylor. Old Zach, who at this stage wanted no part of citizen soldiers, asked the War Department to take them back. At the same time he belittled the New Orleans scare. Long years at out-of-touch frontier posts had made him rumorproof. Taylor always waited for the facts to catch up.[3]

On September 16 an embarrassed Washington allowed that Gaines' volunteers might be sent home again, "to mingle with their friends and relatives, from whom a sense of duty to their country had so suddenly separated them." So suddenly that none of them knew anything about soldiering. Even so, Gaines had a friend in Taylor's own camp. West Pointer Hitchcock could never, of course, sanction action without orders, and yet he was happy to find somebody besides himself who thought

[3] Later, Captain Robert E. Lee spent a few weeks with the army, long enough to learn from Taylor that rumors of overpowering enemy strength usually proved false.

the force at Corpus Christi, as a threat to the whole of Mexico, looked puny.

5

The puny force went about its job of homemaking throughout the fall of 1845. A newsman writing in August liked what he saw. "When the eye first rests upon this camp, clustered with a thousand white tents, along the shelly margin of Corpus Christi Bay, irresistible shouts of admiration follow!" There was security too, as well as beauty. On the extreme left, near the village, the New Orleans volunteers (of the short stay); on the far right Twiggs' 2nd Dragoons; in the center the 3rd, 4th, and 7th Infantry. Texas Rangers picketed a short range of hills inland. The whole line covered about a mile and a half, with a 300-yard fieldwork on the right, six feet thick.

Now back to the newsman's idyl: "The cool nights invite weariness to repose, disturbed neither by the promenading flea, nor the buzzing mosquito." Lieutenant Meade liked the shell beach and the bathing, though being Meade he had to find something to fret about—lack of wood and the brackish water. Captain E. Kirby Smith got tired of pork and beans; also of the "perfect state of monotony."

Nobody seemed to agree with anybody else on what he found in Corpus Christi at the beginning. Only three houses, according to the New Orleans *Picayune*; Kirby Smith had it a dozen. One house, Lieutenant French said. Captain Henry gave it between twenty and thirty, mostly sheds with grass roofs. Grant guessed in terms of people—fewer than a hundred souls. Hitchcock let it go as a very small village. If all these eye-witnesses had hit camp the same day, only the most abstruse equations would ever arrive at the truth about anything in

22

Zach Taylor's little army. As it happened, they all were putting down what they saw at different times in the first frantic days of landing.

More important was the change that took place once the army began to settle in. Trader H. L. Kinney's small ranch lost its isolated character in a hurry. Surgeon N. S. Jarvis took over one of the few frame buildings for a hospital and medical storehouse, *with guard*; whiskey was a popular remedy. Ordnance, commissary, and subsistence arranged for supply depots. Wheelwrights threw up sheds for repairing wagons and gun carriages; blacksmiths whanged away in areas of their own; corrals for the horses, mules, and oxen sprawled over acres; and artillery and wagon parks elbowed for extra space. The slaughtering pens lay beyond camp. Add the parade ground, and Taylor's war machine had eaten up miles of landscape before it ever fired a shot.

The village of Corpus Christi itself, on the extreme left, housed the complex of nonmilitary: lawyers, business "agents," hairdressers, photographers, sutlers, gamblers, whores, and plain hangers-on. The list included wives and sometimes children of the soldiers.

The weather held beautifully through most of autumn, so that "weariness reposed" fairly well. The hunting held up, too. The glut of food on the wing, on the plain, and in the bay no doubt delighted commissary. Geese, ducks, turkey, and jacksnipe in the thousands; plenty of deer; and from the water pompano, red snapper, and green turtle. All of it was good sport as well as good eating. The luxury of shooting and fishing helped offset high prices for staples like potatoes at $5 a pound, butter at 37½ cents, and milk at 25 cents a quart. Eggs sold at $1 to $2 a dozen.

Commissary issued its own rations, of course. While Taylor loved economy, he knew well about armies moving on their stomachs. Men in the ranks got bacon, salt pork, beef, bread, flour or corn meal, beans, rice, sugar, and vinegar—all of it free. But on $7 a month a private had little to spend for extras like 25-cent milk.

Besides, where was the paymaster? A soldier correspondent reported more than half the army on hand, and half of them without pay for six months. Was the War Department trying to prove that American troops were not mercenaries? "Unfair!" the Paymaster General countered. Only 48 unpaid out of 3789 men by the end of November. The correspondent stuck to his story. Forty-eight payless soldiers could howl like half an army.

By December the cold began closing in on Corpus Christi. It melted in the daytime, froze over at night. Forty-degree drops in the space of several hours, and canvas crackling with ice in the wind. On some mornings Captain George A. McCall's orderly would pour boiling water on the tent flap to let him out. Lieutenant Meade lined his tent and had a chimney place built in. Rugged Lieutenant John F. Reynolds stopped sleeping on the ground, moved into a bunk and muttered about the lack of wood—sticks only for cooking and "so crooked they wouldn't lie still when you put them down."

Now came the "northers," an old name for an old curse of the west Gulf region. But what was a norther to an old campaigner like Zachary Taylor, who had lived through prairie lows in Minnesota? "I do not deem it necessary to hut the troops," he assured Washington. But sleazy canvas leaking in every rain must have got under the skin of Surgeon J. B. Porter. "It is a peculiarity of our service," he wrote, "that men are better paid, better clothed and better fed than those of any other army in the world; while they are worse lodged, both in peace and war, than any other troops." In one dripping tent he was treating the wife of a 3rd Infantryman and her two children, one with cholera.

A board of officers condemned the tents, but still they leaked. Men made the best of it by facing them south, packing dirt walls around them and piling on chaparral to cut the whipping winds. Taylor finally got lumber enough from New Orleans to floor some of the tents, but that was all. Zach hated to spend money, and lumber was $60 a hundred feet. Penny-pinching years in a peacetime army, too much accounting for the last canteen strap, guidon, ridge pole, or the extra mouthpiece for a bugle had done their work.

Through midwinter the northers bit harder than ever. More sickness moved in. Dysentery, diarrhea, and catarrhal fevers put men on their backs and filled the hospital. At one point 30 per cent of the army showed on sick list. Policing of sanitation broke down. A whole army with diarrhea was too much for the privies, Surgeon Porter observed. Taylor should have done more about it than he did, but in the army background of the old frontiersman bad conditions were normal.

No doubt of it now, the Corpus Christi that the general reported healthy in October was getting out of hand. The peak of the sickness found his 22 medical officers too few for the job. One of them advised Lieutenant Meade to get out of the country. Men were beginning to desert. The early euphoria of autumn tailed off into grousing.

Where to turn for relief? A place to drink made a good start. An early newsman with the army put the count of local grog shops at 30. Corpus Christi had become quite a town. Its original settler, Mr. Kinney, estimated the population at around 2000 civilians. Whenever the wind and rain slacked off, soldiers shook the tarantulas out of their boots and left the soggy tents to hunt excitement. Corpus Christi looked promising if you read the advertising in Sam Bangs' *Gazette.*

25

The ex-Bostonian was a wise printer. He had bought a press in Galveston and hurried down to set up a paper. It was a good move, judging from his paid columns:

F. Gonzales was offering 40 boxes of claret of very special brand—St. Julien Medoc.

F. Helmuller announced 40 boxes of chewing tobacco—Hong's, Clark's, Henry's, Robinson's, Moore's, and A. Cabanes's.

D. Wolf & Company would faithfully attend customers desiring dry goods, clothing, and liquor.

John P. Kelsey would thankfully receive all orders for horses, mules, and breeding mares and fill them at the lowest rates.

William Mann & Company had on hand 50 barrels of whiskey, 20 of cider, 15 boxes of lemons; also port, claret, and sherry.

Conrad Meuly had coffee and hot drinks, bread, and pastry of every variety constantly on hand.

J. R. Mills could supply beef, pork, mutton, and venison; also could supply steam boats and shipping at the shortest notice.

These notices read like a going town even without adding the "Great Western Eating Saloon," the "Stop That Ball!" bowling alleys, Kilgore's Oyster Parlor, or "All the Comforts of Home" in the Kinney House.

Lieutenant John Reynolds sent his family in Lancaster, Pennsylvania, a copy of the *Gazette*. "You must not imagine from this paper," he warned, "that we have all the luxuries and amusements it would lead you to suppose upon a mere perusal of the advertisements." Reynolds added a new list of items on sale—carved furniture, music boxes, jewelry, and notions. It was nothing but junk stacked in a row of canvas sheds. He wrote off the eating houses and grog shops as vile. Corpus, he said, was one of the rowdiest, cutthroat places he had ever seen. To go out at night was to tempt being robbed, or even shot down. "There is no law of any kind—save the Bowie knife &c the pistol."

A correspondent agreed with Reynolds. All the thieves and murderers of the United States and Texas had poured into Corpus Christi, a run of "bloated and sin-marked visages." Why not invoke martial law? he wondered. The gambling, drinking, and whoring were going too far. Taylor held off. For one thing, tee-totaler and tent-hugger that he was, the old general never saw most of the carousing. Some of it, of course, he accepted simply as release for the kind of soldiers he knew so well. If helling around a little got them through the days of waiting, then good.

But Taylor did crack down on the worst excesses, especially those involving officers. His 2nd Dragoons had first ridden into camp after a boiling 500 miles from Fort Jesup. (Correction: 501½ miles; Lieutenant George Stevens measured the distance.) Some days they had made 25 to 30 miles, nearly all of them at night to escape the sun. They damned the new government saddle at every step. Faulty design cost 60 horses injured, 60 men on foot. This had one virtue. By slowing the pace it gave the men a chance to know the ladies along the route. "The ladies, God bless them, always enthusiastic," a dragoon remembered. Too many balls and parties brought the unit into Corpus still looking for fun, and they had it.

Result: one captain forced to resign, two standing trial.

Taylor's officers generally steered clear of the night life, theater excepted. The *Gazette* of January 8, 1846, announced the opening of a "substantial and commodious theatre in this flourishing town . . . under the joint management of Messers Hart & Wells, who are daily expecting the arrival of an effi-

cient auxiliary force to their present popular theatrical corps."
First performance: James Sheridan Knowles' *The Wife, a Tale of Mantua*. Following the play Mr. Wells would dance; then more singing and dancing would be topped off with "the laughable farce *Loan of a Lover*."

The Union Theatre got mixed notices, running from "a fair company of actors" and "very clever" to "a company of strolling actors, who murder tragedy, burlesque, and comedy, and render farce into buffoonry," a "low-flung company."

Either the auxiliary professional talent was late in arriving, or the harsher critics won out. Anyhow, army amateurs moved onstage. Production manager was "Prince" John Bankhead Magruder. Once he talked Ulysses Grant into playing Desdemona, but Othello threatened to walk off. Lieutenant James Longstreet lost the role through overweight. The West Pointers never said how much the saloon and refectory adjoining the theater fired their thespian urge. And critics apparently spared the results.

6

As recreation the theater was not enough, and time went slow for the officers. They kept asking for books and newspapers from home. Colonel Hitchcock had one of the few libraries in camp. In his tent Captains William Bliss and Charles H. Larnard spent evenings arguing over Spinoza, Schiller, Kant, Hobbes, and other cerebral fare in the colonel's collection. It was Hitchcock's only pleasure in army life— leisure for good talk, good reading, and his own writing.

Writing became an escape in itself, usually letters but sometimes diaries and journals. Families in the states could thank tough Corpus Christi for keeping good men in their tents.

Instead of finding trouble they wrote long and frequent accounts of life in Texas (or on foreign soil, if their politics leaned that way). They described strange firsts like Mexican "themales," fandangoes, señoritas smoking the cigaritto, other-world dress, and semitropical flowers, vegetation, and climate. Many writers omitted mention of the maguy wine and native girls bathing in the raw.

The West Pointers also asked questions. Four years of Thayer-motivated study had made the best of them intelligently concerned about their country. What was Dan Webster or Tom Benton saying in the Senate? Was "Old Man Eloquent" Adams in the House still baiting Polk on Texas? Was the President still baiting Great Britain on Oregon? Had Mr. Slidell managed anything yet? And the Mexican, Santa Anna— where was that rascal and what was he up to? These men from the Point were good citizens. They still had to prove themselves as soldiers, but they stood just off-scene in a most sensitive area. If anything broke, it should not take long to find out.

Daytime in camp at Corpus Christi presented no major problem—or only one. Drill. *Drill*. DRILL! Too much of it, Captain Henry moaned. Meade said his ears rang all day long with drumming and fifeing. Grant recalled it all later, but being Grant, he wholly approved.[4]

In promoting drill, Taylor was merely complying with a polite suggestion from the War Department. The Adjutant General in Washington saw the assembly of so many troops as an opportunity, "while resting on your arms, of practicing a regular system of field and camp instruction." Old Zach set

[4] Justin Smith, the best known historian of the Mexican War, accused Taylor of slighting drill at Corpus Christi. Army historian William A. Ganoe went further: Taylor neither knew much about war nor believed in teaching it. See Appendix I for Taylor's defenders.

about doing exactly that, as he dutifully reported to his superiors. But he reminded them that regiments cut up for long years into small detachments would hardly be ready for large scale evolutions.

Parceling the United States Army in fragments to man over a hundred posts was traditional. Dragoon officer Richard S. Ewell had fixed the formula: learn all there was to know about handling 40 men and forget everything else. Even Taylor's understrength regiments looked big when seen together for the first time. Units up to brigades in size would have to be maneuvered by book alone. No wonder Hitchcock, who did know the book, aired his ego on the subject of drill.

The Adjutant General in Washington added one more suggestion. He thought proper "dress" should be observed by all officers. This hit Taylor himself, the worst offender. His garb and manner led to all kinds of stories, some probably true. In one of them, for instance, a new lieutenant appearing to pay his respects saw an old man out behind headquarters cleaning the general's—it *must* be the general's—sword. "A dollar to clean mine too?" he asked. "Sure thing." The old man turned out to be Old Zach. In another story two young officers in search of their general ran across a shabby old farmer. "How's crops, old fellow?" "Oh," he answered, "purty good." Before moving on, one officer said, "Give our love to the old lady." That evening they caught up with the shabby old farmer in his headquarters tent.

Lieutenant Grant liked Taylor's messy dress and copied it as far as he dared. But only Taylor could assemble an original Taylor get-up. Any kind of head covering, from local sombrero to oilcloth cap; any kind of coat that suited the weather, linen or wool, of accidental color and cut. His pantaloons lacked the regulation stripe; loose socks showed his calves; and any boots would do. Everyone who saw the general remembered his costumes. Did he affect his dress to bother the shine-button, torso-tight men from the Point? Probably not; he had cheated on regulations for years. Out on the country's fringes who cared? Taylor simply wore what a man over sixty felt good in.

He put on his finery just twice, once for a grand review at Corpus that never came off, and once for Commodore David Conner. Zach knew the Navy—all spit, more spit, polish, and braid; and he came aboard turned out in his best. But Conner had heard about Taylor too, and as host he showed up in mufti to save embarrassment. After *that* reverse in roles, Taylor put fancy garb aside for all time.

To his men, indifference to army punctilio was only a part of the general's appeal. Soldiers who wrote for newspapers at home gave him a good press from the start. They compared him most often with Andrew Jackson. They liked his ripe judgment, his practical common sense, his proved courage— even his stubbornness. They also liked his accessibility. In good weather he held daily court, stocky bulk astride a campstool in front of his tent. No appointments needed and no meddling staff officers to insulate the general from his men. When Taylor had the time, he talked freely to anybody about anything, including his crops in Louisiana.

Except for some mild carping from Hitchcock and one or two others, the word going back to the states was high on Old Zach.

For all his plainness and affability, Taylor was under heavy pressure at the turn of the year. Over him hung Polk's and much of America's drive for land, for the geographic sense of one country between two coasts. Taylor served as southwest agent for this ambition, or policy. So far it was peaceful, and his command went by the innocent title "Army of Observation."

Meanwhile, Taylor observed. To the south, a country

31

played its game of changing governments. Antonio López de Santa Anna had run through his luck, along with too much Mexican wealth, between 1840 and 1843. In '41 worshipful citizens had made a worshipful ceremony of burying the hero's foot. Santa Anna had lost it three years before at Vera Cruz when the French tried to force payment of some debts. But bitter citizens of 1844 dug up the saintly foot and dragged it through the streets. Their savior had misused the presidency. Out with dictator Santa Anna. In with José Joaquín Herrera. By the end of 1845, Herrera was out. He had looked too eager for a deal with the greedy country in the north. Along with Herrera, Mexican honor and pride also shook off Slidell, Buchanan's persistence, and Polk's hope for conquest by way of purchase.

That was the view south. Looking north toward his own country, Taylor saw the new American state of Texas. In nine years of declared independence she had balked Mexican efforts to reclaim her. The Santa Anna of the Alamo in 1836 won nothing from Texans but hatred for his cruelty, then lost at San Jacinto. Earlier attempts had never got as far. Mexican land grants to American settlers had helped make the difference. Beginning with the Austins, father and son, in 1821, newcomers took root (a feat which the parade of governments below the Rio Grande could never bring off for themselves). Part of Taylor's job was to protect a quarter century of American success in Texas.

In January 1846 the War Department defined another part of the general's job. "It is not designed, in our present relations with Mexico, that you should treat her as an enemy; but should she assume that character by a declaration of war, or any open act of hostility toward us, you will act not merely on the defensive, if your relative means enable you to do otherwise." The sentence seemed to be hedging. Northern Whigs in Congress would have revised it to read: "To obtain Polk's objective, we may have to fight Mexico, but make sure she starts the war."

To 47 per cent of Taylor's regulars a war against Mexico to protect American interests would be ironic. They were immigrants. The Irish alone totaled 24 per cent of the army. Next in order came the Germans, with 10 per cent; then English, 6 per cent; Scotch, 3 per cent; and a scattered 4 per cent for Canada, Western Europe, and Scandanavia combined.[5] Foreigners from the old world and still foreign to the new. Yet here they were, on the brink of a foreign invasion. They were part of the President's policy, helping to expand a country in which so far hardly any of them could afford to buy an acre of ground.

They would help, that is, if they measured up to West Pointer Albert Sidney Johnston's opinion of them: "A large number write their names; so that there can be claimed for them, *for their class*, a high degree of intelligence. It is said many of them are foreigners; this is true, and in that respect they represent very perfectly the population of the country." While admitting that such soldiers could not expect to associate with refined persons, he thought they ought to be as much respected as they were despised. "When called upon for duty they do not count the cost."

To make them good soldiers took doing, but both the old-line officers and the West Pointers knew how. Always keep soldiers busy cleaning rifles and equipments, drilling in the dust or mud, or on parade, or mounting guard, or policing the grounds. Put them to tending horses, repairing roads, paint-

[5] The percentages, based on a total count of 5-year enlistments in the Regular Army from 1840 through 1845, are taken from the records of the Adjutant General's Office, National Archives, Washington, D.C.

ing, building, gardening. Tie offenders across wooden horses. Hang signs around their necks and stand them on barrels for everybody to see. Run them behind wagons, tied to the tailgates and carrying weights. Slip poles crosswise between elbows and knees tied close to their chests, and stuff gags in their mouths. Brand them, shave their heads, drum them out of camp. Slap them in guardhouses and threaten the worst with the rope or the firing squad.

Johnston's kind of private lived hard. He ate his share of tainted and moldy food, and drank plenty of bad water. He came down with smallpox, yellow fever, malaria, typhoid, diarrhea, consumption, dropsy, and apoplexy. To shore up his health or forget he was sick he usually got drunk. Liquor was about the only medicine he knew, and his doctors often agreed. In the end, if he survived and behaved, he might make a good soldier.

If there was irony in sending this tough and half foreign army toward Mexico, there also was irony in sending Taylor himself, at least at the start. Riding down from Fort Jesup in '45, he had sounded like a good Whig protesting Democratic ideas of aggression. Seven years before that, sighing for retirement, he had sounded like an old man, a general out of sympathy with the administration and tired of soldiering. But now Colonel Hitchcock began to accuse Zach of ambition: "I think the general wants an additional brevet, and would strain a point to get it." He even thought Taylor was losing respect for Mexican rights.

If true, this was quite a switch. The "new" Taylor was bound to promote the policy of Democrat Polk. The President would have his instrument.

CHAPTER II

A FOREIGN CITY

By the middle of 1846 Taylor had what looked like an army—on paper:

	Officers	Privates	Total	Sick
General Staff	24		24	
2nd Dragoons, 10 companies	41	555	596	80
Artillery, 12 companies	81	842	923	97
Infantry, 50 companies	200	2336	2536	324
Total	346	3733	4079	501
Total absent	58	140	198	
Effective present	288	3593	3881	

The phrase General Staff had a good sound but mostly it covered adjutants, assistant quartermasters, surgeons, paymasters, engineers, and ordnance. No intelligence section, and with under 600 cavalry, the army would be operating almost blind in strange country. Of the 12 artillery companies, nine were serving as infantry. That gave Taylor only three companies (or batteries) to man the field pieces.

35

Field artillery had made an abortive start in 1808. On July 4 of that year a battery of six horse-drawn guns and their ammunition wagons galloped up and down Pennsylvania Avenue in Washington. A demonstration aimed at impressing Congress ripped off two salutes, each a half mile apart in less than half an hour. Everybody cheered. Within months the same Secretary of War who had interrupted appointments to West Point canceled the bold experiment. He ordered the horses sold at public auction and impounded the guns. From then until 1837 no gunner climbed onto a caisson or limber in America. Meanwhile Napoleon's light artillery had been careening all over Europe's terrain.

In 1837 a dedicated officer named Ringgold got his chance. He nursed a mounted 4-gun battery into such high efficiency that the War Department showed it off to stir recruiting. Eastern parade grounds learned to admire the burnish and patina of its bronze 6-pounders. Over the next 20 years Sam Ringgold labored to combine the best of the French and British models. The result was Battery C of the 3rd Artillery, already a great name in the peacetime service.

In Taylor's army nobody was working harder to match Captain Ringgold's standards than Braxton Bragg. To succeed he drove his men close to mutiny. The one windfall left over from Gaines' rejected heroes was artillery horses, of good stout American breed. When Taylor shipped those first volunteers back to Louisiana, he wisely hung onto their animals. The choice pretty well expressed his feelings about citizen soldiers. Now Bragg at last had horses to haul his guns and mount his men. The new battery gave Taylor three of the five in the entire United States Army. Lieutenant James Duncan led the third. Duncan lacked Ringgold's military flair and some of Bragg's drive, but his battery was good enough to belong.

Mere proficiency, though, never satisfied Bragg. No matter what weather, his E Company (also 3rd Artillery) daily scarred the plains in formations from line to column, by right and left wheel, by countermarch, passage of carriages, changes of front, intervals of distance, limbering and unlimbering of pieces, sighting, and loading by the motions. Any skill that sweat and a nagging eye for minutia could improve, Bragg would achieve.

The field artillery needed all its skill to win over Old Zach. What he had seen of it in earlier wars left him cold. Since then oxen had given way to horses, soldiers took over from the hired civilian drivers, and now they rode in the saddle or on the limbers and caissons. But none of the changes was battle-tested. Besides, Taylor remembered the artillery officers' weakness for the easy life. He liked and admired Ringgold, and he liked Duncan—as persons. So far his good will did not include their guns.

A correspondent in the army wondered about the artillery, too. The general's pleas to Washington for recruits to fill up his regiments had brought in a trickle of new men, nearly all Irish and Germans. Some of them went to the batteries. But why expect illiterate foreigners to begin riding like Cossacks in the matter of weeks? "The military authorities say that very few soldiers are fit for the light artillery arms—that it requires picked men, bold and expert horsemen—and these only become good light artillerymen after long practice in riding, driving, managing, and attending their horses, and in using the sabre."

What bothered the writer even more was to see both officers and men out foraging for their animals. Artillerymen had to leave off drill and, taking on quartermaster chores, "pick up the scythe to enjoy the perfumes of new-mown hay." Lieutenant Reynolds made the same point, without the imagery.

"We are actually making hay," he wrote home in shocked surprise.

Still, doubts or no doubts, field artillery was about the only new look the army could boast. With few exceptions the infantry lugged aging flintlocks, courtesy of General-in-Chief Scott. He liked them as tried and tested weapons.[1] By the 1820s American woodsmen and hunters had gone over to percussion. Instead of the clumsy jaw that held the flint, a hammer set off the priming powder by direct blow. And the powder had moved in out of the weather, enclosed in a copper cap. The government arsenals had been turning out percussion arms since 1841, most of them smoothbores (24,825 compared to 7618 rifles in 1846). But, percussion was too complicated, said Scott. His caution was in the old army tradition—fight the next war with the weapons of the last. The dragoons and Sam Walker's Texans got hold of some carbines and Colt's revolvers, and a few officers had Colts. Otherwise Taylor's small arms had all the look of earlier wars.

2

The old look included the army's colonels and the next man in line. General William J. Worth held second command. Good service in the War of 1812 and later against the Seminoles in Florida had won him a brevet as brigadier. Although no West Pointer himself, his years as commandant of cadets at the academy in the 1820s had publicized his glitter and hard

[1] General George B. McClellan made a similar choice in the summer of 1861. He decided in favor of muzzle-loading rifles for all Union infantry, although both breechloaders and repeating arms had been improving for 20 years. Not till the latter half of the Civil War did the newer small arms see much use.

efficiency. He symbolized all the military snap that Taylor lacked. "The Ney of the army," an awed correspondent called him. But Worth had serious faults. He went in for spells of temper, heavy drinking, and often—possibly from cause to effect—periods of bad judgment.

Worth came to Corpus hoping to supplant Taylor at a time when rumor had the old general about to retire. Nothing could have hurt the army more. Worth's admitted talents needed a steadier head. But by keeping Worth under control, Taylor could make good use of him. Both Worth and Lieutenant Colonel William G. Belknap were the same age—fifty-two. The other field officers carried more years: Colonel David E. Twiggs, fifty-six; Lieutenant Colonel James S. McIntosh, fifty-nine; and Colonel William Whistler, sixty-six. Each of them, a writer said, "was prepared to fight in 1846 as his army had fought in 1812."

Next to Worth, big-necked, big-voiced Twiggs was best known. His good humor got better results from his men than McIntosh managed with all his ripping profanity. Colonel Whistler had a reputation in the Army too. Over the years his feats of strength and endurance made legend, but of late his best feat was a capacity for drinking. It would soon cause him trouble. Another old-timer, Jacob Brown, had come up through the ranks over a 34-year stretch. At fifty-eight he was sure he still had two more campaigns left in him.

For all its old weapons and aging leaders, the army at this stage looked good to several of the younger officers. It impressed Grant as a most efficient force. Lieutenant John Sedgwick called it the best organized and equipped the country had ever sent into the field. Captain Henry said: "There is a 'physique' and 'morale' about our 'little army'. . . . I feel more and more convinced that we can contend with an immensely superior force." Pride and spirit like this might even save Winfield Scott's bet on the last war's weapons.

Considering the manpower available, Taylor seemed to have a good command. He still was short of officers, especially at field rank, but at company level the Military Academy had provided real potential. There were names worth remembering:

Richard H. Anderson	Henry M. Judah
Philip N. Barbour	Fitzhugh Lee
Bernard E. Bee	James P. Longstreet
Jacob E. Blake	George A. McCall
Braxton Bragg	John B. Magruder
Robert C. Buchanan	J. K. F. Mansfield
Don Carlos Buell	George G. Meade
Silas Casey	John C. Pemberton
Abner Doubleday	Alfred Pleasonton
Arnold Elzey	Theodoric Porter
Samuel G. French	John F. Reynolds
Robert S. Garnett	I. B. Richardson
George W. Getty	Randolph Ridgely
Ulysses S. Grant	Samuel Ringgold
William J. Hardee	E. Kirby Smith
Alexander Hays	William S. Smith
Daniel H. Hill	George Stevens
Joseph Hooker	George H. Thomas
Samuel P. Heintzelman	Earl Van Dorn
Bushrod Johnson	

More West Pointers would join Zach later,[2] and not all of those listed would complete his graduate seminar and field practicum. Carried far enough, the course was sure to invite attrition, but even the earliest casualties would not be forgotten.

[2] See Appendix II for complete list.

One crack in the army's good morale developed from a fight over brevet rank. A law of 1812 permitted the President of the United States, with Senate consent, to promote an officer for gallantry in combat or other meritorious service. The rank remained largely honorary because most brevet captains went on serving as lieutenants, most brevet majors as captains, and so on. Only rarely did a vacancy or reorganization give an officer enough troops to qualify him for his brevet rank and pay. Taylor, for example, was a brigadier by brevet alone, yet the size of his present command more than met the requirements of his brevet.

The system had its detractors within the Army, officers who held that brevets were meaningless. In fact, Taylor himself favored actual rank over brevet. So in planning a grand review of the troops he named Twiggs to head it. Twiggs' commission as colonel predated Worth's. But William Jenkins Worth exploded. He, not Twiggs, would lead the review. He, not Twiggs, had earned a brevet for gallantry in Florida. A brevet brigadier ranked any colonel, he argued.

The dilemma put Taylor in trouble. From Washington, General Winfield Scott had recently instructed the Army to honor brevet rank wherever possible. And Scott's circular upset Hitchcock. He got off a hot circular against brevets and rounded up 158 signatures from officers of all ranks in camp. ". . . to give precedence to brevet rank in violation of law and reason . . . is the assumption of a wrong principle—the principle of the despot!" It was exactly in line with this opinion that Taylor had chosen Twiggs over Worth. Now it looked like a mistake. Argument was breeding dissension and hurting morale at the very time the army might be moving.

The general called off his review. Of course the dispute buzzed on among the officers. Honest doubts about brevets no doubt influenced Taylor in rejecting Worth's claims, but

he also had some doubts about Worth himself. After the ruckus over rank, give-and-take between the two was not likely to improve.[3]

3

Sure enough, the army was about to move. A dispatch from the War Department reached camp on February 4, 1846. The general ought to take up a position on or near the Rio Grande as soon as possible. Taylor answered that he would lose no time in getting off. On the 9th he sent a small wagon train 60 miles south to test the roads for travel. A month earlier Lieutenant John Reynolds had reported the whole country between Corpus and the Rio as "perfectly under water and the roads impassable." In looking for snipe, he said he found the prairies literally drowned out. But by now the wagons bumped over roads fairly dried out under the warming Texas—or was it Mexican?—sun. Once Taylor picked his route, he could start his 180-mile march for the Rio.

What would happen to Corpus Christi when the army left? No more theater, no whiskey parlors, oyster bars, bowling alleys, and no more *Gazette*. No town. Old Zach meant to cut clean. Except for a guard to protect public property and help to care for the sick, he was ending the boom for Kinney's ranch on the bay. Supplies would begin shipping direct from New Orleans to Point Isabel. Taylor had fixed on the small

[3] From the beginning until they were given up before the Spanish-American War, brevets caused as much harm as they did good. The current practice of awarding ribbons and medals may be open to abuse, but at least it ended the confusion and battling over rank.

port for his new base. It lay on the mainland nine miles above the mouth of the Rio Grande and inside Padre Island.

Corpus fought for its life. Its weapon was rumor.

No. 1, February 9: General Paredes with 2000 Mexican troops on the way north to attack.

No. 2, February 11: Taylor's little force threatened by 20,000 hostile troops.

No. 3, February 13: Paredes ordering out army of from 60,000 to 100,000 to retake Texas.

Taylor reacted in character. He hoped his government would not credit the wild rumors growing out of "personal interests here at Corpus Christi." Army boom towns died hard, but they were an old story in the history of wars.

Six months in camp make soldiers restless. Captain Kirby Smith was glad to learn that they would be pulling out. Lieutenants Meade and Reynolds wanted to see more of the country to the south. Major John Monroe herded the walking sick aboard a convoy provided by Commodore Conner. The siege train with its four 18-pounders and a field battery also loaded for Point Isabel. Dust clouds hung over corrals where Mexican *arrieros* roped wild young mules for branding and breaking for harness or for lugging packs. Lieutenant Grant worried about the army teamsters, foreigners who volunteered as drivers but had never held reins in their hands. These were Mexican mules—foreigners themselves. Grant decided the men would be teamsters before they got through.

At last, final inspection of troops and equipment. It included a grand review under Inspector General William A. Churchill. Detailed and thorough, a young officer called it. Colonel Hitchcock thought otherwise. Tangle-footed commanders further entangled bewildered privates. One brigade, he noted, was not maneuvered at all, and another only slightly.

He did admit that Worth seemed to know something of brigade movements, though his 1st was clumsy.

The colonel got after Taylor again. "General Taylor knows nothing of army movements. We ought to be the best instructed troops in the world, but are far from it, except the regiments, which as regiments, are instructed." It was the case of units too long isolated in scattered detachments. As a drillmaster, only Hitchcock suited Hitchcock. "I can do anything with the 3rd Infantry, for every officer and man knows his place and duty."

On Sunday, March 8, 1846, at 10 A.M. the march for the Rio began. "The roads are in good order, the weather fine, and the troops in excellent condition," so Taylor informed the War Department, and medical reports bore him out. Colonel Twiggs led off with the 2nd Dragoons and Ringgold's battery. On Monday, Worth took out the 1st Brigade and Duncan's guns. Colonel McIntosh started the 2nd Brigade next day and, on Wednesday, Whistler's 3rd, Bragg's artillery, Taylor and staff closed up the rear. A train of 307 ox- and mule-drawn wagons rattled along behind the columns. Altogether an army of 3554 officers and men were tramping ahead on disputed soil to serve an administration which drew back from quite committing it to war. President James K. Polk showed sense in hoping for more by negotiation than by anything Taylor's little army could achieve by force, if it came to that.

The army in motion started two kinds of record-keeping. Taylor set down the official one day by day. On March 10 he passed the rear brigade, hoping to camp with the 1st, some 14 miles in advance. He wrote next on the 18th from Camp "El Sauce," 119 miles from Corpus: "The 2nd Brigade camps to-night 7 miles in my rear. I shall concentrate all my force on Little Colorado, 13 miles in my front, so as to be prepared for any contingency. I am happy to say that all the corps of the army are in fine condition and spirit, equal to any service that may be before them."

Old Zach's men could dead-end in confusion on parade evolutions by brigades, but marching in four columns on full alert, they looked good to a general who knew the value of morale. Foreigners or not, so many of them, they had learned the essentials. An order "To the right by column" still gave them trouble, but they could take to the road in respectable alignment. And like all soldiers moving from here to there, they were curious. What would "there" turn out to be? In peacetime "there" usually seemed the same as "here," yet even cynical regulars would always trade old boredoms for new ones. If fighting broke the routine—well, it was high time something broke.

With Taylor's dispatches toting up miles covered, indicating brigade positions, encampments, etc., the officers in their letters and journals rounded out the story. Lieutenant Sam French recorded the first night's stop, in a beautiful place covered with hyacinth, a place enchanted and drowsy, except for rattlesnakes. "That night I slept on the ground and dreamed a great centipede was crawling over me."

Aside from snakes and a Lieutenant's bad dream, the first four days out went pleasantly enough. Columns passed through farmlands with their cultivated fields, and skirted tree-fringed lakes. Masses of flowers colored their route—spiderwort, fireplant, lupin, and phlox. The striking Spanish bayonet reminded Kirby Smith of ships' masts in the distance. He and others gave up counting the herds of antelope and wild horses.

March 14 brought a change. The road underfoot turned to sand with the sting of hot ashes. Lagoons had shrunk to caked rings of brine. Drinkable water lay a whole day's march behind. Seeing men somehow stagger along without it, Grant wondered why certain officers insulted them as "dumb foreigners." They were good soldiers. Even so, many began to lag and drop out. A pulsing, vertical sun crisped every step of the way ahead. Straggling mounted. Then Surgeon Madison Mills gave credit to Bragg for practically saving the army. Somewhere along the way he had searched out a safe source of water.

Trust Bragg. It took live men and horses to maneuver his guns.

Next day it took Colonel McIntosh to half-kill off his command. Kirby Smith said he marched and countermarched the brigade in midafternoon heat for over an hour. Not many of them had the strength to pound tent stakes by time "Old Tosh" found wits enough to let them camp.

4

On March 20, General Worth's 1st Brigade reached the Arroyo Colorado. It was a salt river, or rather lagoon, about 100 yards across and barely fordable. Excitement sparked through the column. This might be something. Staff officers, men, and camp followers threaded back toward the rear with the news. Twigg's advance had been warned by a Mexican party of horse before reaching the river: an American attempt to cross would meet resistance.

Taylor also had been warned earlier, in a chesty proclamation by General Francisco Mejía, commanding troops in the city of Matamoroş. It was across from this city that Zach intended to plant his army. The Rio Grande would lie between, but in Mejía's words that river would "witness the ignominy of the proud sons of the north. . . . We shall fight, and the crown of triumph shall be the merited reward of

[our] valor and discipline. *A las armas! Viva la nación Mejicana!*" Now it looked as if the Mexicans meant to fight even for this river, Little Colorado, 30 miles north of the Rio.

Meanwhile the Americans' 2nd Brigade had moved up, so Taylor began giving orders. By 9 A.M. he had the 2nd deployed into line on right of the 1st Brigade. Two field batteries covered the point of crossing, where men cut away the 30-foot banks to the ford.

Next the general sent Captain Joseph Mansfield to parley with a Mexican scout still on the north bank. Taylor's General Orders No. 30 had already circulated for some days among the towns below the Rio Grande. Without Mejía's heaving rhetoric, it assured all Mexicans of Taylor's peaceful intentions. His only purpose was protection of Texas soil. Neither persons nor their property would be harmed. Mansfield repeated these statements to the scout, but added his general's warning that any Mexican who tried to prevent a crossing would come under artillery fire.

The scout carried the message back to the other side. In moments a great blowing of bugles shrilled from behind a screen of chaparral on the bank. Shouted orders picked up along the Mexican line—that is, if there really was a line. If there was, and it stood, Polk might get his war right here. Old Zach tested the degree of fight waiting across the stream. The first troops splashed into the ford, Captain Charles F. Smith at their head. Then Worth spurred his horse to beat the scramble of dripping blue uniforms up the rise of the south bank. The American Ney made his gesture in the grand manner, but saw it peter out in anticlimax. All that bugling and the shouted commands faded to a dusty scatter of Mexicans, under 300 in number. They broke without firing a shot. A band soon got across to strike up "Yankee Doodle," and a shaky peace hung on a while longer in the Rio Valley.

47

Taylor sent off a detailed report of this "first occasion on which the Mexicans have shown themselves in an attitude decidedly hostile . . . It also furnished," he went on, "an excellent opportunity for instruction of the troops, and for displaying their discipline and spirit, which, I am gratified to be able to say, were everything that could be desired." The old general's practicum was entering the examination stage.

The army had seen its leader under pressure for the first time. He meant business. Somehow brigades that could never maneuver to suit Hitchcock had taken position quickly, no tanglefoot about it. Field guns covered the crossing, in battery, unlimbered, matches lighted. Obvious enough moves, but they took sudden shape out of weary, sun-punished men. Few of the troops had ever fought. The hint of a battle in front had jumped nerves all along the columns. To form an effective line from this force, jam up against a river, showed a sure hand. Confidence filtered down through officer levels to the ranks. Old Rough and Ready. The boys in 1837 had named him right.

After its first alert the army went into camp south of the Arroyo for two days while the wagons caught up. Getting them and the teams through neck-deep water was a chore. Ropes hitched to tongues and rear axles steadied the wagons from both banks. Stubborn mules were yanked over before they could balk. Unique military engineering, but successful. March 23 saw the columns on the road again, four abreast at intervals for deployment at any threat. Captain Henry thought his general "showed great wisdom in all his arrangements." What Colonel Hitchcock wrote at the same time seemed hard to believe. He admitted that the army presented a fine appearance. The brush at Little Colorado had even impressed him.

Now the country improved. It looked more like the first

days out, with acacia in bloom and scenting the air, with grass, and more small game. About 18 miles north of Matamoros, Taylor left Worth in command of the march and turned ten miles east to his new supply base at Point Isabel. The escorted convoy had made the run down the Gulf without trouble, but Mexicans beat Conner to the base. They burned the customs house and destroyed several other buildings. In addition, Mejía sent a delegation of about 40 men to protest any farther advance by the Americans.

By this time Old Zach was tired of trifling. He had begun his march in an amiable mood toward the people south of the Rio. He still did not hate Mexicans and never would, but threats of resistance and burning villages annoyed him. They hardened the temper of his mission. Taylor was accepting a shift in title: from "the Army of Observation" to "the Army of Occupation." Occupation of what? Of southwest Texas, his government had been saying all along. Now in good conscience Taylor was taking his command to the north bank of the Rio Grande.

5

Under General Worth the army pushed eight miles closer to Matamoros, then waited for Taylor's return. Midmorning of March 28 brought the muddy Rio in sight, about 200 yards across, deep and fast-running between 20-foot banks. Captain Henry saw Matamoros as a "fairy vision before our enraptured eyes." One lieutenant thought the wide, right-angling streets and intersections had all the look of civilization again. For Sam French it was the promised land, a city of green foliage, with tropical plants surrounding white houses. Every-

49

body stared through homesick eyes. They were seeing their first city since New Orleans, almost a year ago.

Colonel Belknap had the honor of running up the first flag, the 8th Regiment's. It took over an hour to find a pole for raising the Stars and Stripes, and it raised Meade's hackles as well. Worth instead of Belknap got the credit. That general had not come up till after his brigade arrived, "and you can readily imagine how easy it would be for General Worth to have done it with his own hands when I tell you the pole was over thirty feet long, and required a big hole to be dug ere it could be sunk, &c, &c." In this same letter home Meade had been telling his wife a lot about Worth, and then he summed up: "He is a gallant and brave soldier, but he wants ordinary judgment; he is irritable and deficient in self-command."

The Americans got the flag up, and their bands played a concert of patriotic airs. From over the river watchers crowded the rooftops above a racket of their own making—music, bugles (Mexicans loved bugles), barking dogs, and a din of church bells. The uproar rolled across to the Americans on the north bank. Quite a reception, though what exactly did it mean? Mexican girls swimming naked in the river and waving at strange soldiers—what could be more friendly? But fieldworks looming above the water somehow contradicted the promise of flashing brown bodies below. Adding two careless dragoons who wandered from camp and fell into Mexican hands, the gay welcome from Matamoros seemed more apparent than real.

No man for scenery, even unclad señoritas, Taylor at once sent Worth over to talk with General Mejía. The Mexican refused to honor a visit by second of command but permitted Romulo Vega to meet the American party. In a scramble of English, French, and Spanish the two sides painfully managed a degree of communication. Even the spotty report of exchanges showed a brittle edge. Worth began by asking to see the American consul in Matamoros. Vega refused permission:

WORTH: Is the American consul in arrest or in prison?

VEGA: No.

WORTH: Is he in the exercise of his proper function?

VEGA: (*after consulting aides and translators*) Yes.

WORTH: Has Mexico declared war on the United States?

VEGA: No.

WORTH: Are the two countries still at peace?

VEGA: Yes.

Once more Worth insisted on his right to see the consul. In response Vega had questions of his own. Why was the American army here?

WORTH: I am well aware that some of the Mexican people consider it an aggressive act (interrupted at this point), but the American army was ordered there by the government and there it would remain. Whether right or not was up to the respective governments to decide.

When Vega broke in again, Worth answered that he had come only to state facts, not to argue them. He cited General Taylor's awareness of the city's need for commerce and of his respect for Mexican laws, customs, etc.

VEGA: Is it the intention of General Taylor to remain with his army on the left bank of the Rio Grande?

WORTH: Most assuredly, and there to remain until otherwise ordered by his government.

VEGA: We feel indignation over the presence of the United States flag on Mexican soil.

WORTH: That is a matter of taste. The United States flag is there in a peaceful attitude, only to protect United States territory on the left bank.

All this was in Worth's best style, arrogant, authoritative.

The lines fit the man, and he impressed the Mexicans. Old Zach they already knew about, and punned on his looks—"like the lowest Mexican *tailor*."

The interview finally ended on Worth's third demand to see the American consul. U.S.-Mexican relations were faring no better at the point of military contact than they were in the hands of civilians in the two capitals.

In the next days Matamoros followed its routine undisturbed by the guests across the way. Well, not wholly undisturbed. Soldiers began swimming the river. Taylor posted guards to stop them. They shot one deserter on April 4, another on the 5th. Meade blamed the two dragoons captured the first day. After Taylor had secured their release, their stories of fine treatment went the rounds. The delights of capture tempted others. One night 14 men went over. Henry saw what happened to one man. A perfect bit of marksmanship sank him at almost 200 yards. Only a rifle in good hands could have made the shot, a skill that impressed the captain. But by the middle of April the Matamoros *"Gazette"* was claiming 43 Americans won to the Mexican cause, and expected momentarily "Old Taylor, body and soul."

Nobody accused the Mexicans of planting bathing girls as a lure, though they did try other tactics. They knew the heavy foreign makeup of Taylor's army and rightly guessed at the large number of Roman Catholics. Matamoros played the Church to the hilt—bells for Mass, festivals, saints' day parades, music. They must have invented a new saint a day. The Americans could hear and see most of the celebrations from their side of the river; many a soldier felt an old-world pull.

A proclamation in English came over next. Stressing God and Christianity again and again, it read: "The most of you are Europeans, and we are the declared *friends* of a majority of the nations of *Europe*. The North Americans are ambitious, overbearing, and insolent, as a nation, and they will only make use of you as vile tools to carry out their abominable plan of pillage and rapine."

First bathing girls, then saints' days, now proselyting.

The desertions gave Taylor a problem. He had gone to all the effort of training and conditioning an army only to have a potential enemy begin draining off the results. The leak had to be plugged. But with the United States and Mexico still technically at peace, how justify the shooting of men for trying to cross the Rio? They were not deserting in the face of an enemy. Congress might howl over Taylor's action. Meanwhile the general decided to go on shooting and hope for the best.

In time Congress did get wind of what went on. A House resolution asked "whether any soldier or soldiers of the United States have been shot for desertion or in the act of desertion; and, if so, by whose order and under what authority." Of course there they were, on the record, the first two victims of Taylor's tough policy:

No.	Name	Rank	Reg't	Co.	Where born
1	Carl Gross	Pvt	7th	I	France
2	Henry Lamb	Pvt	5th	D	Switzerland

Why these deaths? Because, Taylor answered, the Mexicans had already assumed a state of war and were using every device to encourage desertion in his army. Soldiers found entering the water were first warned to return. "How far I should have been justified," he ended one dispatch, "in seeing our ranks daily thinned by the insidious arts of the Mexican general without resorting to the most efficient steps to stop it, I cheerfully leave to the decision of the War Department."

6

Congress dropped the inquiry on desertions, and Old Zach turned to other matters. Within days he had lost two of his brigade commanders. He had to relieve Colonel Whistler of the 3rd for drinking. And from the 1st Brigade, General Worth had to leave because of pride. That old ruckus about brevet rank erupted again. In faraway Washington, Polk had reversed Scott by deciding in favor of actual rank. He found his general-in-chief's support of brevets both exceptionable and insubordinate. Maybe the U. S. Army should do away with a general-in-chief and send Scott to some post on the northern frontier. The result of Polk's ruling, as it affected Worth, meant that Colonel Twiggs now superseded him.

General Worth would have none of it. He would resign. He would regretfully "cease to belong to that beloved service and profession which I have idolized for thirty-three years. I can no longer remain in it with honor or self-respect."

The 8th Infantry lined up in farewell. A teary-eyed Belknap bussed the parting brigadier (by brevet), who mounted and rode down along the blue front. Ney was taking his leave—this officer about whom it was said "The fables must be searched to find . . . a more sparkling eye, more gallant bearing, or one who was more prodigal of himself where the clang of arms was loudest."

Meade damned Worth again. Taylor, he said, had used every argument to hold Worth, including private information about a Mexican movement. "Still he went off." Colonel Hitchcock reacted too. "So Worth leaves us while the very atmosphere is animated with rumors of attacks on us." Then the grandson of a Revolutionary hero asked a rhetorical question. How would one of Washington's officers have fared had he aban-

54

doned his post in the presence of an enemy over a petty grievance?

Four days later, on April 12, Hitchcock followed Worth out of camp. After nine or ten miles in the saddle, he switched to a bed in a wagon. He was off for a two-month sick leave.[4]

Another problem for Taylor was multiplying Mexicans. Their troops had numbered about 3000 in and near Matamoros from the time the Americans arrived on the left bank. Then on April 11 General Pedro de Ampudia brought in 2000 infantry, 200 cavalry, and six fieldpieces. The cavalry and guns were under General Anastasio Torrejon. Four hundred more irregular horse under General Antonio Canales and 500 Matamoros volunteers gave the Mexicans a total above 6000. At best, Taylor could count on half that number to oppose them if fighting broke out.

But for the three fieldworks across the Rio the American general had an answer—a fort of his own. Engineer officer Mansfield began a survey the day after the army encamped. Construction had started on April 4 with plans for a fully enclosed area 800 yards in perimeter, walls to be nine and a half feet high from ground level and 15 feet thick. A ditch eight and a half feet deep and 20 feet wide would surround the work. Taylor meant to stay.

Ordnance set four 18-pounders in bastions facing Matamoros and bearing on the main plaza. Even so, Mansfield's fort was in a bad location, in a U of the river exposed to enfilade from above and below. But Engineer Meade felt all right about it. He said "at the first gun we shall rattle them about their ears in such a manner as will soon silence their fire." By April 11, Captain Henry reported good progress on construc-

---

[4] A Worth biographer, Edward S. Wallace, says Hitchcock had his leave extended for months and missed all the fighting in Taylor's campaigns.

tion. Kirby Smith reported the flies and wood ticks that took part. Another month would pass before the last sand-filled barrel was set in place to protect the powder magazines. Soon all the fort would lack was a deserving name.

The Mexican bluff at Arroyo Colorado and the burning at Point Isabel convinced Taylor that he camped in hostile country. General Ampudia removed all doubt. On April 12 he ordered the Americans to begin moving back to the Nueces River, and across to its north bank. Otherwise they stood on Mexican soil, and arms alone must then decide the question.

So far Taylor had been patient. Put a Napoleon or an Andrew Jackson in his place, the New York *Tribune* wrote, and "we should have had a murderous battle ere this." Just the same, Old Zach was staying put. "I shall not retrograde from my position," he informed the War Department. ("Retrograde" sounded more like Adjutant Bliss and certainly less belligerent than his general's next act.) At Taylor's request Commodore Conner blockaded the mouth of the Rio to choke off Ampudia's supplies.

A blockade was an act of war, as Ampudia quickly pointed out. Taylor in turn defended it as necessary in the quasi state of war the Mexicans had assumed. Again, exchanges between generals only matched the failures in diplomatic channels. In the City of Mexico, President Herrera had lost out to Mariano Paredes. By the end of March, John Slidell, still facing closed doors in an unfriendly capital, warned the new president's foreign minister. "Surely it cannot be necessary to remind your excellency that the menaces of war have all proceeded from Mexico. . . . The question has now reached the point where words must give way to acts."

The message had the sting of an ultimatum, but all it got in reply was a weary refusal to rehash old arguments. That and Slidell's passports.

Taking a tough stand against the United States made some sense at the time, or at least it did to the Mexicans. They still looked for America and Great Britain to tangle over Oregon. They also thought Congress would resist war below the Rio Grande. Their reading of speeches by Webster, Benton, Adams, and John Davis told them so. The Northeast would never stand for a war to fatten slave territory; even powerful Calhoun of South Carolina had turned against war. And in Britain and France there was talk of mediation, or intervention if needed, to favor Mexico in any crisis.

Besides, Mexico had the most soldiers, 32,000 compared to 8500 for the United States. Any war to come would take place on home ground with all its advantages. Over the years local infighting had given native troops a sharp edge in combat experience. In fact, the London *Times* saw good prospects for Mexico as of spring 1846:

> Nothing can be more ridiculous than the contrast between the zeal of the Americans in provoking war, and their real state of preparation for it; and a defeat will probably be sustained by the American forces, worsted by troops whom they have affected to despise, before the people of the United States have learned that bluster does not win battles, though it may begin brawls.

7

One thing sure, American zeal was being tested down on the Rio Grande. The calendar of events kept moving in one direction—toward war:

> *April* 12—Army chief quartermaster missing. Good quartermasters hard to find. Col. Trueman Cross one of best.

57

Did not return from ride out of camp on 10th. With army 800 miles by sea from nearest home base, loss doubly felt here.

April 14—Army on full alert. Great stir in Matamoros all day. Taylor expecting Mexican reaction to blockade off river mouth.

April 21—Body of Col. Cross found, bullet in head. General suspects guerrillas. Captain Henry says big funeral: flag-draped caisson, slow procession, three volleys above grave, flag run up, then back to camp by lively tunes. Typical military funeral: "no time for grief." But Taylor wants murderers. Search party out (20 men). Ammunition and muskets wet in rain. Lt. Theodoric Porter and one man killed in fight. Growing Mexican pressure reported.

April 23—Proclamation by President Paredes. Says new policy of defensive war: "So many and such bitter outrages can be tolerated no longer."

April 24—Larger party sent out, 63 dragoons, Capts. Seth B. Thornton, William J. Hardee commanding. Tricked into ambush by Mexican guide 28 miles up river. Attacked by Torrejon's regular cavalry. Casualties: 16 killed, 47 captured, including captains. Thornton a reputation for recklessness. Avenging Cross expensive. General Mariano Arista now in Matamoros. Tall, red whiskers, freckles—odd for Spaniard. Popular in city; plenty of wealth and political savvy. His orders that put Torrejon across river. New commander now offering 320 acres to every U. S. deserter. Number of Americans going over said to be near 200.

April 26—Taylor: "HOSTILITIES MAY NOW BE CONSIDERED AS COMMENCED." From Texas General wants 4 regiments volunteers—2 mounted, 2 foot. Wants 4 more regiments of foot from Louisiana. Total to be 5000 men. Hopes soon to prosecute war with energy; carry into enemy country (Mexicans claiming Taylor there now).

Polk had his war. The declaration, when it came, would merely confirm what had already begun.

With Mexicans on the north bank of the Rio, Taylor had to think of his base at Point Isabel. On April 20 he had authorized two companies of Texas Rangers to act as scouts. They were under command of Captain Sam H. Walker. The ex-Marylander had fought well against both the Creeks and the Seminoles, then later for Texas against Mexico. Ever since Taylor had been on the river, Walker had been after him to enlist his 75 men. Taylor held off, not from doubts of Walker's courage or ability, but because the Rangers stood for irregular warfare. They lived off the country and drew a thin line between legitimate booty and plunder. They laughed at discipline. Old Zach, though, had his mind changed by what had happened to Cross. Let guerrillas fight guerrillas.

So the general sent the Rangers out on reconnaissance between the army and its base. No discipline, no thought of pickets to protect themselves at night. Lack of simple precautions on March 28 cost Walker 15 men. That was bad enough, but for a man who worshiped good weapons the list of items lost must have hurt:

12 Colt pistols	6 waist belts
4 carbines	6 wipers
3 rifles (North's)	1 spring vice
12 bullet molds	2 army chests
12 boxes percussion caps	28 powder flasks
6 boxes cartridges	&c

"I certify that the above list of arms were in the possession and care of 15 men of my company . . . and that all these arms were lost." All of it modern equipment, painfully acquired.

That night Walker reached Point Isabel and asked for volunteers to ride through to Taylor—"at the risk of his life," read *Niles' National Register*, and like "a son of the old Mary-

59

land Line of Revolutionary days." Sam Walker made it too, with six men, and warned the general that communications between the army and its base were in danger.

On the last day of April a Mexican brigade and four guns under General Ampudia crossed the Rio Grande ten miles down from Matamoros. Now Taylor would have to cover Point Isabel. With Walker's warning he had reason to know that Arista's presence meant more than the defensive war of the Paredes proclamation. First Torrejon, then Ampudia. Zach Taylor's little army found itself pinched both from above and below.

One comic lift broke into the April build-up against the army. Five days after Colonel Cross disappeared, Lieutenant Edward Deas, 4th Artillery, decided that the quartermaster was a prisoner in Matamoros, or so he told friends. He, Deas, would swim over and search the colonel out. A valorous act indeed—till a newspaper got the story:

It appears that Lieut. Deas was officer of the day, and it was customary for American bands to perform the national air when the "Star-Spangled Banner" was lowered for the evening. This concert of sweet sounds attracted the attention of Mexicans on the opposite side, and crowds assembled on the banks of the river to listen to the strains of the music. Among them were many ladies. Lieutenant Deas became enamored with a certain Mexican beauty, and signs and tokens of affection passed between them; on the same evening [April 15] like another Leander, he plunged into the Mexican Hellespoint after his Hero.

A river came off misspelled, but not the facts, according to Zach's reaction. His report barely shielded the cause of the officer's absence: "Lt. Deas, 4th Arty, was laboring under mental alienation at the time he committed the unfortunate act."

The phrasing was pure bliss, Captain Bliss, and a euphemism like "mental alienation" deserved to roll down through the years. Almost cleansing words for any soldier pulled off base by the hot eye of a woman. But with Deas a prisoner, Old Zach struck his name from the rolls. War was a serious business and no time for lovesick lieutenants to go swimming off on romance.

Not that Taylor had worked himself into a state of nerves. A captain passing through New Orleans to recruit men in Texas told reporters that "The old general is as cool as a cucumber." Judging from other news, he needed all his calm. Texans were so cold to enlistment they would be lucky to fill half their quota.

New Orleans papers peddled gloom. A clip from an officer's letter said: "You will believe me when I tell you that this army will have the d——dest hardest fighting that ever an army had in this world. . . . I tell you, sir, the enemy have been entirely underrated, and this army has put itself in a trap."

Another writer, on May 2, sounded worse: "You need not be surprised to learn that General Taylor's army is destroyed or made prisoner within ten days of this time." Arista, he added, was an excellent soldier, and our government was stupid to send Zach down to the Rio Grande with such a tiny force. Of course both letters came from men with the army. Their timely appearance in print was hardly coincidence, given the slow response to Taylor's call for men.

But the *Picayune* of the same date, which seldom used anything larger than 5-point heads, broke out in bold 10:

THE ENEMY IS UPON OUR SOIL! LA VOLS, THE HOUR HAS ARRIVED!

New Orleans had just got word of the Thornton-Hardee brush. This news, along with the 10-point heads, brought results. The Louisiana legislature promptly raised $100,000 for enlisting and equipping volunteers. Tents went up in Lafayette Square. The area between Canal and Poydras Streets swelled into one great encampment, with bands, speeches, and a great rush to the colors. In time the exploding urge to rescue Zach Taylor's little army might even reach Texas.

There was action down on the Rio as well. Early on May 1, Arista marched out of Matamoros with a brigade and eight guns to join Ampudia at the crossing below. At 3:30 that afternoon Taylor started for his base at Point Isabel, 25 miles northeast on the Gulf. Some 2200 men beat through wet, waist-high grass until after midnight. Young Grant called it the hardest going he had ever known. Meade called it senseless. The Old Man must be asking for a fight. Otherwise why hogtie the army's movements with 250 empty wagons? There were plenty of rations in camp.

Not according to Sam French. The lieutenant always spoke well of food, and he worried about Arista's force downriver. From there to Point Isabel was only nine miles. Mexicans were about to curtail and diminish the pleasures of the table, French was sure. "In plain English, rations were getting short."

Taylor had left strength back at the fort opposite Matamoros: the 7th Infantry, Bragg with three 6-pounders and a 24-inch howitzer, and Captain Allen Lowd's four 18-pounders. He also left the sick and the wives who had followed their men down from Corpus. The "Great Western" was there—a mountain of woman who was already becoming a legend for courage. She laundered for some of Bragg's men, and they were proud of her.

The now completed fort could rely on 500 troops to keep Mejía's 1400 Mexicans pinned down in the city till Taylor's main force returned. That at least was the idea. Supplies and ammunition good for a week or better ought to allow time enough. And although Zach had split his army, so had Arista. Of course the Mexican leader could afford it; he had a big edge in numbers. But luck was with the Americans on May 1. Arista's men found only two boats for crossing the river. The day they lost should be all Taylor needed to reach his base.

The old general was showing plenty of confidence in his army. He had lost his second in command when Worth took his injured pride back to the states. His chief quartermaster was dead. Colonel Hitchcock, who knew all the evolutions of the line and how to maneuver whole brigades, had gone off on sick leave. By now the highest actual rank left in the army was that of colonel, and two officers held it—Taylor and Twiggs. The commander's star as brigadier was by brevet only. At that, the total effective fighting force fell under 3000.

Then why all the *sang-froid* or whatever mood gave Taylor the courage, or the recklessness, to make his move?

The general felt good about his men. With skilled help from the young West Pointers, months of drill and discipline had shaped a lean, hard tool. The toughening had sloughed off the invalid and inept. The 3rd Infantry, for example, dropped ten per cent in strength from January through March of 1846. In April the regiment lost only three men, solid proof that conditioning had taken hold.

So far the army had missed the yellow fever. The V*omito*, or "black vomit," was supposed to kill off Taylor's soft Yankee soldiers. Mexico's defense minister had counted on it as a special weapon, but it gave out in the cool breezes wearing in from the Gulf. Finally, no one had to tell this general that one way of keeping an army healthy was to keep it well fed. With the short march into Point Isabel early on May 2, he aimed to take care of its stomach.

CHAPTER III

PROFESSIONALS ONLY

On the day Taylor first saw the Rio Grande, March 28, James Polk made a hopeful entry in his diary. With the new Mexican president hard up for funds, he might be open to some kind of treaty. Slidell's offer to buy territory still stood. What Polk had in mind at this point, if Paredes resisted, involved Santa Anna. Since 1844 the ousted dictator had been living high in Havana. But along with cock fights and women, he managed a busy correspondence with his homeland.

In February of 1846 an agent from Santa Anna had dropped in at the White House. He brought a suggestion for the American President. A tough policy toward Mexico would force Paredes to negotiate. Let the Mexican people feel the threat of military power. Then let the United States offer some payment in advance on the territory it sought. Santa Anna expected soon to return there, Colonel Don Alejandro José Atocha went on, as a friend of the present government. Meanwhile he had kept in close touch with the country and well

64

knew its desperate need of money. He thought a half million American dollars would make a good start.

For Polk a good start meant his dream of getting New Mexico and points west, including Upper California. To Santa Anna a good start meant Paredes in trouble—for selling off Mexican land. By all logic the next move would be a call to the old hero of Tampico and Vera Cruz. Save the Republic! Santa Anna would be in.

Polk listened, but Atocha left for Cuba without a message. Dealing with Santa Anna hinted at too much cloak-and-dagger. Better to go easy. Better, Polk decided, to wait until he settled the Oregon boundary. First he wanted Congress to pass his resolution ending the agreement of 1827 (joint American-British occupation of the entire territory). The President was still looking John Bull straight in the eye and expecting no trouble.

In the Senate, on March 30, Daniel Webster made the right sounds: "I am of opinion that this question must be settled and settled shortly, on the parallel of 49°." That suited Polk exactly, though the lingering echo of "Fifty-four Forty or Fight" kept him from saying as much. And there still was fight in the Northwest. Senator Cass showed it in following Webster the next day: "The American title now held embracing the whole territory between the parallels of 42° and 54° 40' is the best title in existence to the entire region." Carried too far, the President was afraid this sort of talk would stir up Great Britain just when a Mexican solution was hanging fire.

By April 7 Polk knew that Slidell had failed in the City of Mexico. It called for bearing down, and when his Oregon resolution went through on the 23rd, he was ready. Great Britain would never fight for Oregon south of 49°. She had trapped out the best furs; she already felt the heavy pressure of American population in the territory; and she had too many other problems. At this stage speak softly to the lion and Oregon would come out all right.

So far, good. Now Mexico.

Slidell's bad luck in Mexico helped Polk at home. Newspapers began to banner American rights and dignity, insults to her honor. Talk about war caused less shock in Congress, though nothing was done in the way of preparing. Nobody in Washington made a move toward gathering intelligence about the country to the south. Down on the Rio, Taylor had a few land maps, but no two of them agreed within 20 miles on anything. Mexican climate was largely mystery.

Before the end of 1845 both War Secretary Marcy and General-in-Chief Scott had put in for more troops—a new regiment of artillery and three of infantry. At the same time they argued for more strength in existing units. Not full strength, of course; they knew better than to ask for that. Nothing happened, not even after Taylor's warning that the Mexicans were showing fight. All the administration granted him was permission to levy volunteers from Louisiana and Texas—that is, if he could establish the "approach of a considerable Mexican force." Then he might send officers 900 miles by boat to New Orleans to recruit citizen soldiers. How many would sign up, when could they be armed and equipped, officered, and shipped down?

In the spring of 1846 that was Taylor's problem. Behind it lay politics. As a Whig, Scott weighed light with the Democratic administration. Worse yet, he looked like a front runner as presidential nominee for '48. His availability did not endear him to Polk. Thus, while Taylor was running into more and more Mexicans down on the border, the President and the general-in-chief barely communicated. Scott offered no information, no advice or suggestions, and no program. In turn the President asked for none. Instead, throughout the month

66

of April he worried his diary about Democrats too busy politicking for the coming elections and about powerful senators like Benton and Calhoun who talked against war with Mexico.

In May, Slidell reached Washington. He came back bitter "over injuries so long endured." The President must act. Agreed, said Polk, but there had to be some excuse, some hostile move against Taylor. As the Lord knew, Mexico's refusal to pay admitted debts or to recognize the annexation of Texas gave cause enough. Yet Congress and the country would hang back unless or until they saw evidence of aggression against the United States.

The evidence was already on the way north, contained in Taylor's April 26 report of the attack on Thornton's and Hardee's dragoons. It would be May 9 before Polk got it.

2

On May 2, Zachary Taylor had led his tired men into Point Isabel. Loading the wagons would take some days; the army set up camp to wait while Mexican labor brought off the guns, ammunition, clothes, and food from the ships. At the mouth of the Rio below, Conner's four frigates, four sloops, and three brigs still bottled commerce upriver. But Matamoros had an answer of sorts. On the 3rd it began shelling Taylor's fort across the water. An echo of gunfire bounced up along the Gulf to the army's base. It shocked Lieutenant Grant into confessing "I felt sorry that I had enlisted."

A story in the Matamoros "Eagle" of the 4th would have depressed him more. It claimed all kinds of destruction to the Americans and their fort. "They had not the courage to load their cannons." How overrated their artillery had been—their great 18-pounders against Mexican 8s. "A ball scarcely fell before the children ran in search of it, without fear that another, directed by the same arm, might strike in the same place." The *Eagle* admitted only three Mexican dead by the end of the 3rd. Its estimate of Americans killed was 56.

Taylor's garrison had its own reporter. At the end of the bombardment he filed his version for the papers at home in the states:

On the morning of the 3rd at daylight the Mexicans opened their batteries on our fort, or rather our grand entrenchments; from that moment it was right hot work until after 12 o'clock, when both parties had to cease until their guns would cool. Were you ever shot at, in front with a 12-pounder, on a flank with a 6-pounder, and a shell directed to burst over your head? If not, try it, just to properly enjoy a brandy toddy after the gun cooling begins. Well, after refreshments the ball continued. . . . It was only 23 minutes after we commenced our fire before one of our 18-pound shot struck their 12-pound cannon directly in the muzzle, and knocked it, head, back, and stomach into the air 20 feet, and it was accompanied by legs, hands, and arms. Seven Mexican officers were wounded, and 8 privates who were around their piece killed. We have not heard from their 12-pounder since.

What could old Major Brown add to that? When he made his official report on May 4, the fort's commander left out the brandy and flying anatomy, listed one fatality, and regretted that Bragg's 6-pounders fell short of effective range. The next days would leave defense to the four 18s.

Up at his base Taylor had heard the guns. Several officers advised him to break off loading and rush back to save the fort. Instead he sent Sam Walker and four others to get through if they could and learn how Brown's men were doing. Captain

Charles May of the 2nd Dragoons was soon back. Too many Mexicans between the base and the river, he said. When Walker was still out on the morning of the 5th, Meade began to worry. The fort must be cut off from all sides.

Later that morning, though, Walker did get in—the only one to make it. He reported that Major Brown could hold out as long as he had food and ammunition. The major was being stingy with his 400 rounds for the guns, and not at all bothered by an attacking force in rear of the fort. This information satisfied Taylor and relieved Lieutenant Meade, who was sure the works could never be carried by assault. Engineer Meade gave full credit to Engineer Mansfield for both design and construction.

While he was about it, Meade went on to review prospects in general. A hundred and fifty recruits to fill old units and four companies of the 1st Infantry had shipped in and would be kept at the base for defense. This gave Taylor about 2300 men to take back to the Rio. The one weakness, Meade thought, was in cavalry. The general had only 200 dragoons compared with an estimated 2000 Mexican lancers. As for artillery, he rated Ringgold's, Bragg's, and Duncan's batteries far ahead of anything he thought the enemy had.

Finally, as for chances of fighting, Meade said the army was anxious to whip the Mexicans before the volunteers began pouring in. West Point pride coming through. Captains Barbour and Kirby Smith were saying the same thing. Let professionals, men and officers both, do the job. End the old American fear that standing armies threatened a nation's freedom. The first Congress had leaned on it in 1776, to General Washington's annoyance. "The jealousy of a standing army," he insisted, "and the evils to be apprehended from it, are remote." But the prejudice survived even the sorry evidence of the second war with Britain. With a small ready force at last in being by the end of the '30s, a congressman from Virginia still had wide support for his fear of an army "enervated by the inactivity of camp," and "a moth on the public treasury . . ."

West Pointers knew all this history too well—this waiting till war struck and then relying on citizen soldiers to fight it. So now let the new professional army make the test, they argued. Given victories, it would lay an old ghost.

May 7 saw the last wagon loaded and swung, or cursed into column. Colonel Whistler had a stack of somebody's books tossed out of a wagon to make room for a keg of whiskey. Why lug books to a battle? An officer demoted for drinking could at least be in on the fight—if properly fortified. Taylor put Major John Monroe in charge of the base, then wrote out the orders for marching. They were brave words that brought cheers in the reading: "It is known that the enemy has recently occupied the route in force; if it is still in position the General will give him battle. If his orders and instructions are carried out he has no doubt of the result, let the enemy meet him in what numbers they may."

It was time to relieve the fort on the Rio Grande. Point Isabel could now take care of itself. Commodore Conner had added 500 sailors and marines to strengthen the base. (But of what use they would be to Taylor, Captain William Harwar Parker of the Navy had his doubts. He had seen them in small-arms drill on board ship, so ready to load and fire and so dangerous to themselves. Once on land, a naval lieutenant could only think of "Double Up!" to form his men in two ranks. Point Isabel was going to be safer if Taylor met the Mexicans somewhere else.)

Seven miles out from the base Old Zach went into camp. Ahead of him stretched the prairies his army would cross to reach Matamoros. The road cut around water-filled ravines, or *resacas,* and bore through dense clumps of chaparral. At sunrise of the 8th the columns started on again, slowed by the heavy train, two 18-pounders hauled by oxen, and two unmounted 12s banging along in wagons behind. The day turned hot, with drinking water as hard to find as always in this semi-arid land.

Eleven miles more brought on the first brush with Arista's troops. The Mexican general had camped at a small pond named Palo Alto, then moved back for better water. Now he advanced in two lines reaching a mile in length across Taylor's front and splitting the road at right angles. On the American side "the long roll sounded, hearts beat, pulses kept time, and knees trembled and would not be still." So French recalled it, and he wondered what made Arista hold his fire.

In the strange, quiet interval Lieutenants Jacob Blake and Lloyd Tilghman rode out ahead to reconnoiter. This was boldness to the point of suicide; the two topographical engineers moved into musket range of the Mexicans. Still only silence. They took in the whole enemy front, like guests at a grand review, then cantered back to report. Mexicans left secured in a swamp fringed with chaparral, which screened cavalry and two guns. From that flank massed infantry and guns straight across front to tree-covered knoll on right. This flank also secure. Except for exposed main strength, enemy position good.

For Taylor and his men all the months at Corpus Christi and the weeks on the Rio Grande pointed to this sultry afternoon at Palo Alto. They were committed to fight their country's first battle against another race of people. They were part of its first standing army—men recruited and trained in peacetime. At company and field level they would be led largely by a new officer class, the West Pointers. The light artillery was new. In all, four impressive military firsts.

Both generals were defending their native soil, each fighting for the most righteous and glorious cause, his homeland. Taylor's government said the southwest Texas boundary ended where Texas claimed it, on the Rio Grande. Arista's government said the line reached north to the Nueces, the river John Quincy Adams had accepted in 1819. Whichever side won, justice was sure to be served.

3

Between 1:30 and 2 o'clock the Mexican general rode out along his front. "*Viva la Republica!*" roared up behind him over the din of brass bands. The cry called for a speech, and oratory was in character for the Spaniard. On the American side Zach was in character too. Slumped sidesaddle on Old Whitey, one leg hiked over the pummel, he chewed tobacco and talked casually to anybody that came up. A platoon sent to find good water filed quietly back from a stream and passed out filled canteens. Then the general began deploying his regiments. Facing south, they took position:

RIGHT   *LEFT*
5th Ringgold 3rd   2   4th Arty Battn Duncan 8th
Infy   Batt   Infy 18-lbers Infy (as infy)   Batt   Infy

Taylor set up his wagon park on the left to rear of his line. The 2nd Dragoons served as guards. It put both the park and horsemen near the road, which ran southwest between the two armies. Where it intersected his own line, the general wisely placed the lumbering 18s. These stations gave the road to everything that moved on hoof or wheel. Taylor had to protect his supply train. Meade called it a "complete incubus," and some officers had advised leaving the wagons at base to give the army more freedom to maneuver. But in his single-minded way, Zach thought otherwise. He had hauled those wagons up

72

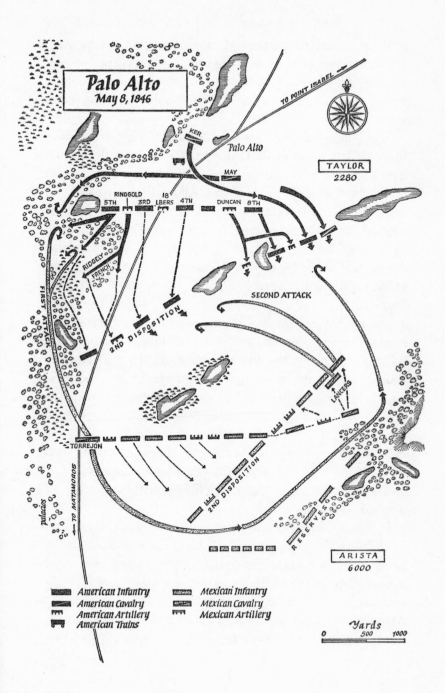

Palo Alto
May 8, 1846

TO POINT ISABEL

Palo Alto

KER

MAY

TAYLOR
2280

RINGGOLD   18
5TH   3RD LBERS   4TH   DUNCAN   8TH

RIDGELY
FRENCH

SECOND ATTACK

2ND DISPOSITION

FIRST ATTACK

LANCERS

TORREJON

2ND DISPOSITION

palacios

TO MATAMOROS

RESERVES

ARISTA
6000

	American Infantry		Mexican Infantry
	American Cavalry		Mexican Cavalry
	American Artillery		Mexican Artillery
	American Trains		

Yards
0   500   1000

to Point Isabel for a purpose. He needed supplies for the camp below, and by God he was going to take them there. Nor did he give way to second thoughts when a Mexican 12-pounder arched the first shot of the battle over his line and hit a teamster.

Arista followed the round by sending Torrejon's cavalry from his left to outflank Taylor's 5th Infantry (McIntosh). The Mexicans were after the train in rear. It would furnish the best subsistence they ever had. About 1000 men and two guns worked up through the chaparral for nearly a mile, or most of the distance between the two lines. Taylor countered by moving the 5th out to front and right in the form of a square. Old Waterloo tactics. It took nerve to advance in that order, with four faces exposed. Hard training must have gone into it.

Then the Mexicans broke from cover in a rush of leveled lances, flapping pennons, and raised carbines. The 5th Infantry's square caught the shock in right and rear. They held, waited for short range, and had the firepower to drive Torrejon off. He fell back on his two guns to reform his squadrons. But guns called for guns. Randolph Ridgely and Sam French swung forward with two pieces from Ringgold. His subalterns had waited years for this test, and they unlimbered and whirled into battery alongside the 5th. They hit Torrejon's second try at close range. His men fell away without getting off a round in return.

By now artillery fire along the whole front was sparking fires in the shoulder-high grass. A choking, acrid wall of smoke screened the two lines. For almost an hour neither side could see the other. Both used the blackout to change front. Pivoting from center, Arista wheeled his right forward and his left back. At roughly the same time, Taylor conformed by sliding his own front forward on an oblique to his right. About 4 o'clock the smoke thinned to show the new positions: like hands on a watch reset from quarter of three to twenty of two.

Taylor thought the retired Mexican left looked weak. Besides, he also could spare some cavalry. He picked a squadron of dragoons under Captain Charles May. In they went, the captain all flowing hair and mustachios. Sabers high, they made a hard ride from the wagon park down along the chaparral. But over the same ground, May had no better luck than Torrejon. After losing six men wounded and six horses killed, he pulled back.

It was Arista who had cavalrymen to waste, and this time he threw them against Taylor's other flank. Stopped on the right, then try the left. But Duncan saw them start out, backed by columns of infantry. He got permission to move down left in front of the 8th. He unlimbered at an angle just beyond but held fire till the lancers moved into case-shot range, and caught them point-blank. A flying shudder of steel raked horsemen back onto infantry and enfiladed their scrambling retreat. "Duncan's fire was really terrible in its effect," Captain Barbour said. Praise from the infantry, no less.

Field artillery was beginning to make friends at Palo Alto.

Arista kept pouring in cavalry now at Taylor's center. He had to knock out those booming 18s on the road. The Americans countered again with a square. Colonel Thomas Childs moved his musket-toting artillery battalion out of line and forward. Short ranges seemed to be the answer, so he waited for a distance of 50 yards. The 18-pounders and Ringgold joined in. The lancers peeled off, faded, but every Mexican piece that could get a fix turned on the American guns. Men began falling around them. Captain John Page lost his lower jaw. Another ball dropped Ringgold and his favorite mount, Old Branch. The artilleryman was hit in the thighs just below the crotch—an ugly wound.

The Mexican general, though, had given up. At 7 o'clock he drew back out of range and went into camp. With dark coming on, Taylor's men also quit. Now, who had won? Meade supposed the enemy must have got rather the worst of it. Grant thought losses might have evened out. Anyhow the groans and screams of wounded men ripped through a night otherwise moon-soft and beautiful. Captain Henry said the surgeons' saws kept busy.

On sunrise of May 9 one of the wagons beating back over the road to Point Isabel carried Sam Ringgold. Navy surgeon Jonathan M. Foltz came ashore to help if he could. The Pennsylvanian probably knew Ringgold as a grandson of John Cadwalader of Philadelphia, a general in the Revolutionary War. The two men held long talks through the captain's last hours. Ringgold made his final arrangements in good spirits. He had only two regrets. First, he was never able to bring his company up to full strength. Peak efficiency required 100 men. Second, he had labored for years to impress light artillery on the Army. Now, in its first combat trial he was struck down.

Ringgold was proud of the afternoon's work, of his battery's flexibility, its firepower and accuracy. Instead of taking blank aim at masses of men, he said his gunners picked individual targets. But knowing Taylor's prejudice against the arm, he wondered whether the general might now change his mind. Field artillery had been Ringgold's whole life, and he hated leaving without some official word on its performance. The captain died without ever seeing Taylor's report.

4

On the prairie at Palo Alto the Mexican general began pulling out before sunrise of May 9. By 6 o'clock he had his columns on the road south. Either he was retiring on Matamoros or else looking for better ground. If he found it, he could dig in and force the Americans to attack.

What should Taylor do? Arista was between him and the Rio Grande, where Taylor was bent on taking his wagons and even more set on relieving his fort. But some of his officers advised holding off. Why risk an outnumbered army against Mexicans on the defensive? Let them alone until reinforcements came up, troops called from Texas and Louisiana.

Although his own mind was made up, the general held council with the opposition. To attack, 4 votes; opposed, 7. One account had him ending the meeting with an order: "Go to your respective commands, we move forward in thirty minutes." Lieutenant Sedgwick saw and heard differently. As the council of war was breaking off, he said, Captain Duncan rode by and Taylor put the question to him.

"We whipped 'em today and we can whip 'em tomorrow," the artilleryman answered.

"That is my opinion, Captain Duncan." Taylor turned back to his officers. "Gentlemen, you will prepare your commands to move forward."

Another version gave Duncan's lines to Randolph Ridgely, and threw one in extra: "I hope Old Zach will go ahead and bring the matter to close quarters."

No matter who said what, Taylor called in the pickets, and ordered the horses untethered, fed, and saddled. The men ate, and by early afternoon struck out under a cloudless sky. Results of yesterday's work showed everywhere—dead Mexicans, dead horses, a litter of ammunition boxes, wrecked equipment, and weapons thrown away in flight. Maybe the Americans had won after all.

On this march Taylor left the train and the 18s behind with a guard. He pushed on with 2200 men, his column pinched into the roadway by the scrub growth on either side. An advance party of 150 under Captain McCall inched through the thorny cover on right and left, feeling for an enemy line. About 4 o'clock dragoons led by Lieutenant Alfred Pleasonton and some of Walker's Rangers began flushing small Mexican units. Soon McCall was reporting Arista's position to his chief.

It was a good one. Arista had picked the Resaca de la Palma to make another stand. The ravine lay at right angle to and across the road, dropped about ten feet in depth and formed a banana-shaped cavity 50 yards wide and close to a mile long. Chaparral running along its southern edge, or bank, gave protection to infantry and masked the batteries in rear. Cutting through the ravine, Taylor's road was his only approach, a narrow defile swept from above by enemy guns. No more prairie fighting for Arista. His new position canceled out the killing power of American artillery and gave his own a chance.

Ringgold's battery had gone over to Ridgely, and now Taylor ordered the captain to advance along the road. The 5th Infantry beat through the chaparral on his left, the 3rd on his right. The 4th deployed on both sides of the road in rear. Four hundred yards brought Ridgely to the north rim of the ravine and in range of three guns from the Mexican center. But by firing too high the enemy did nothing except expose its position.

Ridgely's men shed their coats, tied their suspenders around their waists, rolled up sleeves and put match to touchhole. Their general sat slouched on Old Whitey close by. When Ridgely's fire seemed to be taking effect, Taylor sent the infantry in under its cover. Both the 3rd and 5th lost all formation in the tangle of growth. The vegetation slowed them more than Mexican volleys until they ran into canister. Arista's guns had them in range from new ground out of Ridgely's reach. To get the guns out of there, Taylor called on May's dragoons.

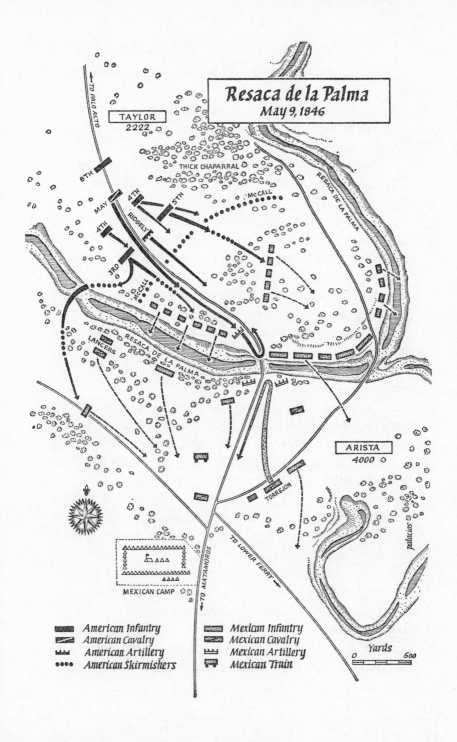

Resaca de la Palma
May 9, 1846

TO PALO ALTO

TAYLOR 2222

THICK CHAPARRAL

McCALL

RESACA DE LA PALMA

8TH

MAY 4TH

RIDGELY 5TH

4TH

3RD

McCALL

RESACA DE LA PALMA

LANCERS

ARISTA 4000

TORREJON

MEXICAN CAMP

TO MATAMOROS

TO LOWER FERRY

palacios

Yards
0   500

- ▬ American Infantry
- ▬ American Cavalry
- ⩊ American Artillery
- •••• American Skirmishers

- ▨ Mexican Infantry
- ▨ Mexican Cavalry
- ⩊ Mexican Artillery
- ▤ Mexican Train

"Your regiment has done nothing yet. You must take that battery."

It was May's second chance, and he brought his squadron pounding down the road in four columns. He pulled up behind Ridgely.

"Where are they?" May shouted. "I'm going to charge."

The captain heard him. "Hold on, Charlie, till I draw their fire."

One round picked the battery out and drew a return of grape shot. Then May went in. The dragoons swamped the first guns and belted on up the south rise of the ravine to take the others. They got a general too, as bonus—General Vega. But May's once-through pass overdid it. He had run through more than he could hold. Mexicans scrambled back to their guns. Ridgely retook them, then lost them again. When Taylor saw them going, he pulled the 8th Infantry up from reserve. "Take those guns and by God keep them!" he roared at Belknap. The men of the 8th did.

Till now the Mexicans had hung on. Up to a point they could be tough fighters. But after a while an officer or two would fall, or a gap open up in their lines, or the infantry would see the overpraised lancers tailing back to the rear. Suddenly the battle seemed hopeless, and they broke.

Here at Resaca de la Palma their general gave them no help. He sat out most of the action at headquarters, writing in his tent. Not even Taylor, he reasoned, was stupid enough to attack his strong position.

Too late Arista saw his mistake. He threw himself into a last-ditch gallop at the head of Torrejon's lancers. For moments they pressed Taylor hard. A few got so close they had Ridgely whipping about with his saber. But Old Zach had reserves. The Artillery Battalion backed up the 8th, the rest of the 3rd came up, also Captain Croghan Ker with the other squadron of dragoons. Duncan's battery had reached the ravine, but held its fire to keep from hitting its own infantry, which was already on the far side.

The Mexican front caved in when the lancers fell away on the left. Then the right collapsed and the whole army took to the rear. Taylor's men followed the flight all the way to the Rio, three miles south. The 4th Infantry got Arista's tent, with all his papers, expensive plate, and baggage. The Spaniard lived high in the field. In their frantic race for the river, the Mexicans left fresh-killed beeves and dinners still cooking—more proof of how secure their general felt.

That bullheaded Taylor!

5

By the evening of May 9 Taylor's garrison on the river would have rocked the banks to salute his returning troops. But sometimes the sight of enemy uniforms is even more exciting. Their wearers look beautiful in flight. Soldiers mounted the walls of the fort to cheer the first of Arista's men, stumbling and sliding down to the water in a gamble to make it across. Hoarded shells from the magazines prodded them along. Seven days and nights without sleep were ending at last. Nobody argued over the wild estimate of 3500 shells lobbing in or over the fort.

May 6 had brought the first pinch. Mexican infantry and lancers worked to within 500 yards of the bastion in rear, then sent in an order to surrender. Captain E. S. Hawkins had trouble with its language and his answer, but managed to communicate a clear American *no*. He spoke for old Major Brown, who had been hit in the leg by a shell. The enemy attempt to surround the fort finally gave Braxton Bragg a target he could

81

reach, though in driving the Mexicans off he lost four of his big Louisiana horses.

Mexican accuracy was improving. By the 8th four mortars were lofting shells in from three sides. One shot knocked out $300 worth of musical instruments. On that day Jacob Brown died, too soon to hear the only music that counted now—the sound of guns to the north. The combat reporter who covered the early part of the week was still turning out copy: "We well knew that it was the general poking it into their short-ribs." And none too soon, with ammunition running low. "We gave the Mexicans an occasional 'crowder,'" he wrote, "to let them know 'the degenerate sons of Washington' were not all dead yet."

As Taylor's force began coming up, Colonel Childs threw pickets out along the river to catch the Mexicans still trying to cross. Most of them escaped by going over far below or above the fort. For the time being Taylor let them alone in Matamoros. Meade and some others laid his delay in taking the city to lack of transport. The War Department had failed to furnish the pontoons the general asked for back in August of 1845. Too much paper-shuffling in Washington. And the Mexicans, in escaping, had grabbed off most of the boats on the river.

Meade was all for bridging the 150 yards of water and marching the army across at once. Taylor had engineers, and although timber was scarce, the troops could have found a supply. But no, "the old gentleman would never listen or give it a moment's attention." It was a Taylor defect, Meade concluded, that he wasted his engineers.

If Taylor had a defect, it was more likely his age and his years on the frontier. Thirty-seven years in service of his sixty-two years of age without ever missing the new hocus-pocus of army engineering. He was old, old army in both habit and

82

thought. You whipped the enemy; you drove him from the field; then you went into camp. You buried your dead, took care of the wounded, replaced your losses (if you could), and restocked your supplies. You sent the government a report of your battle and asked for orders. Whoever heard of tracking a beaten army to the end? Let the enemy go off and lick his wounds. In winning, you picked up enough of your own. Eventually, you might have to fight again, and—well, you had to get ready.[1]

After all, Taylor had just won himself two battles. They left him with only four field officers, and he had captains leading regiments. With neither pontoons nor boats, he would not risk a crossing. So he buried the dead of both sides, put the wounded under care (again for both sides), wrote his reports of Palo Alto and Resaca, added a congratulatory order to his troops, then set off with an escort for Point Isabel. From there on May 12 he informed the War Department that he was conferring with Commodore Conner on a combined move up the Rio Grande. And he promised to lose no time in occupying Matamoros.

Back in camp the army settled down to refight the battles. Palo Alto turned out to be more one-sided than anybody thought, now that the numbers and losses were in. Nine killed, 44 wounded, and two missing out of 2228 for Taylor. The Mexicans lost 200 killed alone, and several hundred more in wounded. Private Barma N. Upton thought he had the answer

---

[1] Failure to follow up victories hung on through the Civil War, with Antietam and Gettysburg as prime examples. High casualties, primitive medical care, lack of transport, of good roads, good maps, and proper communications and equipment—especially for night fighting—all discouraged pursuit. Battles usually ended with darkness. But Taylor was criticized for not crossing the Rio Grande at once after Resaca de la Palma.

for the American casualties: "I found what old soldiers tole me true, that they shoot dreadful careless in battle." By "they" Upton meant both sides. Though higher Mexican losses hurt his case, the armies at Palo Alto actually lined up too far apart for effective small arms fire. It was a picture-print battle, two massed fronts facing each other on a plain and blasting away. Formalized and neat.

When the 5th Infantry and later the Artillery Battalion advanced in formation of squares they looked easy to hit. But the charging lancers had to knock them out by impact. They had to close in. What good was a lance at 50 yards? Musket volleys from the squares kept them off to save what could have been high losses for Taylor.

Everybody agreed that Ringgold, Duncan, and the 18-pounders made the difference at Palo Alto. Arista admitted taking 3000 rounds against his 750. Shell, grape, and canister accounted for most of his dead and wounded. Taylor's field artillery wrote off an old prejudice and won a convert on May 8: "to the excellent manner in which it was maneuvered and served is our success mainly due." Poor Sam Ringgold should have lived to read this. His general had finally forgotten the lumbering pieces of 1812 and the slow-hauled guns that later stuck in Florida mud.

The army had a new weapon, no doubt of it. From now on Old Zach would give it every chance, as he had even over the bad ground of Resaca on the 9th. Chaparral pinched Ridgely into or close to the road and held up his infantry supports. Duncan never did find working room until too late to help. The brilliant guns of Palo Alto simply ran out of space in the second fight at Resaca de la Palma.

May 9 had been mostly an infantry battle, and it took even more out of both sides. Of Taylor's 2222 men, casualties totaled 39 killed and 82 wounded. The Mexicans listed 262 killed, 355 wounded, and 185 missing out of about 4000. The Americans put Arista's loss higher. They counted 300 dead alone on the two fields, and Meade said another 300 drowned trying to swim the river. On the second day Taylor had captured 8 guns and over 100 prisoners, including General Vega and 14 other officers. In addition to the guns, Grant estimated the booty at something like 1000 small arms, 250,000 rounds of ammunition, 400 mules, harness, camp equipage, and musical instruments. The horns and fifes would restock Taylor's band from the fort. The fanciest loot of all seemed to be Arista's personal stationery. For weeks West Pointers filled sheets of it as mementoes to their families and friends.

May 8 and 9 had been good days for Taylor. His men had the best of it in firepower, organization, discipline, and morale. Their flintlocks were at least improved models, 1841–42. Some companies carried percussion muskets, and a few had rifles. By contrast most Mexicans fought with small arms a century old, the Tower muskets of London. With good luck they could hit a man at 50 yards. At 200 a Tower could miss a battalion. As for artillery, the Mexican pieces threw only solid shot, and aim was poor.

Mexican organization was loose. Scattered and largely alien states sent line regiments, sapper battalions, guard units, presidial companies, and auxiliaries. The cavalry rated itself cuts above the ill-served half-breed Indians of the infantry. Some of the troops had come up to Matamoros in early April, under Ampudia. The rest marched in with Arista, who then had to put an army together in the city. The mixed outfits, the split loyalties, and lack of time were against him.

Morale? Not from a patched-up army, from soldiers whose idea of country was limited to local generals and the black-robed priests of the Church. Taylor's men from the British Isles and western Europe were not quite Americans, either;

but they had come of their own choice. Meanwhile they enjoyed, or endured, a built-in allegiance. They were part of the iron-tight unit that Old Zach and staff had coaxed, bullied, and beaten into an army. The few Irish and Germans who skipped over to Matamoros were the exceptions. The recent battles under Taylor showed plenty of pride and morale, two virtues which were practically exclusive with the American side.

6

The two battles also culled plenty of sidelights. The overrated lancers, for one. Another was the Mexican music. Arista's army seemed almost to prefer concerts to fighting. They went on all the time, before and during action. (Up to this point, though, not after. At the end of May 9 the Mexican pace was too brisk, even for lugging the instruments to the rear.)

Kirby Smith had a more grisly note. After Resaca he counted 85 Mexican dead in a single pile stalked by wolves, with vultures wheeling and dipping above, and stench everywhere. Low water in the Rio Grande left bloated bodies at the river's edge, soldiers of Arista's flight who failed to make it. Captain Henry reported seeing stripped and mutilated American dead on the field. He said Arista blamed the women following his army. He could not control them. A strange war was beginning when women of soldiers crawled in under the first lifting smoke to scavenge a battlefield.

Meade made his point once more: the army that won the battles did it without volunteers. Would people in the states please take note.

Somebody else thought being an ox was a charm. Not one

of the 40 yoke was hit during the two days. Old Zach had certainly protected his train.

A correspondent described fat Colonel Belknap leading a charge. He was thrown from his horse and had to be propped in his saddle again. Still game, the colonel grabbed up a standard. When it was shot away, he kept bouncing on with the splintered staff in a whirl over his head. At another time French came across Colonel McIntosh pinned to the ground by a bayonet stuck in his neck. But Tosh was tough and he lived. Belknap and McIntosh were two warriors of 1812. In their day nobody stepped forward until he was led, and it still helped even with Taylor's regulars. Men remarked on the contrast with Mexican officers, who rarely rode out front.

Talk of officers in the advance of troops brought up another name. The whole army saw Lieutenant Blake at Palo Alto on May 8, well ahead of the lines with Tilghman and calmly sweeping the enemy front with his glass. On the morning of the 9th he went into his tent, unhooked his sword and belt and dropped them on a stool. A pistol attached to the belt went off. The shot hit Blake full in the chest. He died three hours later, crying only because of the way he had to go. (But at least the 8th had given him his hour. The two lieutenants on the exploding steamer at Corpus missed even that. These senseless, anticlimactic deaths depressed the West Pointers most of all.)

Any rehash of the fighting had to include the chaparral. It marked a new kind of battlefield, these thickets 100 yards to a mile across, thorn-sharp, meshed with briars, and embedded with prickly pears. One writer marveled that men fought where a rabbit could hardly belly through. At Resaca, Ridgely's infantry supports had to hack out elbow space in order to fire. Even the unhit crawled out of the scrub torn and bleeding like true casualties.

Battles always have their heroes, especially on the winning side. With the army Old Zach stood first in the list. Grant idolized him. Henry proudly watched him on horseback at Resaca, musket balls rattling all around. To someone advising him to move back out of range, he said: "Let us ride a little nearer, the balls will fall behind us." Another story had the general riding into the 5th Infantry square at Palo Alto. "Men, I place myself in your square." Great cheering.

Let men start trading talk like this around camp and facts shade over into legend. But the legend of Taylor's courage had a solid base. As skeptical a soldier as Meade put his chief above that absent model of leadership, William Jenkins Worth. Still it was like Meade to worry the idea through: "General Taylor did omit to do things many considered he ought to have done, but which now turn out to be unnecessary. . . . In military matters, as in all things else, success is the grand criterion by which men are judged."

Sam French used fewer words. He said Taylor's simplicity and coolness had endeared him to all the army. The young professionals like Grant, Henry, Meade, and French were finally judging the top command. Now that the verdict on the first two battles was in, the old guard who missed West Point came off with good marks.

In winning, Taylor did more than merely stay up front with his men and keep his head. At Palo Alto he also kept a tight hand on movements. Meade was only one staff officer who carried the general's orders during the afternoon. One order was useless—instructing the infantry to rely on the bayonet. Neither side ever got that close. Sending May's dragoons down to Arista's left was another wasted effort. A case of too few men. But putting the two 18s in line on the road did wonders. The squares worked out too, an outdated maneuver against an outdated weapon.

At Resaca de la Palma the general showed good judgment in leaving his train behind, in advancing skirmishers before committing himself too far along the single road, and in refusing to waste too many troops too soon on bad ground. French thought Taylor did let Ridgely get too far without his infantry support. As it turned out, though, May was sent in at the right moment. By the time the Mexicans drove him back, Ridgely had the help he needed. From then on the regiments fought their way forward without orders. It hardly mattered, for Zach had made the big moves when they counted.

Hero number 2 had to be Ringgold. He deserved his place less for his short hours at Palo Alto than for his fight to develop light field artillery. Ridgely's four rounds a minute at Resaca were only an end result though they made him number 3, right after the captain himself. What Ridgely did so well, Sam Ringgold had taught. To the extent Ridgely followed the master—and the same went for Duncan and Bragg—the army would keep on proving its new tool. Field artillery owed everything to Ringgold.

How about Charlie May? Hero? He took his 70 or so men in twice, and a cavalry charge always met everybody's dream of hell-for-glory. At Resaca the dragoons swamped seven enemy guns, cutting them out at the peak of Taylor's push. A sergeant captured General Vega. Yet it took Ridgely and the infantry to hold the guns for keeps and to cover May on the way out. May lost a lieutenant, seven privates killed, ten wounded. Twenty-eight horses fell, those good stout animals from the states.

What did Captain May get for his two days' work? Mostly two brevets—that was the kick around camp. French said, "Nothing like blowing a horn and having friends at court." May's good press at home did not impress the Army. Ridgely, for example, looked far better in the two battles and still got only a single brevet. He turned it down.

Two non-heroes soon came in from across the river. Captains Thornton and Hardee were released in a prisoner exchange. An army board of inquiry would have to fix the extent of their responsibility for losing over 60 men by riding into a trap. Present feeling about them was mixed. Brave and aggressive officers, but apparently short on judgment.

Taylor's fort got into the camp talk too. Old Jacob Brown died in defending it, and now it carried his name.[2] The general called his loss "irreparable." Otherwise, in 169 hours of dodging shells the garrison got off easy: a sergeant killed and ten men wounded. The dodging was real. Sentinels on the parapets would spot Mexican battery positions, then work out different signals for each. If No. 2 let go from directly across the river, everybody in Fort Brown knew where best to drop for cover. The system was efficient except for mortar shells. Their high, crazy lobs made their fall points hard to judge.

The garrison's toughest hazard had been mental. Five hundred men watched three-fourths of their army march off, leaving them pinned in a fieldwork with Mexicans on both sides of the river. Food and ammunition rationed at a guess—say two weeks. Would their general come back in time? Suppose he failed to make it? On May 8 the troops in the fort could have heard those first guns at Palo Alto in two ways, good or bad. No wonder Reynolds of Bragg's battery voted for ten battlefields in preference to one more week cooped up on the river bank. Captain Henry, who was not even in the fort, upped the number to twenty just from what the "inmates" said.

Nobody who knew Bragg doubted his feelings. Flying artillery inside a fort! Ringgold, Ridgely, Duncan—big deeds, big

---

[2] Brownsville, Texas, today.

names. In the meantime Bragg had lost the four horses, a wheel from a caisson, and only one brief target to show for it. For his battery's best performance, he could bow to his laundress. By her careful nursing of the wounded, the "Great Western" had won her right to march with Bragg's company wherever the war led. Besides, she boasted the biggest leg in all Mexico.

7

Up at Point Isabel the "web feet and barnacle backs" of Conner's fleet were celebrating the victories. Taylor's staff had trouble keeping them out of the general's tent. If their commodore held them out of the fighting, at least they could whoop it up. "D—n blast my eyes, here is a ship ashore and poor Jack on his beam ends." The reporter who dug out that line had also seen the sailors drill. Worse than soldiers riding into battle on cows, he said, but the tars would have gone in with only knives and forks for weapons.

Navy Captain Parker thought Taylor showed great tolerance for the bluejackets. Of course Old Zach's common touch never left him. When he set out for the Rio camp again on May 13, a man from the New Orleans *Bee* saw him off "dressed in a simple farmer's apparel, and his mode of conveyance a light wagon, driven by a Negro servant." Soldiers, sailors, newsmen—everybody seemed always to see and like the general plain.

With his two victories behind him, no doubt Taylor's homely modesty wore better than ever. It only hid his granitic strength and purpose, which the *Bee* went on to next. "His dander is up since the last engagements, and he seems determined to show them that when the ball is fairly opened, the dancing must not close until the tune is played and the fiddler paid." Not a figure of speech the general would use himself, but it would read well both in New Orleans and farther north.

And farther north President Polk was waiting for Mexico to make an overt act. Or would he wait? May 9 found him leaning toward a declaration of war, but his cabinet meeting broke up with his Secretaries of State and Navy still urging caution. That evening news of the "act" arrived in Taylor's dispatch reporting the ambush of Thornton and Hardee. Thirteen days to bring news of April 26 to Washington. Although by now Morse's lightning wire tapped 1400 miles of country, hardly any of it stretched south. But Polk had the message. Mexicans had crossed the Rio Grande to fight Taylor. Back into session went the Cabinet. By May 11 Polk had a message of his own in the hands of both House and Senate.

"The cup of forbearance had been exhausted," he said, even before this latest act. Now Mexico had invaded American territory and shed American blood on its soil. Her own hostile act had therefore brought on the war in spite of all our efforts to avoid it. Polk built his case step by step. He had to because even the help of 63 killed or captured dragoons allowed for some opposition. He got it. The President had brought on the act himself by moving General Taylor's force to the Rio Grande. In the Senate Calhoun wondered if there was a man who could believe war existed in any constitutional sense of the term. Tom Benton would vote men and money to defend American soil as far as the Nueces River—not one foot farther. Senators Thomas Clayton of Delaware and John Davis of Massachusetts fought the message. John Quincy Adams said in the House that it merely brought to a head Polk's scheme for advancing slavery in the United States.

Polk won just the same. His declaration of war cleared the House 173 to 14, and the Senate 42 to 2. Only antislavery votes of "Conscience" Whigs went against him. The final bill called for mustering 12-months volunteers up to 50,000 in number, and extended militia terms from three to six months. It also voted $10,000,000 to carry out the provisions. To finance the war, Treasury Secretary Robert J. Walker advised raising $12,500,000 through notes and loans. A country recovering from several lean years might cool off in the face of higher taxes.

Senator Webster had an opinion on the kind of troops to be called up. "I would much prefer to have nothing to do with the militia of the states . . . we should organize and commission the regiments ourselves so they fight under one authority." For the Army these words were pure gain. A giant of the United States Congress had reservations about the citizen soldiers of the past. So did Polk, judging from his request for a volunteer force answering to the national government as "beyond question more efficient than any other description of citizen soldiers." Two of the country's leaders had been conning their military history.

Militia practically wrote the record of America's first two wars. Over all, the record was bad. It began in 1776 with General Washington complaining about the inept performance of "men just dragged from the tender scenes of domestic life." They made no bones about being on strictly temporary loan. Any action had better be brief and not too far away. The mare was about to foal, or the boat was bringing nails for the shop, or the stillhouse needed new coils. Soldiering annoyed them; it interrupted the things that counted—job, family, community.

When militiamen fought, they fought as amateurs under other amateurs they had elected as captains, majors, and colonels. Their loyalty stopped at state borders. Congress, of course, found fat political profit in hymning the "bone and muscle of our citizen soldiers," who in every emergency picked up their weapons, bid good-byes to tearful wives and children, then departed hearth and home to defend their country's honor.

But the militia had failed. Too parochial, too lacking in training, too poorly led. Webster's considered judgment deserved a reprise: "I would much prefer to have nothing to do with the militia of the states."

In the meantime all the war excitement had ignited that old recruiting genius, General Edmund P. Gaines. On May 4, before Taylor fought a battle, Gaines had written Kentucky's Governor William Owsley. He said he was asking the President for authority to raise and concentrate 50 battalions of 500 men each on the Rio Grande. This total was five times the number Taylor had asked Texas and Louisiana to furnish back in April. Besides Zach's call had already been authorized.

No matter, Gaines wanted to know how many men to expect from Kentucky. Governor Owsley tactfully stalled him off by praising his ardor while waiting for word from higher up. Kentuckians would never lag, he wrote the general, once he was sure he could go ahead. By this time Gaines was testing the patriotism of the other southwestern states.

The renewed beat of the general's personal recruiting drum had not yet reached Senate ears. Cass of Michigan was still talking about Gaines' first "army," of the Corpus Christi days. The old soldier had acted from the highest motives, he said, but he had acted unfortunately. The few volunteers ever to reach Taylor cost the government $61,500. If Cass had known what came out of it, he might have called it a stiff price to pay for Bragg's artillery horses.

In Louisiana the legislature remembered the early call too, and wholly in praise of Gaines. He had only responded to the

War Department's overwrought appeals for volunteers, if and when needed. Why expect an old soldier to resist phrases like "relying on the zeal and public spirit of the gallant militia," or "from the known patriotism and ardor of," etc.? True, Gaines had ignored the *if and when needed*, but to Louisiana his rebuff was inexcusable. The state's lawmakers voted a resolution of thanks for the general's devotion to country, unrequited though it was.

Now here was Gaines once more.

8

On May 13 Polk made his own move to rescue Taylor. He put Winfield Scott at the head of all troops in or planned for Mexico. Not that Scott impressed him much as a military leader—too scientific and visionary; but after all he *was* general-in-chief. Scott already was talking in numbers like 20,000 volunteers at once, in addition to recruits for the Regular Army. Too many, Polk thought. Generals always magnified their jobs, and Scott especially.

So much talk, so much paperwork. All those logistics: "Supposing the rivers to be navigable in all July for medium-sized steamers, mounted troops can be moved (but costly) from Kentucky and Tennessee by way of New Orleans and the Gulf to La Baca (branch of Matagorda Bay), thence to . . ." and on and on, with more assumings and supposings, until "I come to the second difficulty—can the troops, after getting into position, take up lines of operations beyond the river with any probability, nay, possibility of advance, in the month of August."

Scott was really making sense, but logistics bored the President. So did their fussy, pompous author, with his big Whig notions for the presidential election year of 1848. Then Scott dug himself deeper by writing Taylor on May 18 that he probably would not get down to the Rio himself before September. Why not? the President wanted to know. He informed War Secretary Marcy that the general would either leave soon or be replaced. Why were all generals Whigs anyhow?

Deeper and deeper. Next Scott asked that his orders for assuming Army command be put in writing. No executive, he insisted, ever sent an officer on distant duty of any importance without written orders. Polk, after getting this instruction from his general-in-chief, heard that he was also complaining about officer appointments for a new rifle regiment. They smelled of politics, said Scott.

They did. The President's excuse was the pressure of applicants, "beyond anything ever witnessed." Given so many regular officers of equal merit, he could not choose them all, and to prevent heartburning among them he would be wise to appoint officers from civilian life. Polk's limp rationalization brought howls from way down on the Rio when the word reached there. Meade was crackling: "We did not expect much better treatment from *Colonel Polk* . . . but the Senate has always stood by us, and you may therefore imagine our mortification . . ." John Reynolds called it the grossest kind of injustice and insult.

Scott's curse was his talent for going so far wrong in being right. He did deserve written orders for his new command, and Polk was passing over the professionals with an eye on giving the rifle regiment a safe political cast. But now the general-in-chief felt persecuted. Nobody was going to rush him off to the south with "a fire upon my rear, from Washington, and the fire, in front, from the Mexicans." This line in a letter to Secretary Marcy almost did Scott in. Then he topped even that in trying to crawl free. In a follow-up he said he was interrupting a "hasty plate of soup" to explain himself.

The pages spilled out pity for Scott—a dedicated servant, giving his government all, scarcely pausing for a proper meal, and rewarded only by hounding from his superiors. Both of the letters got into the papers, and a laugh went around the country that scared the Whig kingmakers away from Scott for good. Impaled on his own goose quill, as the phrase had it.

Orders for getting on with the war went out in spite of all the infighting. They directed Colonel Stephen W. Kearny at Fort Leavenworth to put his dragoons on the road for Santa Fe. They called on the Governor of Missouri for 1000 men to follow Kearny. They sent Brigadier General John Ellis Wool to recruit volunteers in Ohio, Kentucky, Illinois, Tennessee, and Mississippi. With regular troops as a nucleus, this force would drive from San Antonio southwest into Mexico.

Polk was not forgetting California. He hoped Kearny could make his way there before winter. But Commodore John D. Sloat's Pacific squadron had been cruising for nearly a year with orders to move into San Francisco and other harbors if Mexico declared war. In November of 1845 the President had hurried a special messenger west with secret instructions for three key persons. Sloat was one; the American consul at Monterey, California, another; and Frémont the third.

Captain John Charles Frémont, Army topographical engineer, had two successful surveys of Western trails and territory behind him. In the spring of '46 he was playing the opportunist in the Sacramento Valley. Nobody would outdo Frémont in promoting Polk's California dream. The President's orders reached him on the same day Taylor fought at Resaca de la Palma.

Now, what about Taylor? That was a question in Scott's letter of May 18, the one promising 20,000 volunteers on the

97

Rio by September. The War Department had not heard from Taylor since April 26. It knew about Torrejon's ambush of the dragoons, but nothing since. Scott was delaying more definite plans, he wrote Taylor, "until I can profit from your better knowledge of the enemy's country, when it is my hope to have the benefit of your valuable services according to your brevet rank and with the column that may be most agreeable to you."

These were kind words for a general about to supersede another in the field—words both more modest and careful than Scott had been writing Marcy and Polk. But with the news of Taylor's two battles in at last, Scott's modesty turned to positive caution. He said he would be ashamed to replace Taylor in command "after that general's gallant victories and before the arrival of competent reinforcements." Kinder words than ever, though only the second clause was honest. Scott would wait for his 20,000, thank you.

The what-about-Taylor interested Taylor too. He asked Washington for further orders on the assumption that the recent battles might have brought a change in administration policy. Secretary Marcy beat him to the question in a letter that crossed the general's. "I am anxious to hear your views as to the measures you propose to execute." Constructive thinking came hard for Washington, so far from the front, so unprepared for a war, so busy with the problems of administration, so shadowed by the politics of 1848.

CHAPTER IV

CITIZEN SOLDIERS

The "simple farmer" general got back to his camp on the Rio in the morning of May 14. He had already impressed the British consul in Matamoros by sending both surgical assistance and medical supplies across the river. This general who could not hate. But he did remember he was at war, and on the 11th ordered Lieutenant Richard Graham with a party to swim over for boats. He also had war on his mind when a Mexican officer rode up under a white flag to ask for a truce.

Too late, Taylor said, though Arista could pull his troops out of Matamoros if he left all public property behind, including ordnance. Taylor wanted an answer in two hours. No answer came. Instead, about sunset Arista's shrunken army took the road south for Linares. According to his official report, the Mexican general was leaving only to save the city from destruction. For the same reason Taylor was willing to let him go. So warfare, old style, carried on.

Now, to get the American army into Matamoros. Zach

99

moved up two miles from Fort Brown to make a crossing early on May 18. At daybreak some 4th Infantry and ten men under Sam Walker went over to reconnoiter. The Colt-toting Texan was proving useful. The 18-pounders and the field batteries covered the move. When it looked as if Arista had gone, more infantry followed Walker. Then Ker's dragoons swam their horses across. Ridgely's battery was torn down and hauled over on barges. After two hours a deputation of Mexican officials rode out in a splash of white—flag, horses, uniforms. Since their army had left, they asked, what kind of treatment might they expect? Taylor promised to protect both persons and property and not to interfere with local civil laws. He had already issued strict orders to his troops against plundering. Occupation of the city would be peaceful so long as the Mexicans cooperated.

At last, Matamoros! The dragoons cantered downriver to raise the flag over Fort Paredes. The army would soon be on the town. "Yankee Doddle. Did you ever hear it, dear reader? I reckon you never did, in a foreign land, just conquered by good, honest hard blows." That was Captain Henry's first reaction. Captain Barbour's was the excellent breakfast he ate, and Captain Kirby Smith's the fine cup of coffee he got that night. The men in ranks would probably name different items once they got in.

Next day most of the army except for guard detachments crossed on ferries opposite the city. One dragoon lieutenant, George Stevens, had failed to make it through the current on the 18th. His body was found two days later and given a military burial. Taylor wrote his regrets of Stevens' death in a dispatch to Marcy; Meade called him a fine officer; Barbour's phrase for him was "amiable and talented." Henry remembered the lieutenant as tremendous in May's charge at Resaca, and his loss depressed West Point classmate Sam French.

Stevens must have been good. Chance accidents between battles continued to pick off promising men.

With Matamoros in hand, Taylor sent his dragoons and the mounted Texans after Arista. They rode 60 miles south over parched land, running across spiked guns, abandoned arms, and all kinds of equipment and baggage. They caught up with and captured a small rear guard, but lack of water and exhausted horses ended the chase.

Some 3000 Mexicans staggered on, killing their oxen for food and hauling their carts and the few guns by hand. Many died, some of the most desperate of them by their own hands. The rabble that holed up in Linares after ten days on the road was no longer an army. What Taylor had begun above the Rio Grande the wasteland below Matamoros pretty well finished off. And for what it might have cost him, a full pursuit could have won him little more.

Besides, Taylor had a new problem. The great stir up north over his battles had young Americans straining to join Old Rough and Ready. Recruiting posters: HERE'S TO OLD ZACH! GLORIOUS TIMES! ROAST BEEF, ICE CREAM AND THREE MONTHS' ADVANCE! Lew Wallace in Indianapolis, up and down the streets with fife and drum and a four-sided sign FOR MEXICO FALL IN! Another young Hoosier hiking barefoot 100 miles from Putnam County to enlist at Evansville, "ready to chaw up a half dozen Mexicans at one meal." Snappy militia outfits on parade and itching to move: the Cincinnati Greys, Montgomery Guards, the Washington Cadets; proud Georgia names like Macon Guards, Jasper Greens, and the Fannin Avengers; in New Orleans the Eagle Guards organizing on the corner of Natchez and New Levee Streets, and the Phoenix Invincibles from Fire Company No. 5.

In Tennessee 30,000 men answered a call for 2800, and some tried buying their way in. At Washington, Captain John R.

Kenly brought in 60 men in 36 hours. Three thousand Ohioans were jumping to move only two weeks after the call. Way up in Maine the Aroostook boys were excited. Connecticut offered double the number asked, and this was New England, supposed to have no heart for the war. Only in Salem, Massachusetts, did a company refuse to join, one unit that held the line against marching down to the ships.

But thousands were on the way, young men mostly, signed up because they were young and itching for adventure. Manifest Destiny, the threat or the promise of new slave states, or Mexican injustice had little to do with it. The pull of simple slogans and the posters got them, with their Halls of Montezuma calling, and the acres of silver and gold only dust deep in Mexican hinterlands, the warm and lazy climate, and always the girls—the señoritas.

2

The volunteers about to swamp Taylor were coming under three different requisitions: (1) Taylor's own, of April 26, on Louisiana and Texas for 5000 men, restricted by law to three months; (2) the 6-months men recruited by Gaines' second call; (3) the new 12-months men authorized by Congress on May 13. The first Louisiana companies under Persifor F. Smith had already landed on Brazos Island, across the inlet from Point Isabel. No tents, no wagons, not much of anything but men. Taylor complained to Washington on May 20 that he had to supply their tents from his own short stock, made shorter yet because the 7th Infantry had cut theirs up for sandbags in the Fort Brown siege.

That was only a minor complaint. By now Zach knew about the new volunteers Gaines had been trying to assemble on his own, complete with officers appointed by himself, also civilians as acting paymasters, quartermasters, inspection and mustering officers, adjutants, clerks, and artisans. Gaines even added chaplains.

Why had all this been allowed? Taylor asked. What was he supposed to do about it?

War Secretary Marcy had been doing his best to discourage Gaines. On May 18 he instructed the general to countermand his orders to the several governors. He had already warned the governors personally to ignore the calls. On May 28 he wrote Gaines again, this time in language that said *STOP!* Small wonder. The yeasty old man had built his private army up to almost 12,000.

Edmund Pendleton Gaines was quick to defend Edmund Pendleton Gaines. Did the government expect the commander of the Southwest Department to sit on his hands and let Zach Taylor's little army be crushed? Suppose Taylor lost? It would be "an indelible stain upon my name." The training of volunteers could never wait on the slow motion of government. He had moved only to correct the lag. He argued that citizens had to learn "the school of the soldier" *after* they got into service, not *before*. There was no time to waste. Anyhow, with the government itself calling up 50,000 men, why pick on General Gaines?

The persecuted officer thought he knew the answer. His old enemy Winfield Scott. Even Gaines' wife said there must be something wrong with a man whose lips could be covered by a button, especially a man as big as Scott. No doubt of it, the general-in-chief was behind it all, cringing and crouching "in and about the political metropolis in moribund thirst for the presidency." Meanwhile, where would you always find the simple, unpretending military leader? Out on the frontier, instead of operating as "chief of cliques" in the nation's capital.

The chief of cliques made a marginal note on one of Marcy's worried appeals for a solution. Gaines' irregularities, said Scott, arose either from insanity or dotage. The remedy: indefinite leave.

That must have done it. On June 2 General Gaines was relieved of his command in New Orleans and ordered to Washington for court-martial. The New York *Herald* of June 2 thought the action too severe, and at least mildly defended Gaines. The Baltimore *Patriot*, on the 16th, was stronger: "Shame on the administration! Shame on the War Department! Shame on his avowed friends! General Gaines acted according to the emergency!"

So did the Polk Administration, with the idea of keeping recruitment and the Army under its own direction. But relieving Gaines did not take care of his mischief. His volunteers, as well as Taylor's and the 12-months men, bore in on Point Isabel, on Brazos Island, and along both banks near the mouth of the Rio. Most of them came from the Mississippi Valley—out of Frankfort or Bowling Green in Kentucky; Jefferson or Madison in Indiana; Quincy or Shawneetown, Illinois; Nashville or Memphis, Tennessee; Fort Leavenworth or Jefferson Barracks, Missouri; Fulton or Washington, Arkansas; and out of Natchez, Mississippi.

The troops shipped down the feeder rivers into the Big Father, and from there on down to New Orleans, already a glut of volunteers from within the city and state. One regiment did come out of Columbus, Georgia; and another from Mobile, Alabama. The movement was largely logistics on the waterways, the country's first on any scale.

The Baltimore Battalion, ordered out of Washington for bad behavior, slipped down the Potomac on a 700-ton steamer built to carry 200 men. Over twice that number jammed her decks, fighting for space among crates and casks of military stores. Captain Kenly called them a tough lot, ex-sailors, fire company lads, and men from fishing clubs. They acted like children. They kept wanting pens, paper, somebody to write their letters, to send money home or hold it for them. They groused about uniforms too large, too small; they needed medicine, and where could they find the doctor? Next, seasickness, sunstroke, shortage of water. Only the money took care of itself: a few hands soon winning most of it. Then fights, knives, blood. Three dead were buried on landing.

From off Brazos Island soldiers lightered across bars in five-foot depths to wade out onto a furnace of sand. Sometimes storms trapped them on shipboard for days in sight of camp. While waiting, they could stare at the ribs of wrecked ships raking the tide. During a blow on May 28 the steamer *Alabama*, with 458 volunteers, dragged two anchors from 70 fathoms into three. Once on the beach, they went under muslin tents "too fine to sift hominy through, but particularly fitted for shower bath purposes." The luckiest arrivals moved four miles west over Madre Lagune to Point Isabel, now "Fort Polk" in honor of the man who got everybody down there.

Men assigned to the other camps had a four-mile march over the stinging sand to the south end of Brazos Island, then through shallow water to the mainland and up along the swampy Rio banks. General Smith's three-months Louisianans made it first, followed shortly by two Texas regiments under former Governor James Pinckney Henderson. A good camp lay just north of Burita, eight miles up from the river's mouth. Like Fort Polk, it enjoyed high ground and a sea breeze. Camp Belknap, across on the north bank, was the worst—a swampland of snakes, ants, scorpions, tarantulas, fleas, and mosquitoes tall enough to drink from a tin cup without leaving the ground. Or so new residents claimed.

On June 3, Taylor's field return put the army at 8000. A

New Orleans *Picayune* correspondent reported 4000 volunteers drilling in the camps. America's citizen soldiers kept crowding in, and without as much as a barrel of flour of their own by way of supply. Their uniforms ran the spectrum in color and modeled the garb of several wars back. One state's dress varied from company to company. Another state furnished no uniforms at all. North Carolina men came togged out in special designs from New York; some Illinois troops wore linsey-woolsey. Anything suited for head coverings: stovepipes with pompons, tricorners with plumes, flat oilcloths, and later, of course, sombreros. Texans dressed in dust, dirty shirts, and Colt 5-shooters, officers the same as their men.

The West Pointers took a first hard look at the volunteers. Their behavior worried Lieutenant John Reynolds, and "still they come," he moaned. Captain Henry accused them of disgraceful behavior too. Captain Barbour said they were ruining the country's reputation. But they bothered Meade most of all. They crowded the guardhouses, shot off their muskets willy-nilly, wasted ammunition and rations, laughed at orders, and got drunk. Give them leave in Matamoros and they made the rounds of saloons, abused the natives, rioted. A volunteer found dead in the streets on May 28; another lying dead in a private house, and both undoubtedly earned their ends.

A non-West Pointer had his say on the subject. "Every regiment of volunteers costs equal to three of regulars, plus loss of arms, accoutrements, and equipage. Thirty-three per cent are sick, and the remaining 66 not worth a straw." That dreary appraisal came from William Jenkins Worth, back on the 23rd from his recent sulk in the states. Old Zach had fought Palo Alto and Resaca without him. But as to that, Worth had an answer. The army had admitted his presence "in spirit." He said "His discipline and inculcations were everywhere manifest."

General Worth had helped win the battles after all.

Taylor gave him his old brigade and shrugged off the whole business with a few grumbling sentences to his young surgeon son-in-law, Robert C. Wood. Worth, he wrote, "has been pampered and bloated for things he never done." But the officer-short army could give a little in favor of a man with Worth's experience. A newsman reported that almost everybody was glad to have the general back again. Soldiers remembered him at the Little Arroyo, plunging his horse into the stream to spark the advance. And Worth could be up front once more if he just kept his temper, rationed his drinking, sat on his conceit—and got another chance to fight.

3

The newsman with the item on Worth was the real thing. New Orleans had been feeding the country spotty coverage from the printers who went down with the first "Gaines Army" in '45. A few of them hung on and continued to send back copy. Published letters of officers, soldiers, and stories picked up from travelers and ship captains helped pad out the record, especially on the battles. But results were hit-and-miss and open to bias. Wild reports made headlines: THE CITY OF MATAMOROS BATTERED DOWN, or, on the untouched mud-hovel village of Burita: ENTIRE CITY REDUCED TO ASHES! The Baltimore *Sun* of May 15 had Walker's little band of Rangers "nobly contesting" with 3000 Mexicans in the ambush of April 27.

The bias cropped up in battle accounts written by officers. For example, complaints went the rounds about Captain E.

Kirby Smith's enthusiasm for Charlie May. Was May that good at Resaca? One volunteer officer blasted away in print against a published letter calling his regiment scum. He prayed that the name of the New Orleans *Jeffersonian*, which ran it, would "ring in disgust from end to end in Crescent City."

A foreign war deserved better handling in the press. It needed trained reporters who had the run of the camps but no ties to any part of the army. By now people in the states were demanding more news. Parents, wives, and the girls and friends of volunteers at the front wanted to know. How are they treating our boy? Are they feeding him proper? Does he sleep on a clean tick? Are they minding his health? Is the general kind? A letter to "Johnny Mc——, Army of Occipation, Tex," carried this postscript: "Gineral Tailor, this is from Johnnys wife. Johnny voltd for his country. Donte forget him."

Some of the boys would scrounge paper, nose up to the stump of a candle, and fight off the insects to pen a word home. But government mail to and from the army moved on whim. Postage could run up to 25 cents and a letter would take months to reach its destination. Communication always seemed to be in cross transit. For so many questions asked, the answers came too late or not at all. What hurt most at home were the chance newspaper listings of soldier dead, to be followed later by their eager, overdue letters from Mexico.

With the war going on, lawmakers also had more stake in the news, both in Congress and in the states that sent their young men off to fight. Nobody could outfret a governor in his concern for our boys.

New Orleans papers like the *Picayune, Delta, Tropic, Bee,* and others played up to the hunger for news, as well as to the profit in supplying it. And they began getting the news out, although a Baltimore *Sun* man thought it would be easier to cover a war in Outer Mongolia than the one in Mexico. They managed by combining the railroads, steamers, stages, the telegraph, and the *Sun's* "60 blooded horses." America, and probably the world, was reading its first true war correspondents. Newspaper professionals now lived with the army and filed almost daily copy. Bad rewrites still appeared: "The prowess of our brave soldiers had made the perfidious Mexicans bite the dust. The serpent of Mexican arms now writhes in death agony in the beak of the American eagle." But from the front crisper, fact-filled, and less gaudy writing gradually reached the states.

James L. Freaner of the *Delta* landed at Fort Polk just too late for the battles. The *Picayune's* chief, George Wilkins Kendall, took even longer because he rode down with 300 mounted Texans on the way to join Taylor. The *"Pic"* would soon send four more men into the field, and the *Delta* would add two correspondents during June: J. H. Peoples, who signed himself "Chaparral," and J. G. H. Tobin of "Tobin's Knapsack."

The *Tropic's* Thomas B. Thorpe apparently worked without a pseudonym, but Freaner had two. He first used the name "Corporal"; then, after killing a Mexican in a fight and taking his horse, he switched to "Mustang." Meanwhile papers farther north began linking up with New Orleans. James Gordon Bennett already had an express to Mobile and west to feed his New York *Herald*. The New York *Sun*, the Baltimore *Sun*, the Philadelphia *Ledger*, and the Charleston *Courier* also strained for early coverage. Before long, copy moving up the east coast would be outrunning the mails by 30 hours.

The invasion of writing talent broke out the news wherever a soldier put foot, volunteer or regular. Reporting began with descriptions of Matamoros itself—how much it looked like an American city, with its right-angled streets and rows of shade trees. The impressive cathedral, the gardens, markets, and the poorer houses built out of canes, brush, and mud were more typically Mexican. People back home read that the population was around 7000, that the city covered an area of two square miles and had both its front and rear on bends in the river.

On May 26 Freaner wrote that the natives seemed friendly, talked against their own government, and were in no mind to fight if they could help it. He said he liked the tortillas, cheeses, and a local liquor he compared to San Croix rum. The women impressed him less. A few he found beautiful, but most were slovenly and lacking in "female delicacy." Generally they wore white muslin skirts, loosely tied at the waist, without bodices and with only chemises to cover their breasts. Freaner saw no stockings in Matamoros.

George Kendall made a first note on the city for his *Picayune*. He had located a place that served mint juleps, and he announced the find as "a long step towards civilization." On June 1 the Americans Hugh McLeod and I. N. Fleeson put the opening issue of *The Republic of the Rio Grande* on the streets. When army opposition to McLeod's editorial policies forced him out, Fleeson carried on with other help. This local paper caught the city as Taylor's men came to know it, and nowhere better than in its advertising:

The Matamoros Lunch House for Judges of Good Liquor —Special! A Supply of London Porter in Pint Bottles.

The Italian Fonda (Angelo Olivia, Iturbi Street)—the Best Cooks, Cleanliness, and Free Circulation of Air.

Mrs. S. Foyle's Goods—Calico prints, Balzarines, Domestics, Capes, Collars, Mosquito Netting, Spool Cottons, &c.

For Gentlemen's Clothing, Tengman & Fellows, Late of Mobile—Cottonmade Gamboon, Summer Tweed, Merino Under Shirts, Palm Leaf Hats.

Mrs. Hamblin's American Hotel (Formerly Arista's Headquarters)—Every Delicacy Served in Superior Style.

Army privates probably felt more at home in the Grand Spanish Saloon or in Dan Murphy's Ten Pin Alley and Bar: "Old Dan Murphy, or the man who was born to be killed by lead or steel." Murphy stocked, or said he did, more cooling refreshments than could be had in all New Orleans, and "Dan abhors a falsehood." The Washington Ball Room, saloon attached, listed a bouncer—"a guard always in attendance to preserve order." Soldiers out of pocket could find the National Pawnbroker's office in Market Square, and plenty of them must have looked it up.

Grog shops and gambling houses that never bought a line in *The Republic* bled endless dollars from Taylor's men.

4

Occupying Matamoros did not mean planting the army in it by any means. Every other day Taylor switched even the guard (two companies) in the main plaza; while there, he expected them to present "a model of discipline and correct deportment." The rest of the force camped a good mile outside or remained across the river. Old Zach let his men go into town only for short leaves, usually in small parties. During their stay they downed "red eye" and "dog hair," watched circus performers and made the rounds of fandangoes. For most of them cockfighting was new sport, but they took to losing as much on the birds as they did at roulette, keno, faro, or chuck-a-luck. Those who wanted women found them. One soldier who was not looking for women found them anyhow, and backed red-faced from a house, still clutching the shirts he had brought for laundering.

What a party of officers found on its first leave was something else—Lieutenant Ed Deas drunk in the street. "Leander" himself, still wet from his swim across the Rio. Later, sobered up and repentant, he got back on army rolls.

Other parties looked in on the Mexican wounded. The sight of them made John Reynolds thank his God for being an American. Who would not, he asked, if he "could have walked through the hospital with me in Matamoros, and beheld the manner in which the poor, unfortunate wounded have been left without proper medical attention and a scanty allowance of provisions, who as you pass along, beg for a 'Picayune' in a tone of pity that would move a harder heart than a soldier's?" Captain Henry saw a dying man holding in his hand the grapeshot that had passed through his body.

In the meantime Taylor was doing all he could, hard up for medics and medical supplies as he was. Of the three to four hundred Mexican wounded, many spilled over into private houses. A reporter found over forty in a room only 21 feet square, and the stench alone a lesson in the horrors of war. Like two other newsmen who had gone back over the ground of Palo Alto and Resaca to describe the disinterred and mangled Mexican dead, this writer was putting down facts that made hard going for glory and romance. Combat had its ugly sides, and the new correspondents were adding it to the record.

Old Zach was one soldier who had no taste for the city. He stayed close to headquarters in camp, where he sat daily on his stool outside the tent to hear complaints from citizens and the army alike. Not only complaints but praise. A delegation from the Louisiana legislature arrived on June 8, bringing the general "a complimentary gift from some of his fellow citizens of New Orleans." Although Zach objected to awards before unfinished campaigns, the honor called for a party. So he set the visitors up with what the press termed "collations." Toasts and cheers for Old Rough and Ready followed. "Here's to

General Taylor—Ampudia has at least discovered that he was a *tailor* who knew how to take his *measure*." Collations must have been the right word.

In the end Taylor accepted the gift, a sword. "My heart feels too deeply and sensibly the high honor that has been conferred on me, my officers and men, to respond to your expression of gratitude and thanks." Even so, his response filled 24 lines of a column in *Niles' National Register*. It took more out of the Old Man than fighting a battle, according to Meade, who was there and enjoyed the party. Surgeon Mills did not enjoy it. "What are two buckets of champagne for four or five hundred officers!" Old niggling, teetotaler Taylor had let the army and Louisiana down.

Whoever was right, the next day more than made up. This time the regular officers put on the party. They held it in the mansion Arista had used as headquarters (Mrs. Hamblin's?), with a band in the gallery which drew a crowd outside to listen. Twiggs acted as master of ceremonies. A reporter rated both the songs and toasts higher than those of the day before. "The festivity was kept up until midnight and right merrily did the wine sparkle." Lieutenant Meade was happy about this party too, and on getting back to camp he added a few lines in a letter to his wife—just to prove he was sober, he wrote.

The top legitimate attraction Matamoros had to offer was theater. The Harts had come down from Corpus to join other professionals fresh from the states. Officers and men saw W. R. Hart in *Dumb Belle* and *Spoiled Child*, and Mrs. Hart in plays like *Fair One with the Golden Locks*, *Maid of Munster*, and *Swiss Girl*. They also saw Mrs. Jefferson, Miss Cornelia Jefferson, Miss Christian, Mrs. Irwin, Edward Badger, etc. "Miss Jefferson won new laurels in *Cachucha*," the *Republic's* reviewer said. He wanted to throw a hatful of half dollars on stage every time she danced. Another performer got cooler notice: "Mr. Fanning, in his peculiar line, is a deserving actor, and, with application to the profession alone, will overstep mediocrity."

Nobody thought of throwing money to Cornelia Jefferson's brother Joseph, but young Joe Jefferson was with the company —all eighteen years of him. In May the young actor had sailed down from Galveston with his mother and sister on a condemned and rickety steamer. At Fort Polk he stood respectfully outside the tent where Captain Ringgold lay dying; then after Taylor's two battles the company opened in Matamoros. The boy found the audiences "the most motley group that ever filled a theater," a rag, tag, and bobtail crowd. Captain Kenly felt the same way. The cultured Baltimore volunteer could never forget the Rangers. They came loaded with liquor, pistols, knives, and spoiling for trouble.

Those Texans. A Ranger killed one of the actors and then simply "sloped away," to quote *The American Flag*, successor to *The Republic*. When still another Ranger murdered a dragoon, he fired the newspaper into declaiming: "It must afford our enemies great pleasure to see us shooting and cutting up one another." The trouble with Texans was history—too much memory of the Alamo and other Mexican cruelties. They rode into the war full of hate and keyed up for fighting. In the lull between battles their tension boiled over into brawls.

At that, the Rangers were only the worst of the volunteers. Old Zach managed to hold his regulars under fair control, but the newly enlisted citizen soldiers were beginning to make a sorry record in Matamoros. For the most part their officers looked on helplessly, if not involved themselves. One night a barmaid who refused to serve a drunken volunteer was run through with a bayonet, or so *The Flag* reported in damning the brutality. As Meade pointed out, Mexicans painfully learned the difference between *tropas de ligna*, and the feared *voluntarios*.

Gaines was right when he said citizen soldiers had it all to learn *after* they signed up. Recruits for the Regular Army, by contrast, began their training at once, at posts in the states equipped to handle them. They quickly got used to drill, hard labor, routine, and the exhausting boredom. Most of all, they got used to merciless discipline. Thus rawer material made better soldiers. In general, the volunteers came from securer backgrounds, and had more intelligence and education. But they descended on Taylor's camps half-supplied, half-equipped, and wholly untrained. The officers they elected seldom knew any more than they did about quartering and feeding troops. Almost nobody knew about fighting.

Fighting was what the volunteers had enlisted for—not to dig wells, hunt firewood, forage for animals, police the camps, shine boots and buckles, salute fellow townsmen, and be ordered round and round, back and forth on a steaming, eye-blinding sandspit. Where was the war? Where were those Halls of Montezuma? Correspondent Freaner took their temperature on the 15th of June. "The most perfect apathy prevails among the volunteer troops here now, and every day the inroads of discontent are more apparent." They needed excitement, he added. Even a false alarm or two would help.

All right, no war—they could make some of their own. The 1st Ohio Volunteers versus the Baltimore Battalion. Cause: somebody on one side took a catfish away from somebody on the other. Cartridges issued, an officer's sword shattered to bits, and a line of battle formed. No casualties.

Next, 1st Georgia versus 4th Illinois. Cause: Illinois Colonel Edward D. Baker had moved in with a few of his men to break up a Georgia scrap. Casualties: one dead Georgian and several wounded on both sides, including Baker with a painful shot in his neck.

All combatants had a crying use for the 4000 New Testaments that went to San Antonio for General Ellis Wool. They also needed the feel of America as a country instead of a jealous accommodation of separate states. For the volunteer of 1846 loyalty was a local virtue, which lost something by export. What could a Georgia cracker enjoy in common with a prairie sucker from Illinois? The same enemy? Well, for Taylor and the country both, that was the hope. Meanwhile the general could only try, as he put it, to get through as best he could and to keep his temper even if the volunteers drove him out of his tent in the end. These soldiers who required a stump speech to get the simplest order obeyed!

5

There should have been a law. In fact there was one. It held to only three months of service the volunteers called up from the states by Taylor and Gaines. Because time began with the day of enlistment, the Taylor men were close to discharge. Gaines had made his call for six months, a period as illegal as the call itself. So unless the 3-months and 6-months troops signed up again for 12, the general could send them home. A great bit of luck for Old Zach, though the Secretary of War hated to see them released "without some employment after their sacrifice."

Governor Isaac Johnson of Louisiana viewed the either-or choice for his boys with what he called emotions of repugnance. After all, to fight for the cause "the judge [had] deserted the bench, the lawyer his clients, the physician his patients, the merchant his counting house, the mechanic his

116

workshop, the minister of the Gospel his pulpit." Secretary Marcy wrote back his thanks for their patriotism, but wondered whether all of them would not be glad to return to their homes.

Taylor was glad, and no matter what Johnson or the other governors thought, the handy expiration dates started the short-termers on the way. Not, of course, without the proper sentiments from their general. General Orders No. 91 read in part:

The Commanding General would do violence to his feelings were he to omit the expression of regret that these brave men have been disappointed in their wish to meet the enemy. . . . The General cannot forget that, with an enthusiasm seldom exhibited by any country, they were the first to flock to his standard. Their prompt and gallant movement to the seat of war will be held as a grateful remembrance by their comrades in the regular service.

A general with political ambitions could hardly do better. Few of the 3-months men wanted to linger in the camps on or near the Rio Grande. Taylor hoped Colonel Albert Johnston's 1st Texas Volunteers would stay on. They looked both hardy and eager, he wrote Marcy. But the only soldier eager to the extent of twelve more months was their colonel. His regiment dissolved, reducing a disgusted officer to staff work with one of the new major generals of volunteers, William O. Butler. All except one company of the Louisianans followed the Texans north. Taylor also mustered out an Alabama battalion and one from St. Louis.

The eager volunteers were mostly those turned back before they could even leave the states. Seven Tennessee companies which had marched to Nashville got orders to disband. Off they went, grumbling. "The scene was one of touching interest," a paper delicately noted. And from another state: "The brave volunteers from Missouri were trifled with in the same manner"—brought to departure points all fired up, then refused muster. Volunteers in Illinois got out a resolution against their governor when he blunted their ardor by dismissing them in the capital. The farther from Taylor's camps, the greater the ardor.

The nearly 8000 volunteers on the way out would make room for the first of 20,000 promised for a full twelve months— long enough to make them soldiers. The seasick 1st Tennessee hove to off Brazos bar on June 23. Lashed about in a storm that held up lightering, they took a week to unload. It was a rough start, with wearing, searing weeks still to go on the beach or the river banks. A dry June turned into flooding rains through the first half of July. The low-lying camps churned into mud. Up went the volunteer sick rolls.

The regular troops, with better sanitation, care, and training, rode out the period in better shape. They had the advantage of hospitals set up by Taylor both in Fort Brown and Matamoros. Surgeon Porter, for example, was optimistic in his June 30 report for the Artillery Battalion. Out of 564 men, he listed 95 cases of diarrhea or dysentery, 23 of bilious fevers, 37 of catarrh, and 62 other cases of illness. Not a very robust outfit by later standards, but as of 1846, in a semitropical climate, the record looked good. Porter lost but one man.

For every sick regular four volunteers were down. Most of the new men had only their tentmates for nurses and the usual daily rations for food. More volunteers died. Lew Wallace kept chart on a man with chronic diarrhea: "His cheeks have the tinge of old gunny sacks; under the jaws the skin is ween and flabby; his eyes are filmy and sinking; he moves listlessly; the voice answering the sergeant is flat. . . . Another week and his place in ranks is vacant."

The recruiting posters and the bands and cheering that sent volunteers off to fight had been silent on this, as well as on the remedies applied to put men back on their feet: calomel, laudanum, tincture of cayem pepper, spirits of camphor, ginger, essence of peppermint, and Hoffman's anodyne. Maximum dose of almost anything, one tablespoon with water. Extreme cases sometimes met better luck—a glass of whiskey or brandy flavored with essence of cloves. But mostly it was essences, tinctures, and spirits against every malady that bad sanitation, indifferent rations, and brackish water could inflict on men in a strange, hot country.

The general disorganization and misery of the camps did enough to break the volunteers down without adding sickness. Taylor worried about their "inconvenience and sufferings," and kept calling on the War Department for more and better medical help. Surgeon General Thomas Lawson shrugged off the complaints: "All I can say understandably on the subject is, that, whether stationary or on a march, in camp; or in the field, the volunteers have been exceedingly sickly."

Taylor already knew that. He also knew the rest of it—that volunteers were not prepared for the privations, the labor, the exposure, guard duty, fasting, self-denial, or restraint. So they took sick, became "melancholy and despondent, with corresponding aggravations of the disease." Still, the surgeon general could scarcely entertain the idea, as he put it, that a man might be broken down in only one year of service.

Not much help from General Lawson: "Why, I would never permit myself to be sick when honor and duty claimed from me active exertion; but whether sick or well, I was never known to quit the field until called off by authority." Statistically the surgeon general sounded better, though not much. As of May he said Taylor had one medical officer for every 164 men. The department considered one to 375 as adequate.

But these were old figures, dating before the influx of volunteers. According to Taylor the ratio was now way off. If Lawson had the figures on file in Washington, Old Zach had the mounting roll of sick along the Rio Grande.

Not much help, either, from the Secretary of War. On July 1 Marcy admitted his concern over having to rush men to Mexico before they could be properly trained. This was an old story in young America's wars: citizen soldiers dumped at the front, green and barely equipped. Some lessons had been learned, of course. The Army now included medical, pay, quartermaster, and commissary departments. Orders, memos, requisitions—papers in the thousands inched from office to office in the War and Navy Building. Out of them all there dribbled some supplies and some transportation, but never enough and never in time. For example, 20,000 men on the way to Taylor, and not a single new wagon.

Otherwise Marcy had good news. He announced Taylor's commission as major general in the United States Army. It came on top of a brevet at that rank granted at the end of May, along with praise from the President—"your skill and gallantry," etc.

6

Before June was out, Old Zach had word of another kind of honor, which began in a series of *whereases* and *resolveds* that started a ground swell around the country. From now on, no important act of Taylor's would escape its impact. On the 11th, a meeting of citizens in Trenton, New Jersey, instructed its committee to report that:

Whereas, for many years past the presidential contests of our country have been managed more with a view of aggrandizing selfish politicians, than of advancing the true interests of the country; and *whereas*, the time has arrived when it becomes the solemn duty of the citizens of this great republic to shake off the slavery of party, and select from among our distinguished men, as candidate for chief magistrate, some one who has shown himself to possess the qualifications for that office, superior to those of mere subserviency to party; and *whereas*, we hold that our commanding general on the Rio Grande has shown himself worthy of our confidence, by his skill and bravery in the field, and by the talent displayed in his modest despatches, after one of the most glorious victories ever achieved by the American arms, and in his whole military correspondence: *therefore*—

Resolved, That we, citizens of Trenton, without deference to party lines, or party questions, as generally understood, do nominate General *Zachary Taylor*, the hero of Palo Alto and Resaca de la Palma, to the presidency of the United States, and that we hereby invite all true republicans to unite with us in this effort to elevate a brave soldier, a successful general, and a true republican to that high office.

Resolved, that here on the proudest battle-field of the American revolution, we boldly raise the standard of the *People's Candidate*, and invite a union of all honest parties, for the sake of our common country, and the true interests of the people.

On June 21, in a letter to his son-in-law, Surgeon Wood, Zachary Taylor set down two reactions. First, he would decline the nomination if offered and even if he had no opposition. The fighting over, he still wanted only retirement and a quiet old age. Second: "Was I a prominent or ambitious aspirent for civil distinction or honors, I might very readily suppose there was an intention somewhere to break me down."

The general was deducing an effect from a cause, and it seemed most logical to him. Interest in Taylor as presidential material automatically prejudiced Polk against him. Soon the country would be asking why the army lay idle instead of marching to new victories. Well, Taylor thought, ask the President and the War Department. Somebody in authority must be holding up orders for prosecuting the war. It was no fault of his if the government kept dumping men ashore on the Brazos without the supplies or the boats to move them upriver.

He could never transfer the army to his proposed new inland base at Camargo without boats. Taylor had asked for light-draught steamers way back in May, and even sent Captain John Sanders to New Orleans with money to buy them. The first boat to reach the river was half eaten away by worms. For $51,000 Sanders had bought eight more steamers by July 4, but they had to be held for caulking, coppering, and alterations. All that money (Zach hated to spend money), all the volunteers, and still no boats.

The general's doubts about the administration had point. Those first feelers of a political boom for the hero of Palo Alto and Resaca did not sit well in the White House. But Polk was no man to fumble a war solely because of it. A successful conclusion in Mexico was essential to his policy. So when June 15 had at last brought a friendly settlement of the Oregon Territory along the 49th parallel, the President began looking to affairs on the Rio Grande. With the summer of 1846, he had shed some of his casual notions of war, if not his contempt for generals. Logistics still bored him, but now he gave Scott a freer hand. Scott loved logistics, though it took two battles, a declaration of war, and Taylor's needling to give him the funds to "logist" with. Brave figures for the start:

2000 wagons at $120	$240,000
10,000 horses, & mules for same at $75	750,000
2000 sets harness at $40	80,000
4000 pack mules at $40	160,000
4000 pack saddles at $15	60,000
4000 yoke of oxen at $25	100,000

(&c, down to horseshoes at $100/1000; nails at 19¢/lb.)

The War Department estimated water transportation alone (including purchase and chartering of steamers) at $1,500,000. Maintenance and subsistence would overreach $2,000,000; total forage $3,000,000. All told, financing the war for a single year brought in a frightening total of more than $17,000,000.

That much war certainly deserved the President's full attention.

Making money available was, of course, only the start. Wagons, for example—the War Department chased down every lead and rumor, and in doing it learned something about the state of one trade:

(1) Report of wagons being made at Georgia State Penitentiary.

(2) Try Savannah too; also Philadelphia, Newark, Troy.

(3) Offer $10 extra to "stimulate the mechanics to greater exertion."

(4) Bad News from York, Pennsylvania: "The wagon business in that part of the country is greatly diminished since the rail road has been in operation."

The same with animals: look for well-broke mules in Louisiana; several hundred mules reported at German settlement near San Antonio; good three-year-olds in Kentucky about cleaned out. Demand was high for horses too. Twiggs wanted 172, of good American stock, to replace battle losses among his dragoon mounts. Taylor was calling for 200 more to fill out the light artillery.

Then—July 14: "The general requests that 300,000 rations be thrown on Camargo in preparation for a march on Monterey."

The calls, pleas, threats, bonuses—all the frenzied shopping around the country came down to this plan of operations. Taylor himself had suggested taking Monterey as far back as May 21. It stood at the head of the long road south to the Mexican capital. It also connected by road to the Gulf. By the route Taylor chose, Monterey lay some 260 miles southwest. As for the stop-off base at Camargo, a bird could reach it from Matamoros by flying 100 miles. But on the snaking Rio Grande a boat often traveled ten miles to cover 200 yards. The army's frantic quartermaster was counting the bird's flight "times" four.

Early in June, Taylor had sent 250 men of the 1st Infantry and two of Bragg's guns up along the north bank of the river to Reynosa. The town stood on high ground and made a healthy halfway station on the way to Camargo. In July more troops started for the new base itself. Those moving by land marched mostly at night to dodge the sun. They strung out along the route, either slogging in river-edge ooze or kicking through layered dust. Other troops jammed the leaky, stinking steamers that fought the Rio's swollen current chug by chug. Between running aground or out of wood to fire the boilers, the boats labored their zigzag way for over a week. In high water they often lost the channel. Ballooning animal carcasses caught up in the flood nudged downstream past the staring men on deck. One bloated cow made a raft for crows.

Taylor finally had got his boats—12 of them—but nobody called the trip a pleasure cruise. Before the army completed its change of base one ship had sunk, one had blown up, and another was lost on Brazos bar before the start. The poor, worm-eaten *Neva* almost made it. Captain Barbour remembered passing the wreck near Camargo.

7

The general himself left Matamoros on August 4. Away from volunteers shooting it out in the streets, or lying sick and sulking in the camps. Away from supply roads under water and a mess of transportation still to be solved. Yet for all he shook off in leaving, there would be more of the same to follow. The old man who kept dreaming retirement was neck-deep in the war—a frontier colonel of 1845 wearing a major general's stars in '46, now charged with moving 15,000 troops from one base to another in alien country. No wonder he could write: "I really consider few if any individual in the army has done more, or that more or as much has been required of them as myself."

Missing punctuation and vague modifiers added weariness to the general's faintly despairing boast. His government could well be asking too much. Yet, if Taylor's judgment and effort fell short of the need, who could do better? Scott sounded good, on paper and from faraway Washington. He had tried his best to arrange for training the volunteers *before* unloading them on the Brazos. He lost that round, though he did send down a top chief quartermaster in Lieutenant Colonel Henry Whiting; also a first-rate adjutant, Major Lorenzo Thomas. They would help tighten liaison between the War Department and the front. It cried for the doing. Old Zach was wrestling a job that outranged anything either in his or his army's past.

Meade put the problem simply. He supposed people at

home wondered about the lack of action along the Rio. They forgot that soldiers could neither march nor fight without means and transportation. So Washington planned an invasion and flooded Taylor with men who were then left to idle "their time here waiting for wagons and pork."

To credit Washington with any solid, intelligent planning stretched a point. Orders had started Colonel Stephen W. Kearny westward by way of Santa Fe to protect the American trade route to California. The word *protect* was a euphemism; Polk wanted the territory occupied, no less. If Kearny could then reach California by winter, he was "to act in such a manner as to best conciliate the inhabitants, and render them friendly to the United States." General Wool was to move south, eventually to join Taylor, who in turn would probably send him west to Chihuahua. Again the aim was political— to conciliate a population Polk hoped to win over.

For Kearny and Wool these were vague, unmilitary instructions. Taylor got none at all. Beyond his own plan for taking Monterey, the campaign was left to him. Of course, now that the government had sent him thousands of men, Polk did want Taylor's views. What did he propose to do?

To all Taylor had on his mind, the administration seemed to be adding the role of general-in-chief. He was on the ground, they said, and could better judge. True enough, if only he knew what to expect from Washington. But Taylor answered in some detail on August 1. He said that whatever happened after Monterey would depend on native attitude farther south. It was hard to subsist troops in hostile territory. If the army found it could base safely on Saltillo, southwest of Monterey, then an advance on San Luis Potosí was possible. Otherwise the government should make the decision on whether to hold the interior line at Monterey and try working in from the Gulf to the Mexican capital by way of Vera Cruz.

"The department must be better informed than I am," Taylor concluded. He did add one doubt. A coastal invasion that had to rely largely on volunteers was risky.

The administration was leaning on Taylor in a situation over its head—how to conduct a war. But in running his own end of it, Taylor in some ways also had got beyond depth. At first he had ordered too few boats to bring off his change of base. He had accepted too much of the sickness among the volunteers as inevitable. He had been too soft on delinquents in their ranks. It was as if the general took poor health and bad behavior for granted. He also kept his pinch on spending. "Economy I consider a virtue and should be practiced by all." Economy in this instance helped to account for the shortage of boats.

Still, granting his faults, Old Zach had managed to put his army on the way to Camargo and had strength and heart enough left to follow it up the river. The work ahead would call for all he had of both.

Back in emptied Matamoros, the editor of *The Flag* began to wonder. What would happen if Taylor should lose the next battle? The general seemed to be shrugging politics off, but it was all the talk up in the states and much of it counted him in. How could he ignore it? How would his luck in the field affect his chances? As for the city, now with the army gone, "all the excitement seems to have left Matamoros and followed the troops up to Camargo." The newspaper would struggle to hang on, hoping for readers among the volunteers still to come down.

The theater died. Young Joe Jefferson, along with another actor, moved from the stage to operate the Grand Spanish Saloon. They ran gaming tables and sold cigars, sandwiches, coffee, pies, and a kind of native cake which a Ranger said they should be shot for displaying. Jefferson's customers were "more numerous than select," and he found that "when the rum was in, the knife was out." When even this clientele moved on, the actor broke off an affair with a Mexican girl and headed north.

For the army it now was Camargo. "As I expected," an Illinois volunteer wrote home, "found it a homly looking place old fences houses fell down all over the place which made it look loansom and desolate." For hundreds of soldiers it soon became worse than that—a graveyard. The city, on the right bank of the San Juan and three miles south of the Rio, almost slid into the summer floods. A third of it went under water. The army arrived to find people homeless and starving, but its coming saved them. Natives went to work as laborers, or sold mules, beef cattle, and other food.

The army itself had less luck, especially the volunteers. Camargo lay too far in from the Gulf to catch the sea breezes. Walled in by limestone rock, a fetid heat hung motionless over the town. Taylor's three-mile sprawl of tents was pitched close to the stream, which served both men and animals for bathing and drinking, waste and cooking. With the general still pleading for medics, the volunteers began dropping from ranks. Captain Luther Giddings of Ohio had the phrase: "The dead march was ever wailing in our ears." Even the birds learned it, so the story went.

Slack sanitation, poor hospital equipment and less medical knowledge, bad water and climate combined to do the volunteers in. When it came time to leave Camargo, only 370 of 795 Georgians would answer roll call; only 324 of 754 Alabamians; 317 of 588 in the 2nd Tennessee. Almost every volunteer regiment listed a third to a half sick. An estimated 1500 died.

The general's regulars stayed fairly healthy, and somehow plans for the next move took shape. Worth had command of the city, and by clamping down on liquor smuggling he reduced the amount of high jinks that had disgraced Matamoros. He also forced out most of the army's loafers and hangers-on, some of them "veterans" of Corpus Christi days. All the while supplies kept piling up on the river bank—supplies with still no wagons to haul them. The army now had fewer wagons than when it left Corpus in early March and yet it had grown five times in size. At least 1000 wagons ought to be on the way, wrote Quartermaster Whiting without much hope. Lack of those horseshoes at $100 per 1000 and the nails at 19 cents was paralyzing the cavalry.

And mules. In the middle of July, Taylor had balked at paying $71 each for good sized three-year-olds, half-broken to harness. By the end of the month the price had gone to $102. Profiteering, no less! All right, Taylor would buy his mules from Camargo dealers at $20 a head. Small and wild, yes, but cheap. How cheap in the long run would have to be learned, but if Zach could not get wagons the pack animals would have to carry the loads.

8

On August 17, 1846, General Taylor staged a grand review of his regulars. The show awed the volunteers, as it probably was meant to do. Captain Giddings enjoyed the music and envied the snap and cadence of the whole line as it wheeled into companies to pass the general and his staff. A good volunteer officer—and there were a few—could see the difference. Giddings could see it in the regulars' camps as well. He envied the clean, carefully laid-out tent rows, the rubbed sheen of small arms and the gun muzzles rimming black circles from under their tarps.

Of course, there was more to the contrast than what the eye alone took in. The same West Pointers who accounted for spit, polish, and the smart parade of their regulars also knew how to keep books. Captain Kenly of the volunteers was grateful for their help. Without it he said he never could have mustered the Baltimore Battalion for pay. So much to record:

(1) Number present and absent
(2) Where and when mustered
(3) Clothing received
(4) Value of equipment
(5) Value of arms
(6) Amount due sutler
(7) Present sick
(8) Absent sick

(9) On extra duty
(10) On detached duty
(11) Under arrest
(12) Transferred
(13) Deserted
(14) Service expired
(15) Died
Etc.

This clerical routine was only the meanest business in conducting a war, and yet it had to be learned. Payday had to come off. As Kenly added, pay alone never made a soldier, but fail to pay him and you might lose him. The men from the Point knew all about payday, including their own.

Giddings, though, still seemed more impressed by what he saw. One morning he watched Bragg's battery at drill. He marveled that horses as well as the men followed every command in the whirl of guns and caissons over the plain. And the volunteer captain knew where the credit belonged:

That will be an unfortunate day for the Republic, when Congress, influenced by motives of fancied economy or the vile appeals of the demogogue, shall consent to abandon an institution [West Point] which has already done much to establish the reputation and extend the borders of the country . . . which is constantly spreading among us that intelligence and skill by which *the people*—in their freedom from the burden of a large standing army—may at any time be

130

converted into the grandest host of soldiers that ever battled in any cause or clime.

Not quite yet, not in this war. But Giddings saw in West Point the sure potential for leading the citizen soldiers of the next. Even Sylvanus Thayer could hardly have improved on his text. The captain's words had extra meaning too, at a time when Polk was staffing new troops with faithful Democrats. Two major generals and six brigadiers, and nary a West Pointer in the lot.

After all, Scott was a Whig, and from Washington it began to look as if Old Zach might be another. So Polk wanted Democrats. The appointments got a wry line from Taylor. "When they arrive," he said, "there will be too much rank I apprehend to get along with, pleasantly." And rank so easy to come by.

The worst of the lot was Gideon J. Pillow, a former law partner of Polk's in Tennessee. Anything West Pointers could do Brigadier Pillow also could do. Like building a fort. He built one at Camargo, with the ditch dug inside. What young Lieutenant Cadmus Wilcox stared at in unbelief was not prescribed in his academy texts. Another lieutenant, he said, mounted a mustang and cleared both parapet and ditch. Fortunately, not all of the new officers looked so silly as Pillow. Major General William Orlando Butler had served under Jackson in the War of 1812; Brigadier John A. Quitman had been in the fighting for Texan independence; and Brigadier James Shields of Illinois had once fought a duel.

Another brigadier general was Thomas L. Hamer. When his appointment reached him in Ohio, he said: "It will cause a hearty laugh all over the state." Speeches yes, but commanding a regiment was out of the question. Yet here he was, one of the faithful who would give the proper coloration to an army saddled at the top by Whigs. After the next battle President Polk hoped for a change in headlines—to Democratic heroes and less Old Rough and Ready.

The advance on Monterey began two days after Taylor's grand review. It aimed first for Cerralvo, 60 miles south. A party sent out ahead to set up a depot en route called the town ideal, with good water and plenty of fresh fruit. Kendall of the *Picayune* was in the van too, planning an "express" to hurry the news back to New Orleans. Meade went along on the march minus tent and baggage. Even the engineers had never looked ahead to moving an army's needs on muleback. General Orders No. 109 parceled out the few wagons (180) along with the pack mules: one wagon for each brigade and division headquarters, three for each regiment; one pack mule for every three company officers, every eight noncoms, musicians, etc. Old Zach was carving the load up thin.

Mules—1900 of them. They carried up to 300 pounds each and Mexican *arrieros* were hired to pack and drive them. Grant's colonel tapped him to help the system work, but Taylor's $20 bargains put a strain on the lieutenant's rule against swearing. Mules bucked or ran off, scattering their loads, rolling on them, snapping tentpoles, throwing pots, kettles, mess pans, axes, picks, coffee mills, chests, and ammunition boxes. Captains Henry, Giddings and Kenly, who were not involved, could enjoy the show. In the end the *arrieros* usually won. Sweating in tight leather jackets above flaring pants split to the knee, they outbrayed, outmaneuvered, and outfought their animals in a daily storm of dust and flying hoofs. Something new and colorful in logistics.

In the White House, James Knox Polk would soon be agreeing with the army's chief quartermaster. How foolish of General Taylor that he should wish to encumber himself with wagons. No, in that country certainly mules were better.

From Washington mules looked good. Taylor, down on the road to Monterey, still thought wistfully of wagons.

Not all of the troops filed out of Camargo. In orders on August 28 the general listed his limited transport and lack of supplies as reason for taking only 3000 of the volunteers. Added to the regulars, they gave him a force of 6000. Too few for the campaign ahead, Taylor felt, but the country was pushing for action and victories. Naturally his government followed the standard practice of passing the pressure along to the front.

In the meantime, for the nearly 10,000 volunteers Taylor left behind at Camargo or on the lower Rio Grande, he could offer only regrets. He knew, he said, that he was disappointing the ambitions of many regiments and officers. Later he hoped to call in more of them if only the government would furnish the means. It was a credit to those cut out from the advance that the general felt the need to apologize at all. In camp they were nothing but trouble, trouble, trouble. Yet at the promise of fighting, some of his citizen soldiers wanted to march.

Taylor had organized the army into three divisions. Of the regulars, Twiggs got the 1st and Worth the 2nd. Kenly was happy to find the Baltimore Battalion under Twiggs—a volunteer force accepted by the professionals. Captain Albert G. Blanchard's "Phoenix" Company went into the 2nd Division. It had been the only short-term unit in its state to re-enlist: "the chivalry of Louisiana simmered down and purified of all dross." No wonder they belonged with regulars. The bulk of the volunteer troops made up the 3rd Division, General Butler commanding.

In the first week of September the last of Taylor's marching men pulled out of Camargo. Camargo—now a byword of the northern Mexico campaign; heat, mud, disease, and death.

Headquarters moved on the 5th. Old Zach had survived a killing summer and at last had his army on the road again.

On the day he set out, in Washington, the President put down some thoughts in his diary. General Taylor, he wrote, seemed willing enough to obey orders but was reluctant to give opinions or take responsibility. Although in Mexico where he could furnish information not available to the government, he offered no suggestions and nothing about his plans.[1] In short, "Gen'l Taylor, I fear, is not the man for the command of the army. He is brave but he does not seem to have resources or grasp of mind enough to conduct such a campaign. . . . Though this is so, I know of no one whom I can put in his place."

[1] Taylor's dispatch of August 26 had not yet reached the War Department. In it he described the defenses of Monterey, the number and kind of troops in the city, and outlined his plans. The slow communications of 1846 would continue to cause misunderstanding between the administration and the army.

CHAPTER V

VICTORY MINUS

Taylor's refusal to add the chores of general-in-chief to his problems at the front left Polk up in the air. As war secretary the solid, plodding Marcy did what a good politician could to master the arcane detail of the military. He got little help from ancient underlings the President accused of being less than lukewarm to the war. Marcy got more help from Scott, probably more than he should have. The ambitious general was happy to fill the vacuum, and he began shaping plans that would make him the logical head of any new operations in Mexico.

But the President had all but written off Scott after the "fire upon my rear" and the "hasty plate of soup." Yet where else could he turn, either at home or down below on the Rio? The dilemma hit just when Polk was taking Mexico's pulse on the idea of peace, and when he was digging at Congress for the $2,000,000 to use as bait. His request had looked good till a Pennsylvanian in the House tacked on a rider. David Wilmot wanted slavery barred from any land that Mexico might give up.

During the storm stirred up over this issue Polk damned the amendment as "both foolish and mischievous." It was the work of anti-war obstructionists. *Niles' National Register* agreed. On August 15, editor Jeremiah Hughes warned Congress against deciding such "grave topics . . . in a fit of convulsions." The President's bill got through the House, but in the Senate a filibuster by John Davis of Massachusetts ran out the clock on the 29th Congress, 1st Session. No money. Instead, Polk complained, only drinking and irresponsibility. Neither generals nor lawmakers would help him along with the war. Well, let it drag out, and the likes of Senator Davis could carry the results on their own consciences.

Polk was feeling sorry for himself: an uncooperative Taylor in Mexico, a trouble-making Scott in the War Department, and a sabotaging Congress in the Capitol.

By mid-September no one was deeper in self-pity than Scott. On August 12 he had informed the President that he was now ready to assume command at the front. "I do this without any hesitation in respect to Major General Taylor, having reason to believe that my presence at the head of the principal army in the field, in accordance with my rank, is neither unexpected nor undesired by that distinguished commander." Polk set him down two days later in equally stuffy words, a rejection which Scott called "vulgar and cold-blooded."

The President seemed to mean what he said about having no one to replace Taylor. Still, he had not changed his mind as to the general's lack of grasp and drive, which he complained of again on September 15. By the 20th he and his cabinet finally took up the subject of strategy themselves. Why not instruct Commodore Conner to take and hold Tampico, a Gulf port some 400 miles above Vera Cruz? Next, send in that

U.S. Signal Corps Photo, Courtesy of The National Archives (artist unknown)

(1) Zachary Taylor, writes the author, dressed up only twice during the war—on one occasion to meet Navy men who had already learned that his attitude toward spit-and-polish was casual, and dressed "down" accordingly. The portrait suggests the hawk-nosed toughness of a general who, fighter that he was, still "could not hate."

WESTERN AMERICANA COLLECTION,
YALE UNIVERSITY LIBRARY

(2)   Captain Samuel Ringgold

LIBRARY OF CONGRESS

(3)   Taylor's low opinion of field artillery changed when a dedicated officer named Samuel Ringgold got his chance. At the Battle of Palo Alto, Ringgold, because of the devastatingly accurate fire of his Battery, emerged as a hero second only to Taylor. (Bottom painting shows Ringgold's weapon in action.)

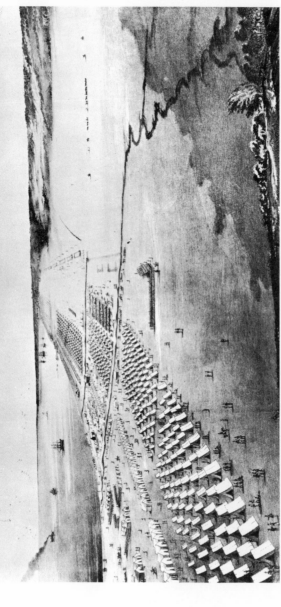

AFTER A DRAWING BY CAPTAIN DANIEL POWERS WHITING, PHOTO COURTESY OF AMERICAN HERITAGE PUBLISHING Co., INC.

(4) The Army of Occupation outside Corpus Christi. "When the eye first rests upon this camp, cluttered with a thousand white tents...irresistible shouts of admiration follow!" wrote an enthusiastic arrival in August. But what followed also were December cold, 40-degree drops within hours, illness and rumor, writes Mr. Nichols.

Library of Congress

(5) *Top left*: President James K. Polk.

© 1953 by Southern Methodist University Press. Reprinted by Permission.

(6) *Top right*: General William J. Worth

U.S. Signal Corps Photo, Courtesy of The National Archives

(7) *Bottom left*: General John E. Wool

(8) Months at Corpus pointed to a sultry afternoon at Palo Alto and a commitment to fight the United States' first battle against another race of people. "It was a picture-print battle, two massed fronts facing each other on a plain and blasting away. Formalized and neat." (From the text.) It took nerve and hard training to advance the regiments in square formation, but everyone agreed that the ox-drawn 18-pounders made all the difference that day.

West Point Museum. Courtesy of American Heritage Publishing Co., Inc.

(9) General Taylor's headquarters at Walnut Springs, after the Battle of Buena Vista. The author writes that Zach's soldiers liked his accessibility. "He stayed close to headquarters in camp, where he sat daily on his stool outside the tent to hear complaints from citizens and the army alike. Not only complaints but praise." Orderly Bingham holds Old Whitey as the general talks with Whiting, Bliss, Mansfield, Bragg, and others.

(10) General Winfield Scott

(11) General Antonio Lopez de Santa Anna

(12) Buena Vista: the triumph of Taylor's campaigns; the battle he needed to bring the war back to northern Mexico and away from Scott; the success that was "an embarrassing fact which no Whig paper would let Polk forget." It was not a pretty battle, and the saber-swinging Mexicans and the Americans relentlessly pushing across the rugged terrain both meant business.

direction any troops not tied up by Taylor or Wool. These plans pointed to an eventual shift of the war from inland to the coast, at least as the start of a new invasion.

Meanwhile Polk had been pushing some personal strategy. On his secret orders of August 16, Conner had passed Santa Anna through the blockade into Vera Cruz. "Old Peg Leg," savior of the Mexican masses, would now befriend America, too. He was all for peace, he told Polk's agent before leaving Havana. As soon as he got rid of the wicked Paredes and his monarchists he would make a treaty to the liking of the United States. For Polk, of course, that meant New Mexico, Arizona, and California far enough south to include the port of San Francisco. In short, his old dream.

To see his treaty through, the President needed the $2,000,-000 still held up in the Senate. But near the end of August the money began to look less useful. Santa Anna stalled. Bad political climate at home, he explained, very discouraging for peace. Better wait till December when a new Congress met in the Mexican capital. Polk's own little strategy slowed to a dead end. *Shrewd, secretive, calculating*—some of the adjectives threatened to backfire. As a partner in intrigue Santa Anna was a mad risk at best, a gamble to stop the fighting before American support cooled off. Congress already was stubborn, and with the dream unfulfilled. *Ambitious* still fit President Polk.

2

So altogether, plenty of trouble hung over General Taylor's head as he worked his way south toward Monterey. He rode along unknowingly shadowed by (1) a thumbs down from his President and commander-in-chief; (2) Scott's itch to take over the army; (3) a switch in strategy to the Gulf; (4) the tricky Santa Anna dumped ashore at Vera Cruz.

Santa Anna was none of Taylor's doing, but in one way or another Zach had asked for the other troubles. First, he had frustrated Polk by not rattling his sword for a drive into Mexico's heartland. Not all of the general's caution grew out of doubt about its success. He was old and tired. His private letters kept repeating the theme. At age sixty-two, field duty came hard. Thirty-eight years in the service had eroded his ambition. Now it took battles to stir him up. The times between only wore him out: volunteers with their delinquent antics and tender health; the cry for boats, for wagons; the curse of mule packs; and always the heat from home to get on with the war.

That was the worst. *"The country begins to be impatient for action!"* And whose paper said that? The Democrats' paper. Polk's paper. In italics on September 14: " *'Old Rough and Ready' has become a sobriquet of the Commanding General. We hope that he will realize the character to the end of the chapter."* And who was pushing? Polk, who demanded results but withheld support.

Now as to Scott. Three times in 1846 Old Zach had written his son-in-law: let the general-in-chief come down and relieve him—release him to look after his own affairs and enjoy the quiet he deserved at this "time of life." Actually Taylor was only two years older than Scott, but with Palo Alto and Resaca hanging from his belt he could relax. By contrast, Scott's heroics of 1812–15 had dimmed in the public memory. Vanity and the ache for applause still drove the general-in-chief. Taylor, then, in his willingness to step down, was courting any trouble it might later make.

Finally, if Polk and the cabinet were switching from Mexico's interior to the Gulf, the old general could only thank himself again. Early in July he had advised against moving south from Monterey. A month later he was admitting the possibility of operating from the Gulf, though with strong doubts.

But in spite of dark rumblings from Washington or his weary old body, Taylor's spirits rose in ratio to the miles he put between himself and Camargo. He was sloughing off the vapors of that caldron, along with the dregs of the volunteers. The harsh winnowing by disease had reduced his citizen soldiers to their hardest core. The residue might even fight. That was what they had joined up for in the beginning, and at last they were on the way. By September 12, as the army climbed the road to Cerralvo, Taylor reported its health much improved, the troops "generally in excellent condition." Five days later they looked better yet—"ready for the most active and arduous service."

Old Zach felt equally good about prospects ahead. He knew General Ampudia had moved into Monterey to join units from Arista. Still he thought a defense of the city unlikely, not with only 3000 regulars there, and as many pickup troops. Meade came back from a reconnaissance to find the army in high morale. Not even the rumors of Santa Anna's return seemed to worry anyone.

The marching went on. The morale went down. Soldiers began to moan about pack straps, the heft of their muskets, the hot scratch of blanket rolls, and the flopping of bullet pouches at their belts. Gun metal burned into hands, and the stony road slashed their boots. Water was short even though Taylor had allotted precious wagon space to carry it. The straggling mounted and more and more men dropped out, their blood "boiling like lava."

But the worst of the march was the beginning. On the sharper rise near Cerralvo the air cooled and the going improved. So did the scenery. Officers jarring along in the "comfort" of the saddle turned tourist. If he was single, Meade wrote his wife, he would spend the rest of his days in this country. Captain Barbour gave up; the surroundings out-matched his power to describe. Quail hunter Reynolds could hardly wait to move up farther. Sam French tried to put it all down. He started with the groves of ebony and Brazil wood, then moved on to a favorite topic, food. Cornfields silk-ripe in the sun and the juicy hues of fruits and melons caught his hungry eye.

These West Pointers were riding to battle, ravished by a countryside. For Captain Henry the spell began with Cerralvo itself, the neatest and most picturesque town he had ever seen. He loved the blue limestone houses, giant trees, and the clear cool stream lined with fig, peach, pomegranate, orange, and pecan. He was hungry, too. If it should get too hot, he said, pick a watermelon and go sit under a pecan tree.

On September 9, Ampudia broke the euphoria with a screaming proclamation. It called on all Mexicans to avenge the blood of their brothers and to drive the invaders from sacred soil. For the Americans it was time to put down the watermelons and move on. Like the others, volunteers Kenly and Giddings hated to leave Cerralvo. Kenly's weakness was the lush gardens, the handsome stone bridges, and *limonada* with a dash of *viño de Parras*.

This was an army, every day thinning out its supply line in hostile country while advancing hypnotic through the beauty around it. Somebody besides Ampudia had to think of war.

Taylor did. Practically insulated by his nature from viewing scenery, he kept probing the route in his front. He covered the pioneers on road repairs with a squadron of dragoons and a Ranger unit. The Texans linked duty with looting. They combed every house in their path, or out of it, and kicked about poor pickings. Not a single Mexican house, they said, was up to the meanest rail-pen stable back home. No starry-eyed gawking from Texas men. Those wonderful groves, for example: "so d——d thick you can't shove a bowie knife through."

Mexican cavalry fell back as Taylor advanced. The Rangers managed one small strike at a rear guard, and that was all until they reined up in sight of Monterey on September 19. Taylor, with his staff and other officers, followed close behind, then Henderson's Texas mounted, then Twiggs', Worth's, and Butler's divisions. Thomas Thorpe of the *Tropic* was along, full of reportorial prose: "The mists still clung around the turrets of its churches, and enveloped its commanding heights; but the ascending sun constantly dissipated the veil. . . . All was silent; not a breath of air stirred; dewy softness rested upon every thing."

Thorpe was working up to the "hot sulphurous smoke" that rolled from a dark colored fort out north of the city. Three shells arched toward the Americans from 1300 yards away. One struck the ground not far in front of Taylor, bounced over his head and ploughed the earth in rear. The Rangers charged down into the plain, where they crisscrossed back and forth almost under the guns. When Taylor called them back the army cheered their riding stunt.

3

That was the first look at Monterey. The army went into camp at San Domingo, a large grove two miles north and slightly east of the city. The engineers picked it for its springs. Giddings said the location reminded him of picnic grounds back home near Dayton, Ohio. Comparison with the home town was the ultimate concession any American could make.

The area covered 100 acres, with brush already cleared from under the live oaks and pecans, fenced for protection and heavy with Spanish moss. The Mexicans apparently liked to picnic, too.

A stream gurgled along through the grove, glinting silver over stones and gravel, shadowed here and there by giant branches. What a shame, sighed Thorpe, to see the ruts of artillery wheels despoiling grass sowed to support flirting girls and young men strumming guitars. The view looking out from the grove stopped even Zach. To the southeast he saw the upsweep of a mountain called Silla, or Mexican Saddle. Others, only slightly less eye-catching, ringed Monterey in an amphitheater opening to the north. The Sierras framed it on the south and Mitre Mountain on the west. To believe Kirby Smith, sunsets washed the three-sided valley with colors unmatched by anything either in the United States or in Europe.

Scenery again. Taylor might succumb, and Giddings and Captain Smith, but not Sam Grant. He swept his glass over the business at hand: ebony groves, sparkling streams, spectacular heights—Grant saw only terrain. This sound military word covered it for him. A good soldier defined ground in relation to offense or defense. To his eye the city was "backed by a range of hills of moderate elevation." *Elevation* also sounded military. The "Black Fort" stood 700 yards north of the first streets, its guns *commanding* the *approaches* to the full extent of their range. Grant's matter-of-fact inventory also noted the fortified heights to the west, which guarded the road to Saltillo. Fieldworks rimmed the eastern end of the city, and the flat, sandbagged roofs of houses with connecting entrenchments fronted the whole. That summed up the scenery for Lieutenant Grant.

Taylor had lapsed into softness but not for long. He sent out his engineers to feel for Mexican strength and weakness.

He could see by now that Ampudia meant to hang on. The Americans would have to fight for the capital of Nuevo León. Monterey shaped a rectangle along the north bank of the little San Juan River. Its main streets paralleled its length, running east and west.

Where to strike? The Black Fort discouraged a direct advance from the north, and the stream saved Monterey from the rear, or south. On the east Mansfield scouted only solid strength—one fort for sure, probably several others. The Mexicans had connected the works by blocking streets with heavy masonry embrasured for guns. They would expose attackers to cross fire. Also, going in on that end would lay a column open both flank and rear to the Black Fort.

Defenses west of the city at first looked even stronger, with its two fortified heights covering the road to Saltillo. But good reconnaissance by the engineer party under Captain William G. Williams found weaknesses. The two fortifications on each hill seemed makeshift. Under-gunned, they would be hard to reinforce. That settled it for Taylor. The main push would aim for the Saltillo road.

On Saturday evening, September 19, San Domingo (now Walnut Springs to the Americans) was an army camp with a difference. The chores were the same. Pickets marched out to their posts, detaching from column at intervals. Hostlers led the artillery horses to water; staff officers cantered about; mess fires started up; wagons were wheeled into park; arrieros corralled their resisting mules—all of it familiar enough. The difference was in the sounds. A before-battle edge rode on everything heard. Taps on a drumhead beat higher, tighter. Bugles shrilled a more nervous vibrato. A sledge smacking a tent stake jumped everybody's nerves. Barked commands and the shouts of roll call echoed back in shock.

Rain came on after dark, pulling men closer to the fires

and the nudge of other shoulders. Only a few of them talked. Huddled in a group of Rangers, Kendall heard somebody repeating an old statistic: it took 100 rounds to hit a man in combat. He had heard it said about the Napoleonic Wars. Another Ranger called such shooting a foolish waste of lead. "I have got just twenty bullets in my pouch, and if I don't kill or cripple just twenty greasers, it will be because they are licked before I have had time to load twenty times, or else because I have been 'sent under' early."

Battle jitters never got a Texas Ranger, but how about the other volunteers? Restless under the soft drip from leaves, they wondered about tomorrow. Big talk and feeling tough had come easy at assembly points back in the states, with the bands, and families and friends waving and cheering along the streets. How could the heady glow of last summer end in this, tossing on a bed of moss in a foreign country, about to storm a city they had never heard of? Well, it would grant A. Moses of Cincinnati his wish: "When I volunteered it was to fight, not to be idle for a year."

Thoughts about tomorrow had their hold on General Worth as well. None of Taylor's good spirits during the march had rubbed off on him. All the way down he kept warning about hard fighting ahead. As for himself, it had to be "either a grade or a grave." Anything to make brigadier. To earn the rank he would have to make up for the two battles he missed. And although Taylor had no reason to reward his pout over brevets, on the 20th Old Zach gave Worth his chance.

Why? First, because Taylor seldom held grudges; second, because he was a good judge of men. He assigned the main attack to his ablest officer.

144

4

Worth took his column out from camp at 2 o'clock on Sunday afternoon. Texans under Colonel Jack Hays covered the advance, as stripped down and wiry as the mustangs they rode. Behind them marched the 5th, 7th, and 8th Infantry, then Childs' Artillery Battalion. His men carried muskets but clannishly hung on to their red-striped pants—in other words, still *artillery!* Duncan's battery and a new one led by Captain William M. Mackall rode out next. Blanchard's Louisiana volunteers closed the rear. Taylor was keeping nothing back in Walnut Springs better than he gave Worth, unless possibly it was Ridgely. Later he added May's dragoons and the Texas mounted regiment under General Henderson.

Captain Kenly saw them off. Once more a volunteer envied the smart cadence and the gleaming arms and equipments, from the bronze 6-pounders down to the last turnbuckle of the carriages. Everything about the regulars stood for class.

Worth's division was the key to Taylor's plan, a plan as simple and sensible as drawings in an elementary text on war:

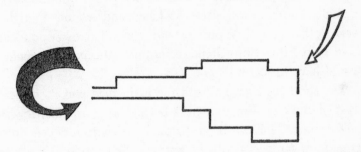

The turning movement (black arrow) would close the road to Saltillo, and with it any chance for supplies or reinforce-

145

ments to reach Ampudia. Meanwhile Taylor would put just enough pressure on the east end of the city to help Worth. In military terms, a diversion.

The advancing column detoured beyond range of the Black Fort, through grain fields and sugar cane. A roadway had to be cut for the guns, which slowed the march to a mere six miles by dark. Riding ahead with a Ranger escort, Worth and Meade swung into a gorge that channeled the Saltillo road. This was a sensitive point to the enemy. Outposts opened on the Americans and drove them back to the main column. It was a dim preview of the next day's job. At night it rained again, colder and harder. In the final quiet hours a lean ascetic-faced captain unknowingly brought his journal to an end. "I feel as calm and collected as if I were in the Astor House," Barbour wrote.

General Pedro de Ampudia agreed with Taylor on the importance of the Saltillo road. He proved it to Worth in particular on the morning of the 21st. Nearly 2000 Mexicans, mostly lancers, charged Hays' Texans and Duncan as soon as the Americans hit the road. But Worth got his infantry up in time. From behind it Duncan and Mackall began looping shells into the target of horsemen. Fifteen minutes were enough. The Mexicans left 100 killed and wounded in the wake of their retreat. Worth lost one man killed, two wounded. Like Palo Alto again—firepower against lancers. The enemy would have to learn.

The short fight gave Worth the main road and its feeders west of the city. But though it bottled up Ampudia, it was only a start. The two heights now lay ahead: Independence Hill, 1000 yards away on the left, and Federation Hill about half as far on Worth's right. To reach Monterey he had to knock out the two fieldworks on each. As usual the fat, black arrow curved like an accomplished fact on the map, smugly painting over hazards still to be met.

Taylor's lighter arrow covered obstacles even worse. His 10-inch mortar and the two 24-pound howitzers took more metal than they threw from their position northeast of the Black Fort. They promised small help to the column about to advance on the city's east end. These men would begin the demonstration to distract the enemy from Worth's approach. The attacking division belonged to Twiggs, but it would leave without him. Twiggs believed in a loose-bowels-safer theory. Take a physic before battle and a bullet would pass harmlessly through the intestines. Even a volunteer had a right to doubt that, and Kenly wondered about the general's purged guts.

5

At 8 o'clock in the morning of September 21 Lieutenant Colonel John Garland took Twiggs' division toward Monterey. Quarry holes and cornfields hedged by shrubs hid the view in front. Garland should have veered left to come in on El Tenería, a fort out on the northeast end. Engineer Mansfield was waiting there for him. This would have pulled Garland beyond range of the Black Fort and kept him from bogging down, first in a ravine, then in a tangle of gardens, narrow lanes, and high stone walls. Instead, Garland's approach brought him in 200 yards west of Tenería where he came under its flanking fire.

A second fort, Diablo, surprised him in front, and the Black Fort had him in range from the rear. Mexican infantry from behind walls, in windows, and on rooftops added their weight of lead.

Unless that Napoleonic statistic held up, 100 rounds per man hit, not many of Garland's men would ever get out. The only volunteers with the column never waited to make the test; young toughs from Washington and Baltimore took off for Walnut Springs. Only some 70 of the 230 in the Baltimore Battalion stuck with the regulars of the 1st and 3rd. Too much ground-shaking *whoomph!* and rattle and orange bursts through smoke that blinded and stung. And more than that—men falling. Those who hung on scrambled for cover. When they could they stuck out their muskets and banged away vaguely west and south.

Taylor sent Bragg in to help them out. Much galloping, coming about and unlimbering, none of it with a target the exposed 6-pounders could hurt. The battery was lucky to get out.

So far only one gain, and it took an officer with the name of Electus Backus to achieve it. The 1st Infantry captain got some 50 or more men up on a roof near Tenería. From there they began picking off Mexicans through the embrasures of the fort and in smaller defense points around the area. If they could hold on and find more help to wear down Tenería, they might give Taylor a toehold on this end of town.

But who said demonstration?[1] A whole division committed and in trouble at that. Now a second division on the way to bail out the first, and just when engineer Mansfield had finally caught up with Garland to order him out. This second column, made up of volunteers, was under General John Quitman. About a half mile from town it stood waiting

[1] Correspondent Thorpe, who was with Taylor, thought Garland was under the impression that his was the main attack, though the general had told him to see Mansfield at the edge of town for instructions. Garland missed the engineer officer by taking the wrong direction in advancing.

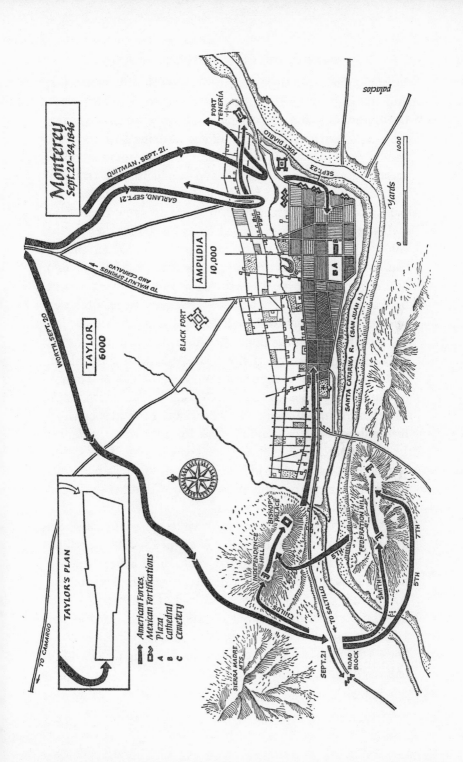

Monterey
Sept. 20-24, 1846

TAYLOR'S PLAN

TO CAMARGO

American Forces
Mexican Fortifications
A Plaza
B Cathedral
C Cemetery

TAYLOR 6000

AMPUDIA 10,000

WORTH, SEPT. 20

TO WALNUT SPRINGS AND CERRALVO

BLACK FORT

QUITMAN, SEPT. 21

GARLAND, SEPT. 21

FORT TENERIA

FORT DIABLO

SEPT. 23

SANTA CATARINA R. (SAN JUAN R.)

BISHOP'S PALACE

INDEPENDENCE HILL

CHILDS

TO SALTILLO

5TH

FEDERATION HILL

SMITH

7TH

5TH

SEPT. 21

ROAD BLOCK

SIERRA MADRE MTS.

palacios

Yards

0   1000

for the order to advance. The men were full of fidgets, fixing and unfixing bayonets, buttoning coats, then ripping them open, checking and rechecking cartridge pouches, swearing. They had seen the scared Baltimores sneaking back to camp. It was their turn next. What would happen to 1200 volunteers on a mission to "save" Garland's regulars? The 1st Ohio, 1st Tennessee, and the Mississippi Rifles had only three companies of Taylor's veteran 4th up front to show them how.

It was costly action when it came. A Black Fort shell drilled through nine Tennessee men on their way in. Their colonel expected the rest to scatter like fowl; instead they held column and drove head-on for Tenería. A third of the regulars went down in front of them, but the Tennessee regiment boxed one side of the fort while Jeff Davis fed his Rifles into an open embrasure on the other. Backus at last had help. What he began and still carried along, the volunteers finished off. The Stars and Stripes soon broke out over the roof of Tenería.

During this time Generals Butler and Hamer had taken the 1st Ohio in near Garland on the right. Their luck equalled his, and once again Mansfield had to order troops out. But by noon, when Taylor heard of Tenería's fall, he countermanded the order. He had his toehold, if only by a nail. One fort down, a tough one still to take, along with other works and a bridgehead over the stream.

Taylor was paying high to pin down troops Ampudia would like to use against Worth. The colonel of the Baltimore Battalion had fallen while trying to make up for his defecting men. Engineer Williams was dead. Captain Barbour of the "calm and collected" entry was dead. Lieutenant Charles Hoskins had borrowed Grant's horse to go in, and he was killed. (Grant had better luck later in the day on another horse.) Well over a hundred men were already down with a half-day's fighting still to come.

At about the hour Tenería fell, some of Worth's division were sitting out west of Monterey. They were trying a mess of green corn, though green corn was not prescribed by Zach's medics. Early in the afternoon they started out for Federation Hill, a steep 1000-foot climb. To take it, Worth sent Captain Charles F. Smith with several hundred regulars and Texans. After fording cold, deep little San Juan, they shinnied up through the first tangled growth. Anxiously their general watched them lose formation; also saw Mexicans moving down the slope. Fire from both their batteries, about 600 yards apart on the ridge, combed the base.

At 1 o'clock Worth ordered the 7th Infantry across the stream, then the 5th, then Blanchard's company. One enemy battery went silent. The other Smith, Brigadier Persifor F., got the second by scrambling uphill on an angle. His men soon drove the Mexicans off the hill and across the water to their works up on Independence. Smith turned their own guns against them until dark ended a duel between the two heights.

The main attack was going better than Taylor's diversion. Worth had lost only 20 men killed and wounded. Over on the east side the cost of Tenería alone was 100 casualties in the Tennessee regiment and half as many in the Mississippi. Fighting in the afternoon increased the cost. The Ohio volunteers of Quitman, after dropping back on Mansfield's order, had bumped into a lancer troop flushed out from the Black Fort. Here the Americans saw dirty work—Mexicans running their steel through the wounded trapped along hedges and fence rows. Because the effect of retreat on green troops was often unnerving, Taylor probably saved lives when he sent them in again.

Back they went. Butler headed them toward the fort called Diablo, but they quickly lost formation under a hammering cross fire. The general took a musket ball in the leg and turned the command over to Hamer, his brigadier. Hamer was hit, then Colonel Alexander M. Mitchell. The drive stalled.

Up to Tenería rode Twiggs, still wobbly from the effects of his "theory." He switched Ridgely from his own battery to the heavier guns of the fort. Taylor sent one of the howitzers down to help. In the excitement of the new buildup Garland regrouped his regulars; they advanced by file, fired, dropped back to reload, moved forward again. They were after Diablo from the rear.

But the Devil fort would not go down. Not for Butler, Ridgely, and Garland combined. The Mexicans caught them from street barricades on the left, the bridgehead south and center, Diablo on the right. They masked their guns and sheltered their infantry. Anywhere in that pocket was hell for Taylor's men. Eight more West Pointers died. Total casualties for the day now bulged to 394.

By 5 o'clock the general knew he would have to settle for Tenería. With Ridgely and Bragg, who finally had a target, driving off two late lancer thrusts, the punched-out divisions took the road for Walnut Springs. The wounded followed in the rain after dark, moaning and screaming with every jolt of the wagons. The guard left in and around the fort spent a bad night too. They widened the ditch, tore down sheds to set up a barricade of their own, and when they could, flopped on the muddy ground to sleep. No blankets, no food— and with a distillery building in their hands, nothing to drink. But the Mexicans did supply fireworks. Rockets flared the sky over Tenería, varied by an occasional shell.

6

Tuesday, September 22, was quiet on the east end of Monterey. Sobered by his losses, Taylor decided to wait for more progress by Worth. After all, Worth's still was the main attack.

Around noon Zach relieved the garrison in Tenería, except for Ridgely. Bragg sat out most of the day in a ravine north of town. Eventually he was driven out when 18-pounders from the Black Fort wore away the ground in front of him. For two days now Bragg had seen little but trouble.

The day's action came from the west. At three in the morning Worth marched 500 troops to the base of the remaining height, Independence Hill. Rain mists covered the start of their painful climb, two feet up, one back. A hundred yards from the crest these driving goat-feet surprised the defenders. After one wild volley in the dark, the Mexicans fled their fort, running their guns down the northeast slope to the Bishop's Palace. Once inside its massive outer walls, they felt safe. No infantry, not even the nasty Texas rifles could reach them there.

Worth agreed. He had Duncan dismantle a 12-pound howitzer, gave him 50 regulars under Engineer Sanders, and up they went. A sweating two-hour haul by ropes found them a spot 400 yards from the Palace. Shells filled with musket balls began exploding inside the masonry. Damned gringos! The Mexicans piled out of their enclosure, some after Duncan, others to retake their fort, and lancers started up from the plain below. Ampudia was making a fight of it to hold his last hill.

Worth countered by bringing the 5th and Blanchard over from Federation. By then the Mexicans had hit a wall of regulars, flanked by Hays' Texans on the right and more under Walker to the left. The howitzer blew open the Palace gate to let one of Childs' artillery companies in. For once his red stripes could put matches to touchholes, an old habit they were glad to pick up again. They turned the captured guns on the beginning enemy flight.

The west end of Monterey gaped open for tomorrow. Casualties: one Ranger officer and five men killed, six wounded. That gave Worth a two-day total of 32. Both fortified heights were in his hands. The general who missed Palo Alto and Resaca was making up for his foolish sulk.

Wednesday morning shrank the space between the halves of Taylor's army to less than a mile. During the night Ampudia had given up Diablo, along with his other eastern defenses. He would make his stand in a two-square area surrounding the main plaza. It pinched him into the city's heart but left him hard to reach through the buildings and blocked-off avenues. And north of the city his men still held the Black Fort.

Worth waited on his side for Taylor to strike. From the west it looked easy and his men wanted to get it over with. What was holding Taylor back? He was closer to the plaza. Finally when late afternoon carried the noise of battle across town, Worth put columns along the two main entering streets. But not for long. In order to dodge the spew of grapeshot they switched to cutting directly through the houses. An old Texas custom—Béxar 1835. Picks, crowbars, axes, and short-fused shells rammed into stubborn walls to hack a path toward the center of town.

Before midafternoon the fighting died out on the east. On his own side Worth found himself going it alone, and he began wondering why. The answer was caution. Taylor still had the 21st on his mind. After five hours of tunneling—there were Texans with Taylor too—had brought him within a square of the main plaza, ammunition ran short. At this point the general sized up his tired men against the job ahead. Too much to ask of them until he heard something from Worth. He pulled back.

Two generals 1000 yards apart and no communication. So with silence on the east Worth broke off too, though he held his ground. Good fighting hours dulled away. By 5 o'clock Major Monroe had worked his 10-inch mortar around the north suburbs from Taylor's sector. His old "soup pot" was good to have and Worth ordered it set up in a cemetery about 800 yards west of the plaza. Too far away for hits, Monroe decided, but close enough for practice lobs. A shell soon grazed a wing of the cathedral, rattling down stone and cement before it exploded in the crowded plaza.

Monroe had the range. Then Worth's artillerymen somehow hoisted two howitzers and a 6-pounder atop the tallest building in the area. They found good targets among Ampudia's massed defenders, some rounds dropping from six to ten men. One good shot on the cathedral might end everything. This church of God held the Mexican ammunition. Meanwhile cavalry stampeded among infantry and scared civilians.

The near panic unnerved Ampudia. Earlier in the day he had asked Taylor's leave to remove the city's women and children. Taylor sometimes was soft but not often foolish. The time lost in getting them out would break his winning momentum, also let the Mexicans recoup. Civilians were the Mexican general's responsibility. Their danger ought to concern him. Ampudia, though, was more worried about his army, and about himself. At 9 o'clock in the evening he asked for an end to the fighting. He would evacuate with the "*personnel* and *materiél* which is left and under the assurance that no prosecution shall be taken against the citizens who have taken part in the defense."

The letter reached Taylor through the lines next morning (the 24th) at seven. His answer was no, but he did feel that the gallant defense of the city called for liberal terms. Let the army lay down its arms, retire to the interior of the country, and agree not to fight again unless properly exchanged.

Ampudia then requested an interview. Taylor met him and his staff at Worth's headquarters. In a newsman's phrase the Mexicans turned out in "barbaric splendor." The fringe of fat epaulets sprayed gold over their shoulders above panels of gew-gaws and medals. And the Mexicans' gall matched their dress. Ampudia wanted to bargain. He mumbled about a change of administration in the country's capital, and so forth. How could he decide what terms would be acceptable to his government?

Old Zach cut the parley short. His threat to start fighting again ended in compromise. Well, not ended exactly; not this soon. For two more days Worth, Henderson, and Jefferson Davis argued against Spanish guile. Example: in all honor the word *surrender* should be changed to *capitulation*—no, still too strong—make it *stipulation*. Further it would embarrass the Mexican artillery to depart without its pieces. First gall, then guile, and now Spanish pride. Who won the battle, after all? Which side had asked for terms? Taylor's staff kept the general from walking out again only by applying heavy pressure to force Ampudia's signature on the final results.

Ampudia got off easy. The Mexicans kept their precious field battery and all side arms and accoutrements. They could lower their flag from the Black Fort to a salute of guns. They had a week to withdraw as far as Saltillo. Further, Taylor guaranteed an armistice of two months, or until both sides could hear from their governments. In return Ampudia gave up the city, its fortifications, two dozen brass cannon, and all public property.

That ended the battle of Monterey.

7

The relieved citizens came out loaded with fresh fruit, corn bread, and wheat bread—practically a native commissary for Taylor's army. The hungry Americans bought everything in sight. On September 26 Ampudia's first troops left the city, the rest following in the next two days. They marched four abreast in mile-long lines, with the usual civilian straggle behind. "Youth and age, beauty and ugliness, donkeys and dogs, rags and finery." Thorpe was making notes for his *Tropic* again. Of the soldiers he preferred the mountain types to those from along the Gulf coast, who seemed to him degenerated by too much mixture of race. The lancers, he thought, would have made quite a show in their flutter of green and red pennons, but undersized mounts hurt their style.

Captain Henry and young Grant watched the departure, too. The captain thought the Mexican infantry looked brawny and tough. To the lieutenant they were an abject lot, pitiful, and as to the war, entirely ignorant of "what it was all about." The officers did agree on the end of the bloodletting. Grant was not for unconditional surrender at Monterey. Except for grumbling Texans who still carried the chips of Mier, Goliad, and the Alamo, Taylor's army went along with its chief. Good to have it over with.

By now the Americans had some idea of Ampudia's strength —at least 7000 regulars and 3000 other troops. He also had the advantage of the defensive, with 40 pieces of artillery (nearly all of them heavier than Taylor's), his forts, smaller fieldworks, street barricades, and the stout flat-roofed houses, every one a redoubt. In fact, with so much in his favor how could the Mexicans have lost? Out on the east end during the first day they gave more than they took, as Garland and Quitman well knew.

As in the earlier battles the Mexican troops began well, but again the first bad breaks shook morale. It hurt to lose the Saltillo road and the two heights on the west. Then, after Tenería's fall, when Ampudia decided to abandon Diablo and its supporting works, morale hit bottom. The general had trouble even getting the order obeyed. His men were already whipped before the final stand in the plaza.

Unfortunately Taylor had no way of knowing how little fight was left in the Mexicans. The cease-fire on the 24th had not included the Black Fort out north with its garrison of 500 men. To bring it down in the face of those 18-pounders would have taken more time and cost many more lives. He had no heart for adding to his casualties of 448, nearly a hundred more than Ampudia admitted losing. What hit Taylor hardest were his 43 officers killed or wounded. Captain Henry, for instance, began September 23 fifth in command of his regiment and ended the day at its head. Another American handicap was shortage of ammunition and supplies, which had to move down from 125 miles in rear.

A final reason for granting terms to Ampudia was Taylor himself. "The consideration of humanity was present to my mind," he said. It outweighed any possible gains to be expected from keeping up the attack. As always, compassion instead of hate. Also, the general could point to the President's instructions from as far back as July 9: "Keep looking for chances to negotiate. We want good will."

Negotiation was exactly what Ampudia had been promising. With a new government under Santa Anna in the making, generous terms at Monterey might lead to peace. Worth thought so, and his name headed the list of signers. Meade was all for trusting Santa Anna too, along with approving the two months' armistice, "for we are not prepared now, and could not have been in less time, to advance." Obviously Taylor's terms were not going begging for support.

The army, in fact, gave its general more credit for his heart than for his head. Doubts about his leadership went the rounds. At the east end of the city Taylor had overplayed his demonstration. He lost too many men. Worth made better headway from the west at only a fifth the cost. "But we were more skillfully directed," Meade said. Most of the praise for the battle was going to Worth. Colonel Baillie Peyton called him "the high comb cock of the army." Worth had no quarrel with this estimate. "I am satisfied with myself," he admitted. It was a satisfaction he did not extend to his chief. In writing his family he accused Taylor of throwing men into action without orders, direction, or proper command. He literally exposed them to murder.

Worth had looked better, certainly. He kept all his troops under close control, foresaw every threat, knocked out key defenses and reached the heart of the city with his columns practically intact. But Worth went in from the easier end. Once on Saltillo road, he had the Mexican works clearly in view—isolated on the two heights in his front. On his right the two forts of Federation Hill carried only three guns between them. To the left, Independence Hill had the four guns of the Bishop's Palace, and two more in the smaller fort above and west of it.

Of course, climbing the hills themselves was a desperate hand-over-hand all the way. The Mexicans thought Worth's men would never make it, and lost heart when they did. Too late they found their defenses too far separated for mutual support and their gun muzzles would not depress enough to rake the American ascent. From the heights even musketry overshot the climbers.[2] The Mexican flight peeled the west side of the city wide open. Worth's approach led through fewer streets, under less cross fire, and beyond range of the Black Fort.

What a difference on the east. Here, four forts (15 guns to the nine against Worth) drew eye-level bead on the American advance. Ampudia could shuttle his men back and forth as needed behind his network of barricades and the bridgehead. The mean-browed Black Fort, which could reach this side of town, added eight more guns to the defense. The Mexicans obviously had tried to compensate for lack of commanding heights like the hills to the west. When Captain Henry looked over the ground after the battle, he wondered how any of Garland's or Quitman's troops survived.

From the beginning two mistakes involved Taylor over his head. First, the engineers had underestimated the defensive strength on their left. The works were cleverly masked, and it took sharp contact to uncover them. Next, Garland's wrong approach put him in such trouble that Taylor had to bail him out—or try to. In went Quitman. So the feint, or diversion, turned into a bigger battle than Worth's. The smaller arrow on the map took over. Tactics backfired. Taylor found himself countering Clausewitz: "Even though we are strong we should direct our main attack against one point only."

[2] In the Civil War battle of Chattanooga, November 25, 1863, these same difficulties helped lose Missionary Ridge for the Confederates. Grant did not think the men under George Thomas could take it. When they did, he demanded: "By whose orders is this!?" If Grant had been with Worth instead of Taylor during the battle of Monterey, the experience might have spared him his sulky remark.

On both the first and third days Taylor went in with his men to help salvage his end of the fight. During the 23rd frantic staff officers tried to call him off, but too many soldiers had seen him and the word went around. Old Rough and Ready, on foot and up front, shouting for an ax to break down some greaser's door! After that there was no coaxing him out. He was the symbol, two thirds of him rugged torso, topped by his hawk nose and the cool gray eyes. Taylor's presence alone added up to another brigade, a volunteer said afterward.

His genius for leading men in battle kept them at it until he could no longer stand the cost: as it "was impossible to accomplish anything in comparison to the loss we were sustaining I therefore drew off the troops in good order." In pulling back he was only following his original plan of leaving the main job to Worth. Meanwhile, if Taylor's losses helped the drive on the west—helped it enough, the sacrifice made some sense. Another military maxim warns that a demonstration has to be convincing. No doubt of it, Taylor's attack was. In any case, Worth had little trouble closing in from the west.

But Monterey tested Taylor beyond anything in his background, including the Florida war, the frontier, or even Palo Alto and Resaca. Palo Alto had been too simple. The next day at Resaca turned into a nightmare of terrain, a blind stabbing through the chaparral. Monterey was something else. It had been stormed before and never taken. The Spaniards tried for 13 days during the war for Mexican independence. Taylor tried and he took it—in three days. Still, officers less jealous than Worth thought he mishandled his part of the battle.

Not cautious enough, too willing to go in wherever the enemy resisted. Well, the last American war had seen plenty of caution: General William Hull at Detroit, General Henry

Dearborn at Plattsburg, and Alexander Smyth. Zachary Taylor patterned after Jackson. Just as Old Hickory had gambled his parcel of squirrel shooters against the 15,000 British at New Orleans, Taylor made his gamble at Monterey. Because he was the attacker he had to accept more losses. But like Jackson before him, he won. Clausewitz again: "No military leader has ever become great without audacity."

As in 1815 the America of 1846 could afford to trade losses for military leaders who gave it victories. Polk's war or not, the country had to win. Allow any hope for Mexican resistance and two things could happen. For one, it would start up the anti-war cry. Also, Britain, and probably France, might begin to wonder. Mexico could well be worth supporting, they would think. Why not test America's claims to Texas or at least keep the territory above the Rio Grande out of its hands.

With so much riding on the result, Taylor's casualties of 13.5 per cent at Monterey could hardly be called excessive.[3]

8

Sights and sounds of the fighting still hung over the city. Giddings remembered how hungry he had been, hungry enough to eat "a priest, a shank, an alderman, or pike." And he later went back to find the spot where he had seen soldiers resting on a fallen mule and putting their coffee tins down on its bloated side. Somebody else pointed to a rock. A wounded

[3] In the Civil War the battle of Antietam cost McClellan's army 23 per cent. Chickamauga inflicted 30 per cent on the Federals, 27 on the Confederates. Fighting units took casualties of at least 10 per cent for granted in even the mildest engagements. Not until World War II were losses of 10 per cent considered high.

man had sat there pressing in his dribbling bowels and croaking out a hymn. Echoes of Ridgely's laugh swelled above the reheard guns of Tenería. Also Jeff Davis shouting: "Great God. If I had thirty men with knives I could take the fort!" Albert Sidney Johnston crackling orders to Ohioans through the din in the streets. Sam Grant feeling over the ground after dark on the 21st to bring in the body of his friend, Charles Hoskins.

One man who would just as well forget Monterey was Braxton Bragg. Other than his small harvest of lancers he never found a target. The first day was typical. The battery went in with four guns, four caissons, and six horses to a carriage. Only one gun had a chance to fire, and they all had trouble getting out. About this time an old Bragg admirer happened along. "A few of his artillerymen, and more than a dozen of his horses, were down in the same spot, making the ground around the guns slippery with their gasped foam and blood."

Not much like the snappy outfit Giddings had watched before. He was amazed at seeing the men, even under fire, refitting teams by stripping harness from dead and wounded animals. Bragg would not lose a buckle or strap.

Sam French had something to say later about the saving of buckles and straps. Earlier the battery had lost two wheel horses from a caisson. Drivers shoved them into a ditch, a mangle of entrails and blood. What did Bragg do then but send French back alone to cut harness. On the way he ran into Taylor, who asked about his errand. "That is nonsense," he said when French told him. Let the lieutenant return to his command. French never forgave Bragg for the order, and Bragg probably never forgave the subaltern for coming back empty-handed.

When Reynolds tried to wrestle the last 6-pounder out, he had to jam the gun carriage up against a house wall to swing it around in the narrow street. It took extra help, and from all sources—volunteers. That annoyed Reynolds more than ever, and left him grumbling about the foolish order that had sent the battery in.

Ridgely's luck with the 6-pounders equalled Bragg's. But once he got hold of the heavy calibers in Tenería, he leveled on Diablo. That made him happy. Over on Worth's side Duncan and Mackall could claim more credit. There they drove off the only serious lancer threat of the battle. The howitzer dragged up Independence Hill broke resistance in the Bishop's Palace, and the end of the three days found the two howitzers and a 6-pounder on that roof near the plaza. There was nothing in Scott's *Instructions for Field Artillery, Horse and Foot* to cover such tactics. Neither did it offer any help for maneuvering in a canyon of houses. "By the left wheel" had a good, authentic ring out on the flat of drill grounds. On the art of handling guns as practiced at Monterey, the manual was understandably blank.

In fact, the battle forced a closer look at the "flying batteries." At Palo Alto they had won most of the glory. At Resaca de la Palma the one battery that found space to work added to Ridgely's fame, but the other could only tag along after the Mexicans broke. Now, in the latest fighting, none of the 6-pounders counted for much in the way they were meant to be used. Shells raised lots of dust and chips from stone and adobe; nothing at all against fieldworks four- to eight-feet thick.

The October 11 *Mercury* of Charleston was blunt about the artillery at Monterey. Why send sixes in "to batter down fortifications that twenty-four [pounders] would have played upon as harmless as a child's bow and arrows." It was from Charleston that Bragg, with George Thomas, Reynolds, and company, had shipped out to show Ringgold how. But the old master had fought his one battle where field artillery could do the most good—on a prairie against exposed infantry. Then after the hat-waving over Palo Alto, Taylor had apparently forgotten the word *field* before artillery. Like the Charleston critic, Reynolds probably was right when he questioned the judgment of sending 6-pounders into the streets of Monterey.

Fire them from roofs!

The newest feature of the army came in for attention too. Reaction to the volunteers was mixed. Meade charged them with losing all organization during the attack on the east end of Monterey. They could not be depended on, he said. Behavior in the Baltimore Battalion seemed to bear him out, with so many of them taking off for camp at the first contact. Their casualties gave them away—23 (five killed) out of 230. But the Ohio regiment doubled those losses. Two West Pointers, Albert Johnston and Joe Hooker, had a lot to do with the better performance here. As staff officers serving under volunteer generals, they steadied the Ohioans.

Volunteer regiments from Mississippi and Tennessee took the Tenería works, though only after the regulars under Captain Backus had softened Mexican resistance. Again casualties measured the effort: 52 for the Mississippi Rifles and a whopping 107 for the troops from Tennessee.

These two regiments were a different breed of volunteers. Ex-West Pointer Davis had drilled his planters' sons, gentlemen farmers, and hunters almost into the ground. And he had armed them with the new Whitney rifle, the absolute best he could find. William B. Campbell's 1st Tennessee, with less class, gave nothing away in organization and morale. State rivalry added something to the performance of both regiments.

Well, if state pride could mean so much, why the bad record of militia in previous wars? The difference between 1776 or 1812 and this war was all-important. The volunteers at

Monterey were 12-months men called by the *national* government to fight a war *already begun*. They were the kind of citizen soldiers Webster had argued for, and so had Polk. They were better material than the boys signed up in peacetime by states or cities to show off for three months on some local commons. Besides, the volunteers who marched out of Camargo in September had included only the pick of 15,000 or more who came south to the Rio Grande. Sickness, death, or refusal to re-enlist weeded out the other four fifths.

This kind of screening at last gave the army citizen soldiers it could use. Fighting screened them further. If too many boys from Baltimore and Washington slunk off, most of the volunteers hung on up front. They needed help from professional officers and fought best alongside regulars. Competition worked here too—competition and example. By themselves the volunteers would have been useless, but for the first time America had a disciplined standing army, small as it was, and a trained officer corps to lead both kinds of troops.

Taylor himself made the final difference in the over-all performance of his volunteers. His example was worth a hundred orders. The men took heart from the old man's easy contempt for enemy shells and bullets. He had Andrew Jackson's talent for making soldiers fight, at least most of them.

To sum up, Monterey produced the recipe for using citizens effectively in war:

(1) Call them up under national control.
(2) Enroll them for at least a year, or for the duration.
(3) Weed out the unfit (though not with Camargo as a model).
(4) Drill them hard and often.
(5) Hold them under the strictest discipline.
(6) Weed out again.

(7) Fight them only alongside regulars led by professionals.

(8) Give them a natural leader whose presence is felt at the front.

For Taylor's purposes the government took care of national control and time of enlistment. Climate, sickness, and human frailty did the weeding. The general's own labors, character, and judgment, with help from the West Pointers, solved the training and leadership. That left number 5, the discipline problem. Old Zach could never be tough enough; few volunteer officers could be tough at all; there were too few West Pointers to go around; and pure citizen cussedness did the rest. Slack discipline also covered sanitation and camp policing, which in turn affected health. Unfortunately not all of the weeding took out the worst material. Good men, too, lay under sod at Camargo and on the banks and mouth of the Rio.

Number 5 would continue to devil the U. S. Army for years. Free Americans simply did not like to be told.

9

Back in the states people liked to be told of victories. During the first week of October news of Monterey veined out over the country from New Orleans. Again glasses clinked in toasts to Old Rough and Ready for President. For some the long casualty lists hurt, but after all the city was ours. Its name looked big in the press. So did General Worth's. The second in command got good coverage both from Kendall and from Haile of the *Picayune*, who acted as his aides during the battle. In Kendall alone he had the top newsman in Mexico and a key paper reporting the war. Copy from the front took nothing away from Worth. The general was aware of it: "If not well poised my head would be turned." Not a word for the man who let him lead the main attack.

Niles' Register of October 17 made up for the omission by praising Taylor's generosity in giving Worth the opportunity "to cull the first laurels from the field." By the 21st the Charleston *Mercury* was knocking the blownup stories about the fighting west of the city. Old Zach still had friends. Yet nobody raised a glass in the White House when first accounts of the battle reached there October 11. The three days were too costly, and both the terms and the armistice were great mistakes.

"He had the enemy in his power," Polk wrote in his diary, "and should have taken them prisoners, deprived them of their arms, discharged them on their parole of honour, and preserved the advantage which he had obtained by pushing on without further delay into the country, if the force at his command justified it." As things stood now, the Mexican army could recruit and reorganize at leisure.

Next day the cabinet agreed. Taylor should have insisted on complete surrender. As for his soft talk about Mexican desire for peace, "we have no information to justify this reason." The general must have been deceived. By going on to capture Ampudia's army he probably could have ended the war.

Armchair strategy in Washington, as always, had it easier to conquer an enemy. But the President was worried. Whig papers were already talking about "Polk's War." Polk had brought on the war, thinking to "swallow up Mexico at a single mouthful," and so on. Instead, the country was spending millions and still no sign that the enemy was giving in.

Polk had reason to be sensitive about the charge. With congressional elections only two weeks off, he could hardly call up more troops, begin new operations, or spend money. Not, at least, until the country voted. Meanwhile Polk had to reckon with two extremes: "Conscience" Whigs shouting Stop the War! and radicals in his own party howling for the whole of northern Mexico. All the President wanted were New Mexico and points west. To get them the war somehow had to go on.

From one direction Polk could report good news. "Gen'l Kearny has thus far performed his duty well." Just follow up his pressure on the west coast by new strategical moves along the Gulf of Mexico. Take Tampico and Vera Cruz, order Taylor to threaten the interior, and even backsliding Santa Anna might be willing to talk peace again.

But Taylor! Not even as far as Saltillo, and graciously permitting a whole Mexican army to march away with its arms. And worse, halting all advance in his sector by granting two months' armistice. What a way to run a war. Taylor— this new darling of the Whigs. Something had to be done about him, Polk decided on October 12:

> It was agreed unanimously [by the cabinet] that orders should be forthwith sent to Gen'l Taylor to terminate the armistice to which he had agreed, and to prosecute the war with vigor and energy. It was agreed that this should be done in terms neither to approve or condemn his conduct in granting the capitulation and armistice. All agreed that the officers & men had fought gallantly and deserved the thanks of the country, but regretted that the victory had not been crowned by the capture of the enemy's army.

There was more, largely setting the errant general straight, and then the President was free to greet dinner guests from Tennessee. His friends intended traveling home by way of the southern route, through Charleston, and he wished them the most pleasant of trips.

CHAPTER VI

THE OTHER ENEMIES

If Taylor could help it, the occupation of Monterey was going to improve on the months in Matamoros. He quartered Worth's division in the city, probably because most of them were regulars, though some talk had it that Worth was being rewarded for his impressive role in its fall. An order on October 5 refused entry to all other troops except by special pass. The beginning looked good, and improved next day when Taylor released a great part of the Texas volunteers, at their own request.

"With their departure," the general wrote Marcy in Washington, "we may look to a restoration of quiet and order in Monterey, for I regret to report that some shameful atrocities have been perpetuated by them since the occupation of the town."

There had been trouble early. Texans still avenging the 1830s between every battle, picking fights to excuse killing Mexicans in the suburbs and outlying farms. Of course Old Zach was careful not to publish his relief at seeing them go.

170

Instead he thanked them for their efficient service and wished them a happy return to their homes and families. A politician drumming up Texas support would not have used pleasanter words. But Taylor still kept reminding his son-in-law that politics was farthest from his mind. As of October 12 he only hoped that linking his name with the presidency back home would not embarrass operations at the front.

The general had problems enough with the army. So far the local food, especially fruit, saved him from a shortage of rations. But his men needed clothes, and too many of them were down to rawhide sandals. No candles, no oil. At Walnut Springs night was really night. Also, the climate was bad; sudden temperature shifts of from 30 to 40 degrees encouraged sickness. Diarrhea and dysentery broke out again.

Put the army on the road, that was Surgeon Porter's solution. March them to Saltillo or farther south toward San Luis Potosí and the sickness would drop off. The wounded, now quartered in Arista's villa, were doing well enough, "but there was culpable negligence somewhere in not sending more medical officers into the field." By Porter's arithmetic one surgeon for every two regiments was not enough. There ought to be four. Unfortunately, in Washington the present number still looked all right.

Drilling went on, sickness or not. It even rubbed against death—a funeral procession passed an infantry band in the middle of "Dance, Boatman, Dance." Twice a day tactics and maneuvers beat the parade ground into dust. Volunteers learned the evolutions of "the school of the battalion," wove from squares into columns, and practiced holding alignment over broken terrain. Giddings was happy to hear even West Pointers dropping a word of praise now and then. The Baltimore Battalion got a tough professional for its head. Good!

Kenly wrote. These volunteers would make soldiers yet. Taylor was remembering their behavior on September 21.

Eventually the general had to let his volunteers go into town. For a while they gawked around innocently enough. Everybody wanted to visit Arista's villa, wander through its marbled halls or on the great sweep of lawn slanting upward from a stream to stone terraces topped by flower-filled jars. Next they climbed Independence Hill to admire the view from the Bishop's Palace. They crowded stores and shops, surprised at seeing Scotch and English owners in Mexican dress. In the cathedral they stared at the paintings, at the dazzle of ornaments above the altar, and listened to the fine organ. The Reverend Mr. Rey, down from the states, had already cleared out the ammunition and restored sanctity with a sermon. Soldiers walked around the captured artillery in the plaza, comparing periods and designs. They even respected the mourning worn by men and women they passed in the streets.

Gradually the eroding effects of occupation began to set in. The novelty of strange new sights wore off and left the volunteers bored and restless. They looked for headier fun. Mexicans soon had a special name for them: "Godamees." The volunteers earned it, helped along by the cheap, raw pulque most of them drank. Worth closed down liquor selling in town, but country peddlers took over on the outskirts.

The resulting hoopla kept most of the better citizens from coming back to Monterey. It countered the image of fair treatment that Taylor tried so hard to implant. Soldiers in conquered territory are seldom good ambassadors, and America's first experience was proving typical. Still, in an odd way, the Mexicans did show their trust in the general himself. They started a market as close to his headquarters tent as they could get. They felt safer there—and no doubt were, Kenly admitted.

More trouble cropped up during the slow days of October.

Catholics in the army were going over to the enemy again. But not "the sons of Erin," Henry insisted. They could not be seduced. He identified the deserters as largely English and German. Occupation brought closer contacts with native priests, who were offering as high as $150 and promising ranks up to captaincies in the Mexican army. The lures drew over 50 more men into its version of a Foreign Legion—the "San Patricio Battalion."

The worst of it was that regulars did most of the deserting. After three battles Taylor's immigrants should have caught the feel of being American, and apparently the majority had. But lulls in the fighting pointed up the harshness and routine of army life. So many men had come overseas to escape just that, and now here they were. A soft-voiced man of the cloth was hard to ignore when he jingled coins, spelled out the luxury of an officer's career, and damned the gringo vandals and unbelievers.

Taylor never lacked for problems. Keeping the army at work, building its efficiency, bleeding the devil out of his volunteers, and guarding against desertion were only a few. He had clothing depots set up at Fort Polk and Camargo. As always, he pressed for more medical help, particularly along the Rio, where sickness was heavier than at Monterey. And he just about buried Chief Quartermaster Thomas S. Jesup in requisitions. Send on the supplies—and WAGONS!

In Washington the administration was busy with its own paperwork. While Old Zach was fighting his late September battle, Polk and the Secretaries of War and Navy drafted new orders. Time for that move on the Gulf. Major General Robert Patterson would take a column of three to four thousand troops into Tampico and eastern Tamaulipas. The move should not, of course, interfere with Taylor's present campaign. To prevent delay, letters would go out to both generals at once: to Patterson, announcing his new assignment; and to Taylor, informing him that the assignment had been made.

The job of finding the ships for Patterson annoyed Polk. "I find that I am compelled to give some attention to these details or the movement of the army will be delayed or embarrassed." War was a tool for promoting a creed like Manifest Destiny, but at the operating level it was only a grubby nuisance.

On October 12, Lieutenant Lewis A. Armistead rode into camp at Walnut Springs. The letter for Taylor on Patterson's command deserved a special messenger. It was quite a communication. Any hope for peace, it said, would have to wait on the Mexican congress in December. Meanwhile the war must be vigorously carried on. To that end Patterson's move was part of a new strategy. Commodore Conner would support him at Tampico and along the Gulf below. All this, the letter went on, gave added importance to a drive on San Luis Potosí. In order to make it, what would Taylor expect by way of reinforcements, etc.? Also, what advice would he be pleased to offer on the new plans?

Taylor's answer put his requirements for an offensive at 20,000 men, half of them regulars, and 5000 additional troops to cover his supply line and bases. His present strength totaled only 3000 regulars and 9000 volunteers, counting all the forces in rear. To move south he would have to have more horses, more transportation, and more ordnance. Every day's march would further extend his line and shorten the enemy's. "It weakens us, and gives them strength."

Even as he listed his needs, he knew they would never be met. The war was moving away from him. Yet in fairness he thought the Gulf strategy was possible, given enough troops— 25,000 at least, 10,000 of them regulars. With his own small force he was tied to the defensive. He could hold either the Rio line or the Sierra Madre range from northwest to southeast through Monclova, Saltillo, Victoria, and Tampico. The march to San Luis Potosí was out.

Besides, the administration had yet to thank him for taking Monterey.

And one thing more. It pained him, Taylor wrote the War Secretary, to remind the government that General Patterson fell under his command. So long as he, Taylor, was responsible for the operations of his army, he claimed the right of making all detachments from it and regulating the time and manner of its service. "Above all do I consider it important that the War Department refrain from corresponding directly with my subordinates and communicating orders and instructions on points which, by all military precept and practice, pertain exclusively to the general-in-chief commanding."

For an officer who seldom worried about Army prerogatives these words bit hard. They bared the raw core of Taylor's feelings. He saw in the administration a purpose, oblique and veiled, but deliberate. Its object was to sidetrack a too successful general. From now on this obsession would color Old Zach's thinking wherever it touched his superiors.

2

On October 27 a senseless accident rocked the whole army. Randolph Ridgely's horse stepped into a hole in the pavement of Monterey's main plaza. The artilleryman was thrown on his head, and death from concussion followed three days later.

Ridgely was everybody's hero. Palo Alto, Resaca de la Palma, and Monterey had proved him beyond doubt. Before his last battle the citizens of Baltimore, in his home state, had given him a sword with solid silver grip and guard, and a

175

scabbard "beautifully chased." The local *Patriot* of September 19 had used 500 words to describe it. Ridgely accepted the sword with a bow to Major Ringgold: "It has been my good fortune to be attached to a corps (new to the army) which was organized and instructed, on soil of my native land, by one of her chosen sons." Ringgold had been Maryland too, and the captain gave the credit to him.

French called Ridgely the fearless and irreproachable knight. It shocked Meade that an officer of Ridgely's coolness and courage should have to die an inglorious death. Taylor, in reporting the accident, said: "His activity and gallantry before the enemy render his death a serious loss to the service, while the melancholy circumstances under which it occurred will make it peculiarly affecting to his family and friends." That was the refrain, the feeling almost of embarrassment, as though a kind of shame attached to these wasted deaths.

Braxton Bragg moved up to Ridgely's "Ringgold" battery. It left an opening. Captain Thomas W. Sherman was in line, but he had been shunted to quartermaster duty.[1] Now he howled, and apparently made himself heard as far away as Washington, because the adjutant general politely informed Taylor that Sherman was available. Bragg was humorless, exacting, petty. Already during the campaign two small explosions had been set off under his bed, fizzled protests against his methods and personality. Sherman also was humorless, exacting, petty; and added a talent for carping insensitivity. The tragedy for both men was that nobody strained harder to lift their units to peak efficiency.

Taylor finally could read his "thanks" for Monterey on November 2. They came in the same dispatch (of October 12)

---

[1] Military writers always warn that this Sherman should not be confused with the *good* Sherman—William Tecumseh ("Cump").

which grew out of Polk's fit over the general's terms. Old Zach skipped through the perfunctory "glory to our arms . . . warmest expressions of gratitude and praise," and lit on the complaints. First, his armistice had injured the government by halting operations. Second, there was not the slightest hint of peace from the Mexicans. Third, the general should be prosecuting the war with all vigor.

Surgeon Mills saw his commander's reaction to the letter. "The old man is very angry," he said, "and flies about like an old hen with one chicken." And with good reason, according to Meade, "for he finds himself called upon to perform impossible things, and has not even the control over his own forces." The President and cabinet were maneuvering his troops from the distant capital, and even naming his commanders. Lay it all to the curse of politics, Meade concluded.

The West Pointers naturally sided with Taylor against the interference. Of course the general himself had been blaming politics for some time, ever since the first cry of "Old Rough and Ready for President." And he still was disclaiming any interest, though a Delaware friend of Taylor's might have noticed a change of emphasis. In a letter to Nathaniel Young back on July 18, the general had been positive enough: "I am not and shall never be an aspirant for that honor." By October 27 he was highly sensible of Delaware's interest in him but hoped the good people would refrain from public expression. "Such a course could only result in defeating their object and in injuring my usefulness in my present position." Again, on November 10, Zach was complaining to son-in-law Wood about the cold notice given his victory by Polk and about how it all stemmed from the recent connection of his name with the presidency. He ended his comment by saying "this is no time for agitating that question, it will be time enough to do so in 1848."

To do so with or without Taylor?

The next day brought more instructions from Washington. They began by admitting that Santa Anna was collecting an army. There went Polk's old "friend for peace." Taylor now was advised not to go beyond Monterey, and by remaining there he could spare troops for the taking of Vera Cruz. So unless the new plan interfered with the general's own operations or weakened him too much, he should prepare to release 4000 men, about half regulars, for the Gulf offensive. The government further suggested Patterson for the command, with Worth to head the regulars.

"Unlesses" and suggestions that proposed specific numbers of troops and named their leaders were meant to be read in the imperative. Taylor could translate War Department jargon. It was telling him that he could now mark time in his captured city while Patterson and Worth took the meat of his army in the new direction of the war.

But the dispatch reached the general four days too late. It so happened that the instructions did interfere with his operations. On November 8 he had issued an order of his own: Worth to march for Saltillo with the 5th and 8th Infantry, Duncan's battery, eight companies of the artillery battalion, and Albert G. Blanchard's Louisianans. Taylor explained his move. Saltillo covered the important defile leading north from the interior; also the route west to Monclova, from which point Wool could join him. The region was a fertile breadbasket; and as the capital of Coahuila, Saltillo was of interest politically. Finally, its occupation anchored the whole Sierra Madre line from northwest to southeast.

That order ought to counter the instructions holing him up in Monterey. Now, about the request for men. He thought the number of 4000 too few for success at Vera Cruz. To augment them he would lead an expedition as far as Tampico himself. The city was essential to operating below at Vera Cruz.

Between the lines in this dispatch of November 12 Taylor was busy talking to himself. This Tampico move would leave the troops in his hands and keep them out of Patterson's. Obviously no Democratic politician had the right to command any force of his. If military activity had to move southeast— and Taylor had been granting the logic—he intended to move with it. Old Zach was going to stay in the war.

3

In Washington, Polk was aiming to take Taylor *out* of the war. The November elections went against the administration. Whigs now had the House, 117 to 110, enough to cause the President trouble. Why make things worse by building up Whigs in the Army? Scott was a committed Whig, and Taylor was beginning to show coloration. With the votes already in, Polk had nothing to lose by pressing the war—nothing, that is, except giving bandwagon rides to wrong generals. Taylor especially. The more Old Rough and Ready looked like the people's choice, the less he looked like the President's man to take over coming campaigns.

Senator Tom Benton knew how Polk felt. Since the elections the two of them had been mulling the question of overall command for the Army. On November 10 they got down to cases. Yes, "Taylor was a brave officer but not a man of capacity enough for such a command." Benton thought so too. Scott? No confidence in him, the senator said. Then he went on. The one answer to the problem was to create the rank of lieutenant general. Let him be a person of signal talents and resources, as well as a military man. Mere bravery was not enough.

A most interesting suggestion—but who?

Well, if Congress could be persuaded to restore the rank once held by General Washington, how about Benton?

The suggestion was Benton's.

If Polk's military innocence needed proof, it came in his response. He would be happy to see Benton at the head of the United States Army. Benton—once a militia colonel in Tennessee and later a lieutenant colonel in the Regular Army. He had never seen any fighting or maneuvered as much as a brigade. He knew nothing about logistics, strategy, or tactics. He was ignorant of Army administration. But Polk was desperate for a Democratic general who would rank both Scott and Taylor. He tried to convince his cabinet, then turned to the Congress, hoping to get through a bill to re-establish the lieutenant generalcy and hand it to Benton. Howell Cobb of Georgia, Stephen A. Douglas of Illinois, Calhoun, Lewis Cass —all of them felt the pressure from Polk. They all kept saying no. So did the cabinet.

The new head of the forces in Mexico would have to be Scott. With Taylor set down by the President himself, there was no other choice. And Old Zach certainly was out. On November 10 Polk wrote in his diary: "I apprehend that Gen'l Taylor's feelings are anything but friendly to the Executive Government. . . . He has no sympathies for the administration and cares only for himself." And this in spite of the great kindness he had shown the general, including the recent promotion. For his own part, Polk added, politics had nothing to do with it, though he regretted that he could not say the same for Taylor.

So it was Scott. The President still had strong objections to him, with his fussiness and giant vanity. But by the 18th even Benton came around to him as the best they could do, although he was reluctant to accept the general-in-chief. Polk called Scott in next morning. Let bygones be bygones, he said, and offered him the command. Then he pumped Scott full of puffs for all good Democratic generals—Patterson, Butler, Pillow, Shields, Hamer, etc. It should give Scott the idea. Here Polk preened a bit: "He was so grateful & so much affected that he almost shed tears."

Like so many vain people, Scott had no defense for a friendly gesture, no matter what lay behind it. The new assignment sent him back to the War Department in a frenzy of ideas. He already had been careful to prepare the groundwork in earlier memos. Taylor and Wool together would hold the Monterey line, from where they could either advance or defend. Meanwhile the officer of highest rank in the Army would direct the main attack on and inland from Vera Cruz.

Now that he had the command in his pocket, Scott was ready to be off. Not too carelessly, though. The general-in-chief had learned a lot during tours of duty in Washington. Before leaving, he put into writing addressed to himself the most precise instructions for conducting the campaign. Marcy's signature would mean agreement and therefore protection once Scott was at the front. But the Secretary refused to sign. Scott would succeed or fail on his own; the government accepted no responsibility. Only Scott's high spirits at the time kept this hitch from being the warning it was.

Another problem for Scott was the general who until now had commanded the American force in Mexico. Taylor had won three exciting victories, he controlled the northern states of the country, and he had put himself in position for further advances. How to ease him down? More than that, how to dilute the shock of carving out so much of his army? It called for quite a letter, even for an old master of the quill:

I am not coming, my dear general, to supersede you in the immediate command on the line of operations, rendered illustrious by you and your gallant army. My proposed theatre is different. . . .

But, my dear general, I shall be obliged to take from you most of the gallant officers and men (regular and volunteer) whom you have so long and nobly commanded. I am afraid that I shall by imperious necessity, the approach of yellow fever on the Gulf coast, reduce you for a time to stand on the defensive. This will be infinitely painful to you, and for that reason distressing to me; but I rely on your patriotism to submit to the temporary sacrifice with cheerfulness. No man can better afford to do so. Recent victories place you on that high eminence, and I even flatter myself that any benefits that may result to me personally from the unequal division of troops alluded to will lessen the pain of your consequent inactivity. . . .

The letter was pure Scott. It showed some sympathy for Taylor because essentially its writer was kind. At the same time, Taylor's solid gains meant little to a man so wholly impressed with himself. Scott had not set foot in enemy country, and he had not seen a single soldier he soon would be leading. Yet never a doubt. The hero of Lundy's Lane could do it all again, and more. Besides, as the letter made clear, now it was his turn.

In closing, Scott added that the government was about to call up ten new regiments. He hoped eventually for others. With such reinforcements Taylor might then be able to resume the offensive. On November 25 the letter started its tedious journey south.

4

Down in Mexico Taylor's army was occupying its third enemy city. Saltillo, evacuated by Mexican troops, numbered somewhere between fifteen and twenty thousand people, all of them more hostile than the citizens of Monterey. Already the West Pointers missed the pleasant picnic atmosphere of Walnut Springs. They missed the hunting (blue winged teal was a favorite bird). They missed the sulphur baths near their old camp. Captain Henry missed the cathedral organist of Monterey. Otherwise, Saltillo's cathedral was bigger, more elegant, had more gilt, more ornaments, bigger statues, and a most impressive altar backed by a wall 50 feet high.

Henry, Giddings, Kirby Smith, and Meade all gave this great place of worship its due. They all praised the well-kept streets, tree-shaded plazas, and fountains that sprayed "a dewy coolness and fragrance." Soldiers strolled a promenade lined with roses, myrtle, and flowering shrubs. The natives, too, looked like a better class than those of Monterey, unfriendly though they were.

It was left for Lieutenant Reynolds to bring in a minority report. What on earth, he wondered, possessed any people to put a large town on the side of a hill without a convenience of any kind except bad water. He granted some appeal to the main plaza, the cathedral, and a few of the public buildings, but most of Saltillo was built of mud. The sooner Reynolds could find a warmer location and decent water, the better pleased he would be.

Saltillo, on a tableland over 5000 feet above sea level, was cold. Wood was so scarce it had to be rationed. Volunteers who had lugged parrots in cages from Monterey, instead of bringing overcoats and blankets, were quick to complain. The sheer effort required to keep warm should have reduced their trouble-making. Yet it was in this city that Surgeon Porter had to admit the first signs of venereal disease. Along with the better class there must have been others. Before long a single regiment supplied several wagonloads of the *hors de combat*, to use Porter's words. In the meantime Worth did his best to police the city, living up to his nickname of "Old Stampede." The melancholy entry about wagon loads in the surgeon's journal was one measure of the general's success.

From headquarters on the south side of the city Taylor concentrated on problems in ferment below. At the least, San Luis Potosí gave him a change from those up north—his long and touchy supply line, heavy sickness in the camps along the Rio Grande, and Washington. In fact, Washington was responsible for his biggest problem to the south. Polk's old "ally" Santa Anna had scraped together an army of around 22,000.

More and more Santa Anna looked like the man to deal with, so, on November 20, Taylor reminded him in a note that the American government had ordered an end to the armistice. The general also added an appeal for peace. Santa Anna's answer was polite; but why, he asked, talk of peace when a foreign army stood on Mexican soil and foreign ships threatened her coasts? In any case, the subject of peace would have to await debate in the National Congress at the City of Mexico in December.

What five months could do when the man was Santa Anna. Yesterday never bore on today, or today on tomorrow. Back in July he was recommending Saltillo to Polk as a good base for Taylor's army. It would force Paredes to fight, would bring him down, and open the way for Santa Anna's recall. Now in November the same army, at last in Saltillo, was the enemy. But with Paredes already out and Santa Anna repatriated, courtesy of Polk, why not? The ex-dictator had judged his people right. The way to power was to carry on against the foreign invader.

At this stage Santa Anna's army had more meaning for Taylor than its leader did. If it moved north, Old Zach would do well to round up a third as many men to meet it. He did have Wool's troops, who had given up crossing the Sierra Gorda range. That obstacle, along with threats of unfriendly reception, ended Polk's wistful hope of wooing the Mexicans in the state of Chihuahua. But even counting Wool, Taylor's returns were not encouraging:

Wool —2500 (at Parras, 90 miles west of Saltillo)
Butler—1500 (at Monterey, 70 miles east of Saltillo)
Worth—2500 (at Saltillo)
Total —6500

Where was the rest of Zach's army? The Washington *Union* said he had 20,000. This estimate resulted from the usual civilian arithmetic. Tote up every man who ever got on the rolls and list him as present at the front, baring teeth and bayonet against the foe.

In all northern Mexico, Taylor's troops actually fell short of 12,000. To reach that figure he had to add 2000 men with Patterson, still at Matamoros; 1000 more on the way to join him later at Tampico; and 2000 held in rear. So at the immediate front the 6500 troops spread out 160 miles from east to west would have to do if the Mexicans moved up.

Subtract one regiment of 500 volunteers. Taylor had no sooner gone back to Monterey in late November than the 1st Kentucky went on a murderous binge. They were out to avenge a comrade, although he in turn was a victim of their outrageous acts. By its own admission the regiment claimed the killing of no less than 40 Mexicans. "Shall we rest quietly in our

185

tents whilst the enemy is lying in ambush and murdering our comrades as they pass the roads?" Then they shot a twelve-year-old and the parents brought him, still bleeding, to Taylor's tent. The general at once ordered the regiment to the rear in disgrace. During the time he kept the Kentuckians there, until they promised to surrender the guilty parties, discipline at the front improved. But the cost in native hostility came high. Tensions rose and precautions around the camps had to be doubled to protect both Americans and Mexicans.

The Kentucky affair worked Meade up to about 2000 words on the rascality of volunteers. His only remedy, assuming there was one, would be to give each regiment a colonel, lieutenant colonel, 10 captains, 20 sergeants, and 200 privates from the Regular Army. Just possibly the infusion might cure these "Goths and Vandals." They were brave enough, most of them, and fairly well drilled by now; but they laid waste to the country wherever they went. They set the Mexicans against the whole army. Meade recognized that a country pledged to small standing armies would have to put up with volunteers. Yet to be useful they first had to be controlled. The lieutenant of engineers was skeptical of the prospects.

On the Rio Grande a young West Pointer was putting down his impressions of citizen soldiers. It horrified twenty-year-old Lieutenant George Brinton McClellan that they died like dogs in the sprawling wallow of their camps. They robbed and killed Mexicans there too, shaming the flag they represented. And the officers! "I found that every confounded Voluntario in the 'Continental Army' ranked me." He classed the Pattersons and Pillows with some of their privates, who broke in mustang ponies to ride and then lorded it over the men on foot. He had a name for politicians wearing stars: "Mustang generals."

5

Taylor had left Saltillo for Monterey with the idea of getting back in the war. Santa Anna, he reckoned, would hardly risk 250 miles of near desert and his raw army to strike at Worth —not for the present anyhow. The defensive line along the Sierra Madre was safe, all the way from Parras on the west through Saltillo and Monterey to Tampico, 300 miles southeast. That left Zach free to travel. But where? The Navy had spoiled his Tampico move by occupying the seacoast city on November 14. It was most inconsiderate.

In one way or another the old general was practically eliminating himself:

(1) It was his own earlier suggestion (holding a defensive line) that tied him to the area around Monterey.
(2) His excuse for marching to Tampico was gone.
(3) He had admitted the possibilities of the Vera Cruz strategy, though with reservations.
(4) That assignment had gone to Scott.
(5) To help mount the new offensive it was clear that Taylor would have to give up the 4000 troops requested.

Taylor, of course, saw these acts and motivations differently. Polk and Marcy were setting him aside. They would not furnish troops for his own offensive. As for Vera Cruz, the plan had already been hatched before his opinion was asked. Then the new command went to Scott. Politics again: "Covert attacks . . . insinuations . . . detractions of the basest kind," Taylor wrote on December 10. The Democrats wanted him out because Whigs were linking his name with nomination for President.

Old Zach hoped they would pick an able man. "I will not say I would not serve if the good people were imprudent enough as to elect me."

He had said it! In this letter to son-in-law Robert Wood he at last had come around. The shock of his admission drove him to his usual cover, hunger for retirement to private life, the little farm and so on. Still it was out. From now on any hint of cooperation or understanding between Taylor and the administration would be a dizzy illusion.

At this level war and politics made a sour mix, a far cut below the war-as-politics thinking of the Prussian Clausewitz. The mix had begun to turn in the relations between Polk and Scott months before. Polk an Old Hickory man; Scott anti-Jackson. Polk a diehard, party-first Democrat; Scott a diehard, party-first Whig. But to Polk a Scott out of contention politically was safer than Taylor. In the new strategy of the war any success for Scott would blur the image of Old Rough and Ready. Two men on horseback would cancel each other out. Not so ideal as a "Lieutenant General" Benton, and yet entirely within the rules, and logical, too. Scott, the general-in-chief, to replace a subordinate who had willingly consigned himself to the defensive.

So Taylor had, but he could define the role in his own way. First he wrote the War Department on December 8. He still planned to go southeast as far as Victoria, he said. As the capital of Tamaulipas and also a flanking position should Santa Anna move north, the city ought to be occupied. Later, after setting up a depot there, he would return with a force of regulars and establish headquarters below Saltillo, a position equally vital to his holding line.

Old Zach also could play by the rules and be logical. He was not violating the defensive—only giving it an "active" character. As active as he could manage, as far away from the dead end of Monterey as he could get, and as close to the new operations as the more than 200 miles to Victoria would take him. No jealous politicians were going to knock Taylor out of the war.

On December 15 the general was off, two days behind Twiggs' regulars, a volunteer brigade under Quitman, and Bragg's old battery under temporary command of Lieutenant George Thomas. Meanwhile Taylor ordered General Patterson to leave Matamoros with three regiments and a mounted detachment, all volunteers. The two commands would join at Victoria. Along Taylor's route the men kicked about 22-mile hikes in the heat of the day. They mixed the juice of sugar cane and green oranges for drinks, laughed at roaring "Old Bull" Twiggs, and burned ebony wood in their campfires at night.

Captain Henry had marched and fought under Taylor for more than a year now, and he still found his general good copy:

> Winding down a hill, our column was halted to let a troop of horse pass. Do you see, at their head, a plain-looking gentleman, mounted upon a brown horse, having on his head a Mexican sombrero, dressed in a brown, olive-colored, loose frock coat, gray pants, wool socks, and shoes; beneath the frock appears the scabbard of a sword; he has the eye of an eagle, and every lineament of his countenance is expressive of honesty, and calm, determined mind.

The captain read like a dedicated Whig puffing a candidate. But he was nearer right on the *determined* than he was on the *calm*. The general Henry admired was anything but calm on this march. He was upset to learn that Patterson had already shipped some of his force down to Tampico, without orders. Also, the Quartermaster Department still dragged its feet in supplying Taylor's wants. The old friendship between him and department chief Jesup was straining. Jesup, who back in July had said "I shall never forget how faithfully and ably General Taylor sustained me in Florida." Now the general would like some sustaining in return.

Taylor's needling from the front had finally brought Jesup down to New Orleans in the fall. Once on the ground, he saw what the *National Intelligencer*, as well as other papers, had been crying about. In this war that was costing millions he found loaded wagons and mules exposed to 100-plus heat on the levees. To ship a hundred or so mules to the Brazos was running freight charges up to as high as $5000. Many animals died on the way and half of those landed died soon after. One shipment of 127 mules managed to put only 22 ashore. The Quartermaster Department was becoming a national scandal.

The mess in New Orleans did not impress Jesup favorably. He exploded in a letter to Washington. Anything Taylor lacked was his own doing. He had failed to make the proper requisitions, or made them too late. It was up to the general in the field to call for the means required to meet his objectives. "If he fail to do so, he is himself responsible." Anyhow a general was expected to use the resources of the country he was in, and "those means are limited only by his own will."

Two days later, from down on the Brazos, the quartermaster general sadly admitted that his department was far from efficient. He regretted the great spoilage of subsistence and public stores. By the end of the year Jesup was all recommendations: rubber sacks for bread, flour, sugar, coffee, and bacon; half-barrels for pork and vinegar; waterproof bags for ordnance; no package for muleback to exceed 80 to 100 pounds. The army in the field cost at least $50,000 a day, he said. Thus, if transport had to be repacked for mules, two days were lost—and $100,000.

As a rule nobody could outworry Taylor over money, but at this stage he was too bitter about Jesup. In writing Robert Wood on December 13, he accused the quartermaster general of coming down to New Orleans for the single purpose of putting himself in the spotlight. He had been angling for popularity all his life, Taylor grumbled.

Zach was beginning to suspect everybody. On the 16th a note from Worth at Saltillo reported Santa Anna moving north. Back went Taylor with the regulars, leaving Quitman to keep the road for Victoria. Then the threat turned out to be rumor, which Taylor had suspected all along. Why was Worth jumping at every false alarm? The general started for Victoria once again. On through Montemorelos and the enchanting town of Linares he rode in a sullen mood. When he brought his regulars into Victoria on January 4, Quitman was already there.

Taylor entered the city with Scott's "My dear General" letter in his pocket, the one sent off from the states on November 25. Here was word that Taylor would lose the 4000 men for sure. Here also were Scott's instructions that he restrict himself to the defensive. The unction spread thin over these hard facts which Taylor was reading 200 miles from where his chief expected him to be—at Monterey. Scott hoped to be in Camargo on December 23, he had said in closing, and would like to confer with Taylor there. Well, it was too late now and Old Zach too far away.

Although Marcy had prepared the general earlier for giving up troops, the finality of Scott's letter hurt. Yet here Taylor was, caught off base by his own orders; he would have to answer Scott. From Victoria he wrote in more humility than he felt. As soon as his presence in the city was no longer needed, he intended to go back to Monterey. "At all times and places I shall be happy to receive your orders, and to hold myself and troops at your disposal."

Victoria turned out to be anticlimax for Taylor. Quitman had made the big entrance a week before, riding into the main square with the battery and his columns close behind. The guns moved into the center, infantry officers stepped one pace front, and "Present Arms!" rolled along the lines. Then from the mayor and party Quitman accepted the keys of the city and ran up the Stars and Stripes. The ceremony ticked off in perfection till an infantry band started a raucous braying among the local donkeys. This dissonance collapsed the shaky parade-ground manners of the volunteers into hoots and shouting.

Patterson, 1600 men, had come in the same day as Taylor, with Lieutenant McClellan still downgrading the Mustang generals. Twiggs, Quitman, and Patterson together now totaled 6000. "We now have at this point a very pretty little army," a *Delta* man wrote on January 4. Six thousand troops and not a hostile Mexican anywhere near. So Taylor had no excuse for staying in Victoria, assuming he should have come at all. Besides, he was running short of supplies. He would wait only until he heard from Scott, who was now reported to be in the country.

6

Scott was in the country all right, straining to catch up with Taylor and feeling equally persecuted. From the moment he went aboard ship in New York to weather a rough, long passage to New Orleans, his luck had run bad. The expected quartermaster mess confronted him there, and worse, the city seemed to know all about the Vera Cruz offensive. Mexico probably knew then too. Having absorbed this news, Scott shipped on down to the Brazos near the end of the month and smack into word of Polk's bill to make a lieutenant general of Benton.

Fired upon in his rear from Washington! In the meantime where was Taylor? Well, he was told, the general had just reversed a march for Victoria and hurried back to Saltillo. Santa Anna was moving on Worth. Scott wrote Washington: "This information has determined me to proceed up the river to Camargo, in order to meet despatches from Major General Taylor, and if this outpost should be seriously menaced, to join him rapidly." Bravely said, but, once in the zigzag of the Rio Grande, Scott learned that Old Zach was off for Victoria again.

Winfield Scott, the general commanding of all United States forces in Mexico, his bulk wedged into a tiny steamer, heading upriver to hear from a subordinate who would not stay put. And to this point only the subordinate had an army.

That had to be changed. How many troops did Taylor have? Probably 7000 regulars and 10,000 volunteers, by Scott's optimistic guess. How many did Taylor need to hold Monterey and the rear? A force of 7000, say, ought to cover it all. Now— how many for Scott? He would take 4000 infantry, 500 dragoons, and two field batteries. They would be regulars. From Taylor's volunteers add another 4000 foot and 500 horse. That made 9000, not counting the artillery. And while he was at it, Scott reasoned, he ought to pick a reliable leader. Worth should be the man.

The general-in-chief wrote directly to Butler at Monterey on January 3. Put all troops from there and Saltillo on the road to Camargo without delay. Next Scott got a letter off to Taylor, enclosing the Butler orders. He had written earlier, he said, on December 20, but regretted that the letter apparently missed

193

connections. "As it is, I am much embarrassed by your great distance from me. . . ." He went on to assure Taylor that he would be continued in the command he had held so long and nobly, even though his diminished force would naturally reduce him for a while to the defensive.

From Camargo, Scott moved down again to the Brazos. There everything went wrong. Not enough boats, not enough seamen at any price offered, and every foul trick of weather. What was keeping Worth's division? Where was his ordnance? Where were the surf boats for beaching his men at Vera Cruz? The hold-up did give Scott a chance to look over the volunteers coming in from the states. Seven out of ten might possibly be respectable, he thought. The rest strained him for words. They were savages, felons, the basest kind of freebooters. It was unjust to unloose them, even upon an enemy people.

The general-in-chief could add volunteers to his troubles, including their political generals, good Democrats all. One of them had opened Scott's lost letter to Taylor. Although it was marked confidential, he read it to his staff before sending it on, a new protocol in Army communications. The officer assigned to carry the letter through to Taylor fell into a Mexican ambush and was killed.

Worse kept piling on bad. Butler sent Scott a colonel of dragoons, William S. Harney. Scott had objections to him and tried to have him returned. Then Harney objected; he wanted to see action. For a change, the administration had a solid West Pointer in Democrat Harney—if only a colonel. Obviously Polk took his side against Scott. After a court-martial that did nothing for Army morale, Harney's transfer was upheld. Further trouble for Scott came in delay on the bill for the new regiments promised in November. He would be lucky to see more than a trickle of the half-equipped raw citizens now being dumped at the mouth of the Rio.

At home, in the Senate, Tom Benton was adding his bit against Scott. The almost lieutenant general reminded his colleagues that he, Benton, had been a lieutenant general back in 1812 when most of the present generals were merely subalterns, and only one as high as colonel. The colonel had been Scott, as probably everyone in the chamber knew, although Benton did not name him because, he said, "I scorn to mention such things." But the senator was *not* scorning to point out that as an officer of nearly equal rank to Scott in the previous war and now a statesman high in the councils of his government, his late bid to head the troops in Mexico deserved more consideration by far than it got. Benton's blunt rejection in favor of Scott still rankled.

Still more. By January 14 the President had decided that his general-in-chief was responsible for leaking the Vera Cruz plans. "He has from his inordinate vanity or for some other cause given it out, so that it has gotten before the public. The truth is neither Scott nor Taylor are fit for the command of the army in the great operations in progress and which are contemplated."

Both generals could plead persecution. But by January 23 Scott at least had his army—13,000 men.

7

Taylor was about to lose most of his. Scott's demands of January 3 reached Victoria on the 14th. They staggered Old Zach. Instead of the 4000 that Marcy and Scott had mentioned before, his chief was taking 9000 men. Taylor fired back at once. Scott's letter of November 25, he recalled, had never hinted at such numbers. Better by far to relieve him and let him retire from the field than take almost the whole of his regulars and half the volunteers "now in respectable discipline." How could he hold his line against the 20,000 of the enemy with the skeleton force left him? "But however much I may feel personally mortified & outraged by the course pursued, unprecedented, at least, in our history, I will carry out in good faith, while I remain in Mexico, the views of the government, though I may be sacrificed in the effort."

That was for Scott. Another letter went to the adjutant general. Taylor asked that this one be put before the President and the Secretary of War. Why, he wanted to know, had they been silent on the heavy withdrawals to be made from his force? A special messenger could have reached him in time to cancel the now wasted march to Victoria. Instead, not a word from the War Department, only semiofficial instructions from Scott. Taylor regarded himself as on duty in Mexico by virtue of presidential orders. Thus he could have refused troops to Scott had he "chosen to be punctilious." Then he said: "While exercising a command I never sought, I have tried to perform my duty without fear or favor," but "I am constrained to believe that I no longer possess the confidence of the administration."

His blunt lecture on record, Old Zach sent a politer note addressed simply to Scott's headquarters. He was taking May's squadron of dragoons back to Monterey, also the field battery and Jefferson Davis's Mississippi Rifles. To the 4733 men leaving Victoria to join General Scott he would add enough troops to more than satisfy the orders.

In a letter to his brother Joseph, Taylor let go. The administration's plan could now be understood, he wrote. It hoped, by stripping his command, to force him out of Mexico either from disgust or by defeat. Only the greatest prudence would save him from the snares his enemies had laid. If Scott had come down with proper orders to supersede him, that would have been one thing. "I would have thought nothing of it, but would have turned over the command or laid it down with much more pleasure than I ever affirmed it." That, of course, would not have answered the administration's purpose. There would be questions as to why he was being relieved. Instead, the scheming of Polk, Marcy, Scott, and Worth would only expose him to censure should he return to the states.

Zach's list of villains continued to grow. Now Worth. He must be in league with Washington. On the orders from Scott, channeled through Butler, Worth had pulled his division out of Saltillo without a word to Taylor. He pushed so hard to reach the Brazos and the new army that Grant remembered the stiff pace years afterward. To his old commander, Worth seemed overanxious to escape, too eager to throw in with the general-in-chief. Just another mean warp in the plot. Depend on it, the administration would stop at nothing to stalemate Taylor on an abandoned front without an army.

However Taylor reasoned, at least one of his villains was more or less in the middle. Scott was a stepchild in Washington. Begrudged the command in Mexico and only half supported, he still was responsible for carrying through with the war. What could he do but prey on Taylor to save himself? The President had planned it that way. Set Scott against Taylor; Taylor against Scott. Again, politics over military.

Proof built on proof. On January 23 Marcy released a sharp order. Let it be clear that Paragraph 650, General Regulations for the Army, must be obeyed! "Private letters or reports, relating to military marches & operations are frequently mischievous in design & always disgraceful to the army. They are, therefore, strictly forbidden." Violators faced dismissal from service.

What dug this ancient order out of the tomb? asked Whig George Ashmun of Massachusetts in the House. Not that he lacked for an answer. The administration was out to get Taylor, "who was probably deemed to be in the way of some political aspirant."

Sure enough, back on November 5, Zach had aired his growing hurt to a friend. For a change he spared son-in-law Wood and wrote an old comrade in arms, General Gaines. Last year's fuss over the rash of 6-months men was easy to forget in all that had hit Taylor since. He bled his grievances freely: government indifference to his successful campaign; its bad temper over his terms after Monterey; its obvious intention to bypass him in future; its exaggerated faith in the Gulf operations—would results justify the cost? Anyhow his own plan was better. Cover all of northern Mexico with a strong defensive line based on the Sierra Madre, then challenge the enemy to "drive us from the country." Sheer frustration would bring Mexico around to peace.

The long letter spelled out Taylor's case for Taylor, as well as his case against Polk, Marcy, and Scott. And it reached the public. The growing halo of Whig favor circling Zach's grizzled head assured its appearance. Opposition papers coaxed the naïve Gaines into releasing it because of the ripe fodder it contained. The letter moved fast. Marcy first saw it in the New York *Morning Express* of January 22, 1847. The Washington *Union*, of course, blew it up. On January 24 Polk read a reprint in the New York *Herald*. And he blew up. Friends tried to calm him by doubting its authenticity. Entirely and lamentably genuine, the President insisted. Exactly what one might expect from Taylor, damning the administration, nursing his own self-pity, and spilling war plans to the whole world.

By nightfall a scared Gaines was on the White House carpet trying to explain. He admitted his error in exposing a private letter, though more of it saw print than he intended. He was terribly concerned. Both the President and Marcy dressed him down and sent him hunching off. "The truth is," Polk sighed, "that Gen'l Taylor is in the hands of political managers." More evidence of his unfitness for command. "I am held responsible for the Conduct of the War, & yet Congress refused to give me a commander in whom I have confidence, & I am compelled to employ the officers the law has provided, however unfit they may be."

At this late date the President was stretching his case to insist that Taylor's letter helped the enemy. But it was a loaded document, and gauging the eagerness of Democratic papers to snap it up, Polk could not have been too sorry about its publication. Yet to accept his own words as sincere was to add one more victim of persecution. Taylor, Scott, and now Polk—all hopelessly impaled.

The letter did clear up one point. Anybody who read a paper knew the reason for Whig Ashmun's query in the debate of Saturday, January 30. Marcy's disinterred order relating to private correspondence waved full in Old Zach's face. Bickering over the "Gaines" letter had broken out after an earlier fight on a resolution of thanks to Taylor and his command for the victory at Monterey. Naturally, in this winter of 1846–47 everything was politics—even to honoring heroes. Democrats agreed to go along with the "thanks" but only as amended to include a "no approbation" of the general's terms to Ampudia. To soften the phrase, somebody moved for "no approbation or disapprobation." Refused.

When the amendment passed in original form, tempers heated up. One member charged anti-Taylorites with rendering the House ridiculous in the country's eyes by "trifling and sporting with brave and gallant officers and soldiers." Another congressman wryly questioned the resolution itself. Why not change "thanks" to "censure"? Why quibble? Go whole hog. "The House *censures* General Taylor and his command for the victory at Monterey." That ought to satisfy the general's detractors.

Yeas 1; Nays 117.

During all this backing and filling, Marcy had worked up two drafts of a protest to Taylor for writing Gaines. Secretary of State Buchanan called one of them too strong. Polk preferred it as the kind of blunt rebuke the general deserved. Also he was glad to hear that the Senate favored airing the entire correspondence between Taylor and the War Department. The public could then judge for itself the unfounded attacks on the administration. "Taylor is a vindictive and ignorant partisan, and after all the kindness and indulgence I have shown him."

8

At Victoria the general was saying good-bye to most of his little army:

It is with deep sensibility that the commanding general finds himself separated from the troops he has so long commanded. To these corps, regular and volunteer, who have shared with him the active services of the field, he feels the attachment due to such associations; while to those who are making their first campaign, he must express his regret that he can not participate with them in its eventual scenes. To all, both officers and men, he extends his heartfelt wishes for their continued success and happiness, confident that their achievements on another theatre will redound to the credit of their country and its arms.

Conventional, predictable—a standard farewell to troops. Delivered in 1847 and by the man who said the words, halting and slow, the message brought tears to many. Both Captains Henry and Kenly were witness. It stirred even Patterson's volunteers, who had never seen Old Rough and Ready. This simple-looking man had fought three battles and won them all. New soldiers had heard all about him before they ever left the Rio camps or the Brazos. Now he visited them at Victoria. "general Tailor Come to see us," an Illinois volunteer wrote, "he is averry old man and very sociable not only to officers but to buck soaldiers also he was not a proud man a tall when he Com to see us he road a muel." A Tennessean said all the soldiers loved the general and would rather die than be guilty of a mean or cowardly act "where he might find it out."

Lieutenant Meade was one of the officers leaving Taylor. To his wife he confessed his regret at "parting with the old man," and thought Washington had treated him outrageously. He had been deprived of his command and left exposed with only a third of his original force. The obvious aim was to break him down, to destroy his popularity. "I trust it will signally fail, and from having the plaudits of the people for his bravery and skill, he will now have their sympathy for the injustice of the course pursued against him." For Meade, who could blow hot and cold on his general, these were warm words.

Zachary Taylor was losing more than the bulk of his army. The exodus robbed him of several chroniclers. Along with Meade, Henry was leaving; also Kenly and E. Kirby Smith. The last three wrote for papers in the states. As expected, the professional newsmen attached themselves to the departing troops. They meant to follow the fighting. Taylor was through. He could only take the shadow of his "Army of Occupation" back to the doldrums of Monterey.

The last week of January saw Taylor on the road. He had the Mississippi volunteers, the dragoons, and the battery under Thomas. Sam French sadly recorded the changed mood.

The march down had been fairly lighthearted; Christmas was typical. On that day John Reynolds had come into camp with some fresh eggs. Eggs equaled eggnog and eggnog belonged to Christmas, but *never* eggnog made of native pulque. French and Reynolds called in the company medic and held him in "house arrest." It worked. A note to the steward produced brandy and rum, with the doctor joining the happy results of his forced prescription.

The trip back was different. A grim Taylor halted at Villa Gran to demand the Mexicans who murdered the December dispatch rider from Monterey. He threatened to levy hard on the town. It took both the mayor and the local priests to cool off the American commander. Next, the wagon train was stalled. Some hours later a gun broke loose and swung across the road. French said Old Zach was so mad he pulled the driver's ear, then waved the piece out of the march. "When he rode away, I ordered the gun into the road, and it was driven on."

Clearly Taylor was no longer the offhand, confident, and affable leader of 1846.

CHAPTER VII

ENCHANTED VALLEY

Monterey and the old camp at Walnut Springs could not hold a restless Taylor long. He was as cold as ever to the rugged pull of Saddle and Mitre Mountains. They were for literary lieutenants who saw clouds "softer than carded wool" disrobing the crests. Hunting was for lieutenants, too. Zach's pulse never rose to the wing beat of pheasant, wild duck, or quail. Shooting yes. He would like to get in some shooting—by his army.

An obliging enemy drew Taylor out of Monterey on February 2. Wool had filled in the vacuum left at Saltillo when Worth decamped to join Scott. Now, from Agua Nueva 18 miles below, Wool was reporting nightly alarms. The Mexicans seemed to be moving up. Scouting parties had made contact only 30 miles farther south. Colonel May lost his baggage in one brush, and two units of Arkansas and Kentucky mounted let a force of Mexican cavalry surround them at night. Ninety men were marched off to San Luis Potosí under enemy guard. John Reynolds was shocked. "They had no precautions against surprise, had no pickets or sentinels and were taken asleep without firing a gun."

Would the volunteers ever learn? For one captain and 17 of his men the story was worse. They fell into a fandango at one of the ranchos, fell out again too drunk to care, and made an easy catch for the Mexicans. Taylor's expressed hope that these losses would teach a lesson must have been weak.

Several days later, on February 5, Reynolds had more opinions. He wrote his younger brother that "General Taylor is perfectly disgusted with the part assigned to him here, of sitting down quietly in front of Saltillo for the winter." And, he went on, it was far from the first ingratitude the government had shown toward Taylor. In Lieutenant Reynolds, Old Zach still had somebody to stand up for him, even with Meade and Henry gone. Another week saw Reynolds reporting on his general again. "He is very impatient under his inactive life and I think if he had a regiment or two of regulars and a few more volunteers he would pull up stakes here and strike a bold stroke at San Luis."

Reynolds closed this letter on problems of his own. Native liquor had reduced him to drinking nothing but water. As for the señoritas: "I have seen only one pretty face since I have been in the country."

Taylor, of course, lacked troops enough for an offensive. In moving down to Saltillo he already was cheating on his orders. On February 7, Scott, who said he was trying hard to forget certain remarks in Taylor's last letter, added a strict order. "I must ask you to abandon Saltillo and to make no detachments, except for *reconnaissances* and immediate defence, much beyond Monterey." On the subject of taking Taylor's troops he reminded the general that he had been left no other choice.

Instead of obeying the general-in-chief, Taylor dropped down to Wool's camp at Agua Nueva. He owed the move to a proper defense of his line, he said, and there he proposed to stay unless "positively ordered to fall back by the government at Washington." To the adjutant general, Taylor explained in more detail. Falling back would hurt troop morale. Agua Nueva lay below the single pass through which the enemy could advance directly. Lack of water and supplies following an exhausting march would force him to fight at a disadvantage or retire. On the other hand, abandoning Saltillo would give the enemy a base from which to operate northward.

Stubbornness and logic about equaled out. According to Army Regulations, Taylor would have to justify his position on strategic and/or tactical grounds beyond any knowledge his superiors could be expected to have at the time. What they might expect depended a lot on how much information the general had given them. Recently Taylor had been less than confiding in his dispatches. A blunder on his part, then, could hurt him. He was gambling that any Mexican attack in force would stick to the main road from San Luis. Santa Anna had choices both east and west of it, though only over rough and wide detours. But if he should manage to outflank Agua Nueva, he could cut Taylor off from Saltillo in rear.

Who was Santa Anna to worry about compared with Scott or the administration? That one line in his letter to the general-in-chief ought to simmer him down. With grim pleasure Zach passed it on to Robert Wood. No sir! He had told Scott, he would never think of pulling back from Saltillo without orders from the proper authority. As for Washington, it would have trouble refuting the case for holding onto Agua Nueva. And Taylor had a new argument. His advanced position would create a diversion in favor of the Gulf offensive. Latest rumors already had Santa Anna moving east to meet Scott, but now with an American force threatening San Luis, he would hesitate.

The last thing Taylor wanted to see was Santa Anna leaving his own front. Wool had brought enough troops from Parras to give Zach an army again, so let the Mexicans come on.[1] The sight of his own 5000 keyed the old man up. He began to feel better. Not once in the whole time in Mexico had he taken a backward step. No government, no general-in-chief could call him off now. To a commander lately reduced to a parcel of dragoons, one battery, and a regiment of volunteers, Taylor's present strength looked good—on paper:

General Staff	41
1st Dragoons, Cos. A and E (Captain Enoch Steen)	133
2nd Dragoons, Co. E (Brevet Colonel Charles A. May)	76
3rd Arty, Cos. C and E (Captains Bragg, T. W. Sherman)	150
4th Arty, Co. B (Captain John M. Washington)	117
Regular Troops, Total	517
Arkansas Mounted (Colonel Archibald Yell)	479
1st Kentucky Mounted (Colonel Humphrey Marshall)	330
2nd Kentucky Infantry (Colonel William McKee)	571

[1] Wool also brought enough politicians, made or on the make, to run a small country. One colonel, John Hardin of Illinois, had Lincoln's support for election to the national Congress in 1840. Polk's first call for troops in 1846 brought Whig Hardin into the war. "He is going wherever ordered," the new colonel orated. "Who will go with him?" The other Illinois colonel, William H. Bissell, had already served in the state house as a Democrat, and after the war he was elected governor. General Joseph Lane, commanding the two Indiana regiments, eventually reached the U. S. Senate; also was the first territorial governor of Oregon and later a governor of the state. Another Hoosier, Colonel James H. Lane, became a senator too and was hotly involved in the Kansas-Nebraska dispute over slavery. Commanding a regiment of Arkansas mounted troops was a former governor of that state, Archibald Yell.

1st Mississippi Rifles (Colonel Jefferson Davis) — 368

2nd Indiana Infantry (Colonel William Bowles)

3rd Indiana Infantry (Colonel James H. Lane) — 1253

1st Illinois Infantry (Colonel John J. Hardin) — 580

2nd Illinois Infantry (Colonel William H. Bissell) — 573

Texas Mounted Scouts (Captains Henry E. McCulloch, John H. Conner) — 88

Volunteer Troops, Total — 4242

Grand Total — 4759

About ten per cent regulars, and not all of them had been under fire. Wool had marched his men 1000 miles without getting off a hostile shot. Of the volunteers only the Mississippians had fought, at Monterey under Taylor. Then why the pickup in the general's mood? He needed one more fight. All the machinations of Polk, of Marcy, Scott, their confederates and connivers would choke out in the smoke of his victory. After that, whether Taylor entered politics or not, whipping the Mexicans meant whipping an administration in Washington which was bent on downgrading anybody who threatened its continued rule. He owed this much to the good people in the states who were begging him to run for President. It was a kind of call. It went beyond his urge to retire, to laze in the sun while cotton fluffed fat and white in his fields.

Let the Mexicans come on.

But with half of February gone, reports from below were disappointing. A *Niles' Register* dispatch of late January reported Santa Anna still in San Luis dunning his congress for money. Meanwhile he went to cockfights or bled his younger officers at monte—to the amount of $34,000, said the awed correspondent. As always, the news lagged behind facts. On January 28 the Mexican general had put part of his army on the road north—the artillery, supply train, a sapper battalion, and the San Patricio Battalion (deserters from Taylor). The rest moved out on following days, and by February 7 the leading division was halfway to Saltillo.

Like Taylor, Santa Anna had been having trouble at home. The government at the City of Mexico accused him of stalling, or worse. They knew about his exchange of notes with the American general. They also knew that his old agent, Atocha, was still busy in Washington. This knowledge made them distrust the slippery Santa Anna, so the pressure was on him to move, ready or not. It meant marching in the driest season over country where water was scarce at best. Northers ripped into his columns, and three men died of cold on the first night out. The number of half-starved, half-frozen stragglers mounted in ratio to distance covered.

Santa Anna knew their condition, but passed it off lightly: "The Mexican soldier is well known for his frugality and his capability for sufferance." Provisions? They would have them soon enough—from the enemy—"once we completely wipe away from our soil the vain-glorious foreigner who has dared to pollute it with his presence." One thing about a Santa Anna army, it could always feed on words.

From the American position at Agua Nueva scouting parties kept feeling for the Mexican advance. They combed every road and mule path they could find to the east, west, and south. In camp Taylor turned the drilling over to Wool. "Old Fussy" had brought his men from Parras in 40- to 50-mile marches, and he had no thought of easing up on them now. He worked the volunteers hardest because they needed it most. They kicked the most too. "We came here to fight, sir! not to clean old iron and groom horses, sir!"

Regular Sam Chamberlain of Wool's dragoons rated the volunteer mounted lower than low. To believe him, not one in 50 of their carbines would fire, and they let their sabers rust in the scabbards. Chamberlain was a casual man with the truth, but even allowing for overstatement, the Arkansas and Kentucky horsemen were far from reliable troops.

Chamberlain had opinions on almost everybody. Wool was a martinet. The general's aide, Lieutenant Irvin W. McDowell, had "the most obtuse intellect in the army. . . ." He laughed at Colonel Marshall with his fat stomach. Charles May was a coward and a fake. The Indian-straight colonel had the look of a dashing cavalry officer, with his long hair and a beard that swept to his waist belt, but he was only an "ass in the lion's skin." Chamberlain was on safer ground with "Battery Sherman." He damned the artillery officer as weak, eccentric, tyrannical—the meanest man in the service.

Soldiers? The dragoon divided the army into three classes: Dead Beats, Old Soldiers, Dare Devils. The first were a dirty lot who spent most of their time on sick roll. The Old Soldiers did well enough in a mechanical way. They were always on hand in camp, kept out of the guardhouse, never drank or gambled. Neither did they ever make sergeant. Now the Dare Devils—first in frolic, first in the guardhouse, first to volunteer for any duty, first in cleanliness of person and equipments, last in the hospital, and *first in the fight.*

No trouble guessing where Chamberlain classed himself, but at least he found some part of the army he could approve.

The best coverage on the weeks at Agua Nueva came from another of Wool's men. Lieutenant Adolph Engelmann of the 2nd Illinois volunteers had read law in his state, and once in the service was alive to every experience it could offer, from the good to the bad. Good things like the Christmas tree he cut, and trimmed with sperm candles, and "some right good cookies" made by a couple of fellows in the company; like days warm enough for swimming; the horse racing and ball games on the parade ground; Saltillo, "the biggest and finest city I have ever seen."

The bad list was longer. "It is hard for a free American to accustom himself to the discipline and aristocracy of the army." Engelmann was tired of Wool's hard marches—116 miles in four days to reach Taylor. He was tired of standing guard after 30 miles on the road. He was tired of company drill in the mornings, regimental drill in the afternoons, and dress parades in the evening. He was tired of Mexican flour and half rations. He had no confidence in Wool or most of the officers under him. They included William H. Bissell, his own colonel. He was seeing too much plundering by the soldiers, though it troubled him when two culprits were drummed out of camp to wander in enemy country without money or weapons.

"With few exceptions," Engelmann wrote his parents, "all the volunteers are mighty tired of this war, and sorry they ever left home. . . . Only real activity can restore energy and morale." For that reason the lieutenant had looked forward to serving under Taylor. He would make a happy change from a general who woke out of a nightmare to order everybody up with guns loaded and not a Mexican soldier nearer than 200 miles. Still, Engelmann's first sight of Taylor was not reassuring—the gray hair, deeply lined face, the same old oilcloth cap, dusty green coat, and frightful trousers. On horseback the general looked "like a toad." A final doubt was Taylor's apparent respect for Wool. It was more than his own men granted him.

Old Zach's judgment would soon be on the line.

2

On February 20, Sam French and another lieutenant went hunting. The day was warm, dreamy, with a peculiar pale sunlight and a silence. On this same day two companies of dragoons and two guns set out on reconnaissance, 400 men altogether.

Under Charles May the 400 moved east, looking for Miñon's cavalry. Taylor could not let the Mexicans outflank him and get into the rear and Saltillo. Near La Hedionda signal fires on several mountain peaks told May to search ahead. He reined up and sent scouts toward a long white lift of dust beyond the hills. May himself then settled down at a rancho for the night. The natives there refused to talk, either from fright or from lack of information. The colonel took no chances. He dismounted his men, posted one gun, and kept all horses saddled.

Both the edgy quiet felt by French and the signals and dust in May's front proved out. Next morning the dragoons rode back into Agua Nueva with the word. So did Henry McCulloch's party of Texans. The captain had seen the whole Mexican army—he thought about 20,000—at La Encarnacion. That put Santa Anna a single day's march away.

And put Zachary Taylor back in the war.

At the moment it only put him in trouble. Agua Nueva dangled helplessly some ten miles below the hacienda San Juan de la Buena Vista, which was Taylor's one defensible position south of Saltillo. He had stuffed the farm buildings around his present camps full of unthreshed grain and other rations. But because Agua Nueva could be turned, Taylor would have to give it up. Giving up supplies so hard to come by in this faraway war was hard on a man who hated to waste a dollar.

The thrifty general did the best he could. All during the afternoon and evening of the 21st, with the Mexicans not 20 miles away, his wagons lugged off every ration and every round of ammunition they could carry. He had most of it out by nightfall, then ordered the buildings burned. Lieutenant James H. Carleton, 1st Dragoons, stood by as the flaming light picked out the valley of El Encantado, blanching the wall of mountains against the dark of their gorges and ravines. The view stirred him to one of the longest sentences to come out of the war:

The noise of the falling timbers, the roar of the flames, the huge column of ascending smoke, the appearance of armed and mounted men moving between the spectator and the fire, with the brilliant light flashing here and there on burnished arms and glittering appointments,—taken in connection with the scattered shots interchanged between still other of our advanced parties and those of Ampudia, the heavy rumbling of our retreating train of wagons, intermingled with the distant trumpet-signals now and then faintly heard in the direction of the approaching enemy,—all conspired to render that cold, deep midnight, one which could never be forgotten.

Old Zach did not linger to enjoy the illumination. He pulled the companies of volunteer mounted and the two of dragoons back to the ranch at Buena Vista. Five miles south of Saltillo, its run-down but stout adobe buildings overlooked one of the strangest positions a general ever picked to defend. Also one of the best.

The army's prose-mulling officer would gasp at the view: a road dropping at easy grade into a narrows alongside a silvered splash of stream; mountains that skied to 6000 feet and squeezed the valley at points to a width of only a mile and a half. About seven miles south of Buena Vista the terrain leveled out onto the plain and rancho of El Encantado, which gave the entire valley its perfect name—enchanted.

General Wool had camped at Buena Vista some weeks before and saw its possibilities, not for brush and pigment or for anapests, but for battle. When Taylor saw the ground later, he agreed. The lie to his south gave him sure protection on his right. Here the stream west of the road fingered out into a network of steep gullies extending almost to the mountains on that side. No enemy could waggle through in numbers enough to worry about. The road itself abutted a high bluff on the left that varied from 40 to 80 feet in height and rose gently toward the mountains farther east.

On that bluff, or plateau, Taylor would make his stand if and when the Mexicans moved up. He had about 400 yards of width nearest the road. From there the plateau narrowed to half the width at the foot of the peaks. The ground allowed Taylor a mile for maneuvering, generally northwest to southeast. A great gouge of ravine protected his rear, another his front. Three smaller cuts broke only part way into the plateau from the road. Artillery both on the road itself and from the bluff directly left could sweep the approaches from the south.

Taylor's defense offered the Mexican general three choices, all bad. He could try bulling his way up the road through the narrows. He could mass a frontal attack against the plateau, or gamble on turning the American left from its upper end. The flank attack on the east was possible only if Santa Anna's infantry and lancers found purchase enough for operating along the base of the mountains.

On the evening of February 21, Old Zach showed his own confidence in the position at Buena Vista by riding the five miles north to Saltillo. He had good reasons for going. Buena Vista's near-perfect ground could actually be its weakness. If your enemy is afraid to risk frontal attack, he begins to think of turning movements. With Miñon's cavalry already probing the passes east and north of Buena Vista, Taylor could not discount the threat. Once bypassed, his army would have to give up its position and scramble for the rear over a single road. Pulling out untried men was hazard enough. To add jerry-building a new defense at Saltillo would only compound it.

The city also was Taylor's supply base. Guarding it were eight companies of volunteers, Captain Webster with two 24-pound howitzers, and Captain William H. Shover with a Bragg 6-pounder. The general could hardly spare more from an army under 5000 in strength, minus 364 sick. Certainly not in the face of McCulloch's 20,000 estimate for Santa Anna. Leaving Saltillo so thinly shielded made Taylor nervous. He held the city against orders as it was, and to lose it would bring the administration down on his head.

The old general needed his battle; otherwise the war would concentrate with Scott by default. But the battle had better take place where Taylor planned to fight it—at Buena Vista.

By Monday morning, February 22, chances at Buena Vista looked good. Santa Anna was making ready to supply the battle. He had judged the American barn-burning at Agua Nueva as pure hysteria. The invaders had lost their nerve. That kind of retreat marked a scared army. "They have fled, they have fled," cried one of the Mexican general's aides. So, as another of his officers put it, "Without giving the troops time to get a drink of water or to fill their canteens, he [Santa Anna] compelled them to continue their advance at the double quick." The order came at the end of frantic marching by already exhausted troops. It added 14 miles more to the Mexicans' desert hike of 35 for the day.

Wool brought the Americans from the hacienda of Buena Vista to take their positions a mile south. They stepped along under a crisp, clear sun. "Hail, Columbia" beat out from a regimental band, and shouts of "Remember Washington" rolled back through the column. The army had a Washington, in fact, though no kin to the one whose birthday was about to earn more than a presidential salute. But John M. Washington had eight guns in his B Company of the 4th. Wool sent him into the road at the pinch of the narrows, along with six companies of Hardin's 1st Illinois. The stream ran close on their right, and the bluff of the plateau shouldered the left. Up there Wool had placed the other Hardin companies, for added support to the battery below.

Next in position eastward on the plateau were Bissell's 2nd Illinois, a company of Texans, and a squadron of dragoons. Farther left toward the mountains stood most of McKee's 2nd Kentucky. On the extreme left the Arkansas and Kentucky mounted held the first slopes above the plateau. In rear Wool kept for his reserve the two Indiana regiments, the Mississippi Rifles, May's dragoons, and the batteries of Sherman and Bragg. Both Taylor and Wool were confident about their right.

Back from Saltillo by nine in the morning, Old Zach rode with his second in command along the lines. The cheers that rolled up called for some words—the fewest possible from Taylor. Wool took pains to remind his own men of how hard and far they had marched to fight their first battle. Cheers again. The army felt good. Even green troops could sense a position's strength. The instinct to survive made up for ignorance about phrases like cordon defense, mobile defense, defense in depth, cul-de-sacs, flanks refused or up in the air. It was enough that they stood on high ground. To reach it the Mexicans would have to expose themselves from below. Just hang on to that mile of tableland and Santa Anna had nowhere to go.

When the Mexican swept his glass left to right across Taylor's front, he must have thought the same thing. An opening American gun did its best to persuade him. Santa Anna lost his horse, and the fall hurt the stump of his amputated leg. But in his favor was the number of troops he could throw against Taylor—only three to four thousand under McCulloch's guess of twenty. More than enough to drive off the spotty huddles of men on the plateau. So at 11 o'clock he sent up a flag and a note. He had the Americans surrounded with overwhelming force, he warned, and he could cut them to pieces. Only his consideration and esteem for their general prompted the wish to spare him. Santa Anna would wait one hour for surrender.

Adjutant Bliss cooled Taylor's sizzling reaction into proper military terms: "in reply to . . . beg leave to say that I decline . . . high respect . . . obedient servant . . ." However expressed and translated, the message was clear to Antonio López de Santa Anna.

3

The Mexican general spent the next three hours deploying his troops. He kept eying the suggestion of shelf along the base of the eastern mountains. If he could put troops up there, he could drive in Taylor's left on the plateau. He might even break through to the hacienda in his rear. Where else could he begin the attack? Not on the American right, where the stream and the lacing of gullies gutted the terrain. Not on the road itself, straddled by artillery. So it had to be the enemy left.

Santa Anna ordered Ampudia's light infantry division to dig for a foothold east of Taylor's line, to get on that shelf. He masked the move by a halfhearted feint at the opposite flank. One of Bragg's guns and some Kentucky foot crossed the stream, feeling as safe as sightseers. Captain Washington felt equally safe about his road. He passed two of his pieces up to the plateau, then another when Wool asked if he could spare it. The general reminded him that he held the key to the army's position. No matter, the captain answered, he would defend it. So a third gun joined Washington's subaltern, John

Paul Jones O'Brien. The lieutenant would find work for them above before this fight was over.

By late afternoon Ampudia's progress gave Taylor something to think about. Neither shrapnel from O'Brien's pieces nor accurate fire from Indiana riflemen could keep the Mexicans from threatening his left. Suppose they pushed on north along the base of the mountains? They would lay open the supplies and the hospital set up at the hacienda. Saltillo lay only five miles farther. The sight of Ampudia pressing his flank put Old Zach on the road back to the city and a last anxious check on his base. There he learned that Miñon had spilled through Palomas Pass northeast of Saltillo. Fifteen hundred lancers could unravel his communications to Monterey.

In leaving Santa Anna's front, Taylor missed a Mexican band concert, and Mexican bands played good music. Sunset inched a bronze wash of color up the eastern peaks of Sierra Madre. Horns and percussion, shouted *Vivas* for Santa Anna, the Republic, and "*Libertad o Muerte*," carried from the plain to the defenders on the plateau. The Mexican leader had just finished his speech. He had offered to spare the lives of the foreign invaders, but in their vainglory they had refused his kindness. Now let them die. Give neither pity nor quarter.

This was an old Santa Anna formula for battle.

Old Zach's ride to Saltillo left his army in the hands of an even more practiced worrier. Wool had doubts about Washington's anchor on the road. During the night he set the Illinois companies to raising a barricade and digging a ditch in the front of the guns. He also called for entrenching on the bluff to the left above. At 10 o'clock he sent the 1st Dragoons back to strike tents and pull camp at Buena Vista. By 1:30 on the morning of the 23rd a wagon train moved into a ravine between the hacienda and the plateau. No loose ends for John

Ellis Wool. By shoring up defenses on and near the road, and by bringing down a store of supplies and ammunition, he could give more attention to Ampudia's insolent foothold to the east.

Both armies waited out the cold, drizzly night without fires. Near daybreak a spit and stutter of musketry rattled along the base of the mountains. Jittery pickets. Lieutenant Reynolds, wrapped in his overcoat on the ground, suffered chills and wondered what the morning would bring. Later he woke to a sun so brilliant "as to remind one of Napoleon's sun at Austerlitz." He followed his bit of martial lore with a breakfast of cold ham and hard bread.

At first Reynolds was worried. The gunners of Sherman's battery were raw, scarcely drilled, and had never seen a fight. Only the drivers were veterans of Monterey, where, like Reynolds, they rode under Bragg. But by 8 o'clock the lieutenant felt better as he took position with Sherman and two pieces on a narrow ridge behind the main plateau. "I never went into action in better spirits in my life," Reynolds wrote. The excitement erased his chills, along with his concern about untested gunners. The young West Pointer's eager mood spoke for the whole army.

The Mexican plan developed logically. Two thousand more infantry joined Ampudia's push against Taylor's left. A battery of 8-pounders worked far enough up the east slope to support the attack there. From his center Santa Anna moved two divisions (7000 men) forward. The first, under Don Francisco Pacheco, filed into a ravine, then rose gradually to front the Americans on the main part of the plateau. General Don Manuel Lombardini took the other division in on Pacheco's right, to fill the gap between him and the 8-pounders supporting Ampudia. To complete the pressure on Taylor's whole line, Santa Anna started 4000 more men up the road for the narrows and Washington's battery. Lancers rode with all infantry, while 2000 troops held to the plain in reserve. Peg-Leg had his offensive grandly under way.

Citizen soldiers from Illinois, Kentucky, and Arkansas stared quietly down on the columns moving toward them. They were seeing their first enemy army. Reynolds' Austerlitz sun lacquered three snaking lines of rifle barrels and equipments. Even the young veteran of Taylor's three battles was awed. "I never in my life beheld a more beautiful sight, their gay uniforms, numerous pennants, standards and colors streaming in all their pride and pomp."

Lieutenant Carleton saw it all the way Reynolds did, the lancers especially—their guidons ribboning back in the bristle of spear points, their drill-ground cadence, and the brilliant trappings of their horses. Dragoon Sam Chamberlain was struck by the lancers' dress, startling blue uniforms faced with red and topped by plumed hats. Farther front, on reconnaissance, Lieutenant Henry Benham of the engineers reported seeing handsome greyhounds leaping and weaving round the horses of the generals and their staffs. Something new in military splash.

No doubt some of the glitter these Americans saw resulted from the diamond-bright morning and pre-battle excitement. No horsemen beating up through the sand and dust from San Luis Potosí could arrive in quite such style. Among the unimpressed was artilleryman French. Santa Anna, he said, was only showing off. The lieutenant probably remembered that lancers paraded better than they fought.

The Mexican objective was clear by now. Santa Anna meant to crack Taylor's center and left. Success would free Ampudia for a romp into the American rear, followed by Pacheco and Lombardini. General Wool was down on the road, still fretting about Washington's position. Somebody on the plateau would have to take charge and move fast. Unfortunately, Brigadier

Joe Lane was the ranking officer within reach. The Indiana volunteer ordered O'Brien's three guns from the left to wheel 200 yards down in front of the line. The 2nd Indiana was brought along in support. Lane wanted a stop for Pacheco's division, already beginning to climb up from the ravine.

Outnumbered ten to one, O'Brien and the infantry stood off the Mexicans for half an hour. But no matter how fast their fire thinned out the advance, new formations kept spilling onto the southern edge of the plateau. When the enemy 8-pounders began to reach O'Brien, from the slope, Lane sent him farther down the plateau out of range. The tough artilleryman made it and even went into battery for a few moments, ripping the Mexicans with small metal. Then his supports broke. One by one, companies of the 2nd Indiana peeled off for the rear. O'Brien got his howitzer and the 6-pounder out. He had neither men nor horses to bring off the third, so had to give it up.

Zach Taylor's battle desperately wanted a general officer who knew how to place and handle troops. Lane had committed three guns and a regiment too far front too soon. Their exposure had ended with a panicky order from Colonel Bowles: "Cease firing and retreat!" Hoosier feet were more than willing. Now the American line was weaker by a regiment and, unless O'Brien could recoup, also weaker by an irreplaceable wild man with the guns. A hole on the left had been opened up for Pacheco and Lombardini across the southeast fourth of the plateau. There they joined to cut off four companies of dismounted Arkansas troops, who found their sudden isolation too much to bear. They followed in the direction of the 2nd Indiana—north.

Still holding a shortened line stood Bissell's 2nd Illinois, a dragoon squadron, McCulloch's Texas company, and two 6-pounders under French and George Thomas. For a while these guns matched O'Brien's work, but weight of numbers soon began to tell. To save their position the Americans gave ground, regrouping in a new alignment across the broad northwest end of the plateau. But a front that had faced south at daylight on the 23rd now looked to the east. And it needed all the help Wool was scraping his reserve to supply. Sherman and Reynolds whirled up with a two-gun section. That made four. Bragg arrived next with his three to make it seven. The detached companies of McKee's 2nd Kentucky came in with Bragg, and four companies of Hardin's 1st Illinois climbed onto the field from the narrows.

Altogether some 1500 of Taylor's men blasted away at the upper plateau. Once more they were outnumbered almost ten to one. A musket ball drilled French in the thigh, but he refused to dismount. Bissell lost 80 men in the fighting here. To hope the troops would hang on was asking a lot.

Down on the road the ratio of Mexicans against Captain Washington was even higher. But the artilleryman had all the advantage of position. His flanks were secured by the stream and gullies on his right, and by the head of the plateau looming above him on the left. The division of D. Santiago Blanco had nowhere to go except into the muzzles of guns and their infantry supports, all of them behind the barricade across the road. Lieutenants Darius Couch, Tom Brent, and Henry Whiting helped their captain rock the valley with iron explosions. The Mexicans who survived veered off into the several gorges cutting into the plateau. The anchor for Taylor's front held firm.

But what was an anchor by itself? Up along the mountains Taylor's left had shrunk. Screened by Pacheco and Lombardini, the troops of Ampudia began driving for the American rear. More Arkansas horse and those from Kentucky fell back. Nearly all of a Texas rifle company went down resisting. The

Mexicans were turning the American position at Buena Vista, not by threading skittish paths beyond the mountains, but smack across the upper plateau. In the buildings of the hacienda a mile or so north, maybe in the American camp, or five miles farther in Saltillo, somewhere they would catch up with the fabulous loot their general always promised them. Santa Anna's underfed army pitched on, full of desire.

4

By morning of February 23 Taylor felt better about Saltillo. For some reason Miñon's cavalry had drawn off, the general did not know why. Defenses looked stout enough to let him go back to the front. His escort included Charlie May and two squadrons of dragoons, Jeff Davis with eight companies of Mississippi Rifles, and a Bragg 6-pounder under Charles L. Kilburn. Before long the shock and boom rolling north to their ears stepped up the pace. They reached the hacienda in time to see the blue press of men along the mountains on the left—Mexican blue, not American.

At 9 A.M., in Lieutenant Carleton's gentlest words, "The aspect of affairs was now most gloomy" on Taylor's battlefield. But Taylor at last was up. He halted the Rifles at the hacienda long enough to fill canteens, then turned them and Kilburn left off the road to reverse the stampede of Hoosiers and Arkansas "Rackensaks." With the dragoons Zach rode on. Men soon saw the familiar head rising out of the ravine onto the plateau. Word zipped along the front, what front the army still held: "Old Zach's up! Rough and Ready's here, boys!" Taylor had picked his moment.

The general talked with Wool and inspected the new line, less than half what he had seen the evening before. The 2nd

Indiana gone, O'Brien out, also the Arkansas and Kentucky mounted; the front bent back quarter circle, his left a funnel for Mexicans pushing to the rear. To make things worse, the San Patricio Battalion had brought their guns on the field. The deserters from Taylor had 18- and 24-pounders, enough weight to blow the defenders off the plateau. Zach's luck helped here. Instead of exploiting their range, they began working within reach of the American sixes and soon lost their infantry supports.

The setback took something out of Santa Anna's men. They began edging back, Bragg after them and ahead of Taylor's advancing muskets. Fight-hungry O'Brien popped up again with fresh guns. Accurate fire, guts, and the general's presence combined at this stage to save the right center. Santa Anna helped by letting the suddenly recharged Americans distract him. Holding Pacheco and Lombardini to a defensive on the upper plateau gave Taylor time to restore some of the damage on his left.

Farther in rear Davis had tried to pick up help for his Mississippians from the routed Indiana, Arkansas, and Kentucky troops. He got little response, though Colonel Bowles did grab a rifle and join the scattering of recovered fugitives. Bowles needed everything the gesture was worth. The ragged left needed more than gestures to repair Ampudia's breakthrough. North of the great ravine behind the plateau a narrower ridge gave Davis a route toward the mountains. Wool promised support and pulled the 3rd Indiana out of reserve. It was a privilege to fall in with Jeff's Rifles, swinging along in the light step "peculiar to Indians and hunters," red shirts hanging outside their white ducks, proud of their special rifles and bowie knives 18 inches long. Even a dragoon could praise this breed of men on foot, as Sam Chamberlain did when he saw them start out.

Ampudia reacted to the threat, the first visible resistance to his plans for mopping up the American rear. Kilburn's 6-pounder answered his opening volleys. Davis waited for fatter shooting at 60 yards, then drove the Mexican infantry back on its reserve. But a heavy force of lancers kept threading north above the ravines. No matter how far Taylor thinned his new left toward Buena Vista, he could see it being turned. The Saltillo road, the wagon park, and the hacienda itself lay ripe for the taking.

Taylor sent Reynolds galloping back from the plateau with two guns. He added four companies of dragoons under May for support. Colonels Yell and Marshall braced remnants of the mounted troops east of the ranch buildings, one of them used as a hospital. Major Monroe shamed more of the earlier rear-runners into manning the roofs and yards. Reynolds pulled up barely in time to lift the pressure from shaky Arkansas and Kentucky volunteers, though not before Yell was killed. Case shot raked the Mexicans backward and Reynolds limbered up again. Next stop the hacienda. Everybody pitched in here. A Kentucky adjutant went down with 24 wounds. But as always American firepower drained the fight out of lancers. They took to the mountains, leaving 35 dead behind.

Shortly after noon Santa Anna, blocked off at Buena Vista, tried for the Saltillo road at a point between the hacienda and the plateau. To make it he had to drive Davis from his perch on the narrow ridge north of the great ravine. Just off its crest the 3rd Indiana and fragments of the 2nd formed a line fronting northeast. Connecting with their left, Davis completed an obtuse angle, or wide V, by facing his men southeast. Its open end was toward the mountain. Sherman mounted a howitzer on left and rear. Soon, in a military display that ignited Lieutenant Carleton's prose again, Santa Anna's lancers moved onto the upper end of the ridge: ranks well closed, troopers riding knee to knee, the whole brigade precise in intervals and direction. "It had a sort of air about it,—an easy nonchalant manner of going into the work,—which could not but recall to one's mind his ideal picture of the cavalry of the olden days."

Success for the Mexicans depended on a simple tactic. Take their losses from the Americans' first volley, then stampede the V before the two lines could reload. On they came, their approach measured, steady—a tempting target of 1500 horsemen. That was the idea, to draw Davis's fire at long range. Many of the lancers knew all about these red-shirted devils with rifles. Two hundred yards and no volley. One hundred yards. The attackers gradually slowed their pace. In another moment they reined up, overlapped now on both flanks.

Halting was suicide. Whitney rifles aimed by Mississippi hunters picked off Mexicans by scores. At 80 yards the Hoosiers had easy targets too. Grape and canister from Sherman's howitzer ripped into the lancers from the left. Only the wreck of a brigade made it back up the slopes to the east.

The road still belonged to Taylor, and wagons rolled down from the hacienda with food and ammunition. Return trips hauled the wounded brought down through the gorges. Mexican pressure never let up on either the plateau or on the narrows below. Santa Anna also kept pushing columns along the base of the mountains. The constant build-up brought May's dragoons and Reynolds down from the hacienda. In a whirling burst of stone and gravel they went in toward the mountains north of the ridge Davis held. Bragg squeezed three pieces in between. The remaining three guns on the plateau swung their muzzles left. Nine guns had Santa Anna's latest drive under fire. They dug in closer and closer as the Mexicans fell back. Shells from Reynolds gouged their right, Sherman ripped the center, O'Brien and Thomas the left. Exploding metal flattened a tortured five to six thousand Mexicans against the base of the mountains.

About one o'clock, in this tight spot for Santa Anna, a white flag among his troops slacked off the American fire. Were the enemy giving up? If so, why the continuing resistance? When a confused second-level parley failed, Old Zach ordered his men back to their muskets and guns. But the break spared Santa Anna's force along the slope. They scattered out of range, most of them to the south.

The Mexican general saw one final move. The Americans had robbed their strength on the plateau to shore up their northern flank. He would hit their center again. He brought his big guns farther down near the east end of the field. From out of reserve a division marched for the same ravine Pacheco had used in the morning. This move, which included a lancer troop, was screened from view above. The new strike would give Santa Anna eight guns to three and over two to one in men. It would, that is, if he could wipe the Americans from the plateau before help arrived from their left.

Taylor, of course, was straining to bring his men back to the main field, to rebuild his old line from road to mountains. Then his obvious tactic was to respark the momentum of Mexican retreat. As a start he pushed O'Brien and Thomas eastward along the plateau. The two Illinois regiments and McKee's Kentuckians leaped forward. A last deadly proof of American firepower could end this battle here and now. It would pry Pacheco, Lombardini, and Ampudia off the slopes for good and put them south on the road for San Luis Potosí.

Everything was right for Taylor except timing. The timing favored Santa Anna. His fresh reserves spouted onto the field, forming in columns to spread across the plateau in front of the American advance. The scattered Mexican divisions rallied from above to join the offensive. They faced Taylor with a combined attack of almost 12,000 men. O'Brien and Thomas riddled the first waves of force, but their hot guns could fire only so fast. Their infantry reeled, rocked back, and groped for cover. They found it by diving for the two nearest gorges dropping west to the road.

Found it, they thought. Then Mexicans ringed their escape from overhead, pouring down lead on helpless troops who could neither load nor fire. Lancers raced up the road to bottle them in. Washington's battery blew most of the horsemen back to open the way out. Some of the Americans stumbled to safety behind his guns. But 20 minutes had filled the gorges with dead. Hardin was down, also McKee, and the son of Henry Clay. Bissell's 2nd took 131 casualties, the 2nd Kentucky 87, and the 1st Illinois 45. No wounded here. The trickle of lancers who reached them ran them through.

With his infantry bled off the plateau, Old Zach was left with the three 6-pounders. Unless help arrived soon, the commanding general and two fine lieutenants of artillery would fall before the press of Vivas-happy infantry. Bragg was beating his way south, his horses so worn-out he had to dump his caissons. From farther in rear rode Sherman and Reynolds. Meanwhile O'Brien and Thomas worked without supports, after every round retiring barely more than the length of recoil. For O'Brien, 100 yards in advance of Thomas, the choice narrowed. He could limber up and move back. He had two men hit besides himself, two horses shot from under him, and too few left to pull his pieces off. To hang on was to lose them. But Thomas was hanging on, Bragg was almost up, and O'Brien could see infantry beginning to scrabble out of the north ravine.

Artillerymen hated to lose guns. O'Brien had lost one in the morning. Now two more? His sole reserve was Captain Washington's generosity. Still, just one last round. John Paul Jones O'Brien whaled away, then limped off. The guns went over to the other side. Bragg was on the plateau, begging for infantry support. No infantry. "Double-shot your guns and give 'em hell!" Taylor shouted. Bragg shoved his muzzles within yards of the Mexicans and let go. Sherman and Reynolds pounded up to unlimber alongside. And finally infantry—the Mississippians and Lane's 3rd Indiana. Bissell added scraps from the battered Illinois below.

The impact began to tell. Case shot and grape mangled the stubborn Mexican front. Davis brought the two regiments out of the ravine on their right flank. The Red Shirts again! Their Whitneys and the Hoosier muskets enfiladed the Santa Anna columns, bent them in on their own left. The Mexicans shuddered to a halt. Bragg, Sherman, Reynolds, and Thomas kept moving up.

The hour from four to five had seen an aborted attack by Taylor, a massive Mexican counterattack, and now a second American drive. This last one did it. Santa Anna fell back on his San Patricio battery. He lingered there with his beaten troops as sunset and the dying light closed out the fighting. Taylor sent out his pickets, ordered Davis's Rifles back to Saltillo, and stepped up the trains of wounded to Buena Vista. Troops ate where they stood, arms at ready. Dragoon mounts remained saddled and artillery horses in harness.

The general was taking no chances. He still held the road and the narrows, had salvaged his left, and won back the plateau. In front of Saltillo during the afternoon, good work by Webster's two howitzers, the Bragg gun under Lieutenant Shover, and mixed infantry had blocked off Miñon's cavalry and chased it back east through the passes. So except for the Mexican battery and troops still on the rise above the plateau, the day ended with Taylor's army on the ground it had covered at the start.

But the cost? Unless Santa Anna had taken far more losses than the Americans, he could gamble the same heavy odds tomorrow. Zach Taylor's little army could not afford to play his numbers game. It already had met four to one, eight to one, and even ten to one at every point of pressure. To offset the disadvantage, Taylor's good position, better discipline, and more punishing fire would stretch only so far.

Nobody from the general down looked forward to daylight through the hours of stinging cold that came on after dark. Four heavy guns under Captain James H. Prentiss and other tired officers, among them Lieutenants Abner Doubleday and James B. Ricketts, arrived at 3 A.M. Their 65-mile push from Monterey was the only good news. Lieutenant Carleton heard the wing beat of night-flying buzzards, marauders settling over the valley's aftermath of battle. Reynolds, along with the other artillerymen, spent most of the night foraging for the horses and bringing up ammunition. Too cold to sleep anyhow, he said. "I had time to think of you all at home [Lancaster, Pennsylvania] and how comfortable you were there little thinking of the critical situation we were in."

Several hours later Lieutenant John Fulton Reynolds, West Point, class of '41, enjoyed his first coffee in two days and watched the sunrise pink the lifting dust of Santa Anna's rear guard. The battle was over. The veterans still with the army had seen this happen before. Arista, Ampudia, and now Santa Anna—the best of the lot, moving south and leaving the field to tough old Taylor. "Rough and Ready was too much for him," Reynolds exulted. "I never saw him so perfectly cool and determined . . . he was in a good humor the whole fight, and appeared perfectly certain of gaining the day."

5

Zach Taylor had got himself the battle he wanted. He had brought the war back to northern Mexico and away from Scott. The rejected general had done it again. A jealous administration tried to kill him off as a political threat by stripping his army and leaving him the dead end of a suspended campaign. Now let Washington worry the meaning of Buena Vista.

Washington would, once it knew.

Having got his battle, Taylor had to win it. He had disobeyed orders in moving so far south to tempt Santa Anna. To lose then would have meant a court-martial, with all its potential for wrecking his military reputation and any hope of other service. In committing the army to fight at Buena Vista, the old general had shown plenty of nerve, but less judgment. He gave the Mexicans at least three-to-one odds over all. He accepted battle 500 miles deep in hostile territory, at the end of a nervous and shaky line to the rear. Losses and exhaustion on the 23rd forced Taylor to skin that line of precious reserves from as far north as Cerralvo. Any weakness at the front would have knocked out communications all the way to the Rio Grande.

The general never once doubted his move. Falling back to Monterey or staying there in the first place, he insisted, would have bottled him up. Santa Anna could have invested the city and gone on to arouse the whole of northern Mexico. We would lose everything, every depot abandoned, "all the artillery & cavalry horses & every animal belonging to the trains . . . destroyed or starved" until "our volunteer army shut up and disheartened must have either surrendered or been cut to pieces."

A frightening hindsight but admissable rationalization by a soldier who wanted his one battle more and was sure he could win it. His own moral force and will, good troops, and Santa Anna's mistakes carried him through. Taylor met a half-starved army at the end of a punishing march. Weak and winded men attacked his strong position. Then when they were turning it on the left, Santa Anna let Taylor take troops and guns from his center to save it. Too late the Mexican general recovered and made his strike against the plateau. By then he had wasted so much strength piecemeal that he lacked the reserves to knock Taylor out before he restored his position.

Also Taylor had the guns. "Without our artillery," Wool wrote, "we could not have maintained our position a single hour." Old Zach was converted all over again. "The services of the light artillery, always conspicuous, were more than usually distinguished. Moving rapidly over the roughest ground, it was always in action at the right place and the right time, and its well-directed fire dealt destruction in the masses of the enemy." Taylor said it simply in a private letter: "Our artillery did more than wonders."

No praise was too high for the "flying" batteries. At Buena Vista they made up for their futility in the streets of Monterey. On the road at the narrows John Washington broke the back of every attempt against the right. He kept lending pieces to gambler O'Brien, and even supplied fresh horses for Bragg. Next, along with Davis and his Indiana help, it was guns that saved both left and rear. At the end, on the plateau, their massed fire was greatest of all—an artillery show like the one that shook a doubting Taylor at Palo Alto. Their officers would be worth watching: Braxton Bragg, Thomas Sherman, John Washington, John P. J. O'Brien, George Thomas, John Reynolds, Charles Kilburn, Robert Garnett, and others.[2]

Most of the army talk after the battle settled on O'Brien. Losing three guns gave reason enough for talk, but all of it was good. The lieutenant lost them in the best tradition of the service—saving a position by sticking to the end, his support gone and the enemy jam up to his muzzles. Out in the open,

[2] Two of the best were lost early—O'Brien from sickness in 1850; Washington in a shipwreck in 1853.

without infantry, guns are nakedly exposed between rounds. Spongers, rammers, loaders, and the men who set matches to touchholes need small-arms protection. So does everyone else in the battery, along with the horses. Let enough men be picked off and the guns are through.

Twice on the 23rd O'Brien kept working after his supports dissolved. The 2nd Indiana failed him in the morning, and his second try coincided with the Mexican infantry attack that drove Hardin, Bissell, and McKee into the gorges. French helped him the first time until he was hit, then Garnett replaced French. O'Brien had Thomas with him through the next attack. Guns but no infantry.

If nobody else worried about giving up guns, O'Brien did. He worried for three full pages in his report to his chief: "You are, sir, well aware that it is often the duty of an artillery officer to sacrifice his pieces for the safety of other troops. Such was my position. I could have saved the guns, had I withdrawn them earlier; but in such case, the day might, perhaps, have been lost." It well might have been, and yet here was the modest lieutenant, fretting over hardware he had paid for beyond reckoning.

Of the artillerists Reynolds covered the most terrain, all to good advantage. He began the day in reserve a mile north of the plateau. From there he moved up to help plug Taylor's center during the opening attack. By early afternoon he was back near the hacienda, driving off the lancers who spilled past the left. In pressing their retreat toward the mountains, he gradually worked to within hailing distance of the plateau. He was there for the final stand. Mobility—to get where the fighting is; what could prove light artillery better?

Lieutenant French lost his mobility midway of the 23rd. For hours he had stuck to the saddle in spite of a stiffening leg and loss of blood. He kept waving the medics off. No sir, he would

232

not dismount. No lancer was going to run him through on the ground. He reached the hacienda on his horse; but after helping Reynolds drive the last Mexicans from the area, he had to give up. Later he rode in a wagon to Saltillo with Davis. The Mississippi colonel had carried a ball in one foot from early morning, and yet refused to leave his command. Next to the artillery his Rifles did the best fighting of the battle.

It was typical of Davis that he insisted on leaving the hospital the morning of the 24th. Again in a wagon, he went out to review his regiment. Just as he had done at the end of Monterey, he dressed his ranks with each man on the same spot he had stood before going into action. Gaps of from one to three places showed in the lines. "The regiment looked like an old comb with the teeth broken out," an eyewitness said. Of his eight companies engaged, only a few over 300, Davis had 40 killed, 56 wounded, and two missing.

During most of the fighting Taylor had kept three of the untried regiments under close control on the plateau. He thought the Illinois and Kentucky infantry did all that could be asked, for which he gave full credit to Wool. Let Lieutenant Engelmann and Sam Chamberlain laugh at Old Fussy, or Lieutenant Lew Wallace hint that the prim martinet ate and slept with his sword on. Taylor liked both the general and the kind of men he brought into the army. They came trained down to the last "Right Face." Luck held them out of battle long enough for drillmaster Wool to get in his licks. The result was important. It demonstrated that citizen soldiers, if given time to learn and proper instruction, could better their spotty record of the last two wars. Of the troops under Wool who joined Taylor, only the Arkansas and Kentucky mounted failed to measure up. The two Indiana regiments had come down to the army directly from the Rio Grande.

Winning generals seldom censure anybody in their battle re-

233

ports. Mere lack of mention usually implies enough, but Taylor charged the 2nd Indiana with falling back in disorder, and other than a handful of men, taking no further part in the action. Years before, he had damned the Missouri volunteers for funking out in the Florida swamps. Now Indiana, a political hotbed. For a man warming up to presidential lures, Old Zach was being careless. State pride was touchy and voters' memories were long.

Lieutenant Lew Wallace came down on special leave to visit the battlefield. Taylor's dark words about the lieutenant's beloved Hoosiers set him off. The only villain, he insisted, was Colonel Bowles. The old amateur botanist never should have been in the service—a dreamy officer wandering about observing specimens of flora while Joe Lane drilled his regiment. At Buena Vista flame and metal undid him on the plateau. When smoke blotted out O'Brien, the colonel "heard no voice of glory calling," and set up his own call: "Cease firing and retreat." What could the 2nd Indiana do?

It was unfair, Wallace complained, to call them the "flying infantry," a phrase going round the camps. Blame Bowles alone and forget his afterthought, that showy gesture of picking up a rifle to join the Mississippi as a private. "Nearby is his own regiment," Wallace went on. "Their colors are his colors. He is entitled to command them. They are the men who voted him colonel with whom he has tented and marched and lived. . . . What is gallantry in a private may be unqualified shame in an officer." Condemn only the officer who let his regiment skulk in rear while he settled for anonymity in the ranks of another.

A mind already made up against the general helped Wallace in his judgment. He never forgave Taylor for keeping his own 1st Indiana in the rear. One time the regiment marched south to Walnut Springs only to be called back before the three days of Monterey. On a second march down he finally saw Old Rough and Ready leaning lazily against the butt of a tentpole, blouse unbuttoned and faded beyond color, hangdown collar without tie, ancient shoes, and a slouch hat pulled low over an unshaven face, dull and empty—"a wooden Indian of the tobacco shops. I did not salute him." Wallace took the general for a teamster, he said, and he never got over the shock.

Nor the shock of what he saw after Buena Vista. Army details carefully dug pits for the American dead, but the natives ordered out from Saltillo took care of their own in their own way. They dragged bodies to the nearest ravines and pitched them headlong under a half cover of gravel and stones. Meanwhile other Mexicans nosed through the scatter of accoutrements, broken muskets, bayonets, cartridge paper, and scraps of uniforms. They clipped the manes and tails of dead horses, good for making lariats and saddle girths. "Commerce goes on," the lieutenant noted sadly. His greatest horror came from seeing the road in front of Washington's battery, the mouths of five guns still staring "with unwinking blackness" on heaped Mexican bodies pulped and shredded by canister and grape double-shotted.

Buena Vista had not been a pretty battle. That both sides meant business showed in their losses. Taylor counted 267 killed, 456 wounded, 23 missing—16 per cent of the number engaged. Cost in officers hit, 20 per cent. The army took more punishment in defending its present position than it had in attacking at Monterey. In Taylor's favor, of course, was the whipping he gave Santa Anna. Surgeon Duncan said the Mexicans lost 3000 out of 15,000. Taylor modestly cut the figure in half. Major Mansfield jumped it back up to 2500 and added 4000 missing. Peculiar Spanish arithmetic by Santa Anna arrived at a claim of three to four thousand casualties for each army. Then by giving Taylor 9000 men, he claimed a third of the enemy in a "Thermopylae" that saw the Americans driven from five successive positions, with loss of two banners and three guns.

Santa Anna felt sure the triumph was being properly celebrated by towns in his rear. In the meantime he admitted that his army would have to fall back for supplies. After a grudging exchange of prisoners, he began a retreat that recalled Arista's miseries in escaping Matamoros. His army filled every rancho along the way with wounded and exhausted men. Twenty thousand or more had left San Luis Potosí beginning on January 28. Some 12,000 got back. Taylor's force was too tired and hurt to follow up the victory, but again, as with Arista, the road south took toll enough.

Old Zach was sensitive about his own losses. They were sufficient, he admitted, "to cover the whole country with mourning." In this fourth battle, though, he could feel better about his wounded. His months of needling the War Department had brought results. For once an army surgeon was satisfied, both with the field hospital at the hacienda and with the base hospital set up in the Saltillo cathedral. "Myself, and so far as I know, all other surgeons in charge of hospitals . . . were provided with assistants, attendants, hospital stores, provisions, etc., promptly and to an extent creditable both to the officers in charge, and to our country." Add another innovation for the United States Army, along with the first effective use of light artillery, and volunteer infantry that would fight—an adequate medical corps.

While Taylor regretted the cost of Buena Vista he hoped the good people at home would be gratified at the results. He flattered himself, he said, on whipping a large Mexican army with his own small force of 500 regulars and about 4000 volunteers. "I had not a single company of regular infantry; the whole was taken from me." Taylor was still feeding his hurt, and nothing nourished it more than getting Marcy's kick about the letter to Gaines, which arrived on March 3. The general who had just won his greatest battle had to keep up his guard against the administration. His long answer came close to exploding. So Polk and Company had dug out that old paragraph about publication of private letters bearing on Army operations. Only the general's high respect for the presidential office prompted submission to the rebuke:

I shall be pardoned for speaking plainly. In the first place, the published letter bears upon its face the most conclusive evidence that it was intended only for private perusal. . . . It was published without my knowledge and contrary to my wishes. Surely I need not say that I am not in the habit of writing for the newspapers. The letter was a familiar one, written to an old military friend with whom I have been for many years interchanging opinions on professional subjects. That he should think proper under any circumstances to publish it, could not have been forseen by me.

The letter said nothing, he continued, that he would hesitate to repeat. No fact or opinion in it was news to Mexican authorities. Obviously the government merely hoped to further its policy of trying to discredit him. "I ask no favor and I shrink from no responsibility while intrusted with the command in this quarter. I shall continue to devote all my energies to the public good, looking for my reward to the consciousness of pure motives and to the final verdict of impartial history."

Polk had already charged Captain Bliss, Taylor's adjutant, with acting like a political campaign manager for his general. This letter, which certainly showed the Bliss touch, would look like sure proof. But Taylor meant every word, whoever set it to paper. He honestly felt let down by his government, and he was sure his case and his record would stand up well in the states.

No doubt at all of how he stood with his army. Taylor's

reputation was more solid than ever. At one time or another during the late battle every soldier must have taken at least one look at the old man astride Whitey on the plateau. A lot of them heard him. At one time, according to Benham, he prodded the reluctant Humphrey Marshall "to stand up to his fodder, rack or no rack." Then when the mounted volunteers hung on in rear: "I wish in God's name they would only come up and show themselves." Still later: "Well done, Jeff! Hurrah for Mississippi!" Somebody else had him hurrahing Old Kentuck: "Give 'em hell, damn 'em!" Of course there was the other "Give 'em hell," the one shouted at Bragg, but it soon formalized into the famous "A little more grape, please, Captain Bragg." Sam Chamberlain said the general sent off a lieutenant of dragoons to "Take that damn battery!" In another account he was assuring a worried colonel that he had the Mexicans just where he wanted them, "and now is the time to give them jesse." Like the more-grape phrase, much of this had the sound of editing—someone purging the language for home consumption. Chamberlain's happy apology for his general came nearer the truth: "The old gentleman was sometimes slightly profane."

One of Taylor's aides had Wool ready to give up at the time Old Zach reached the field on the 23rd. "General, we are whipped," he said. Wool got a steely answer: "That is for me to determine." A variation put it differently: "No, we will decide the battle here! I will never, alive, leave my wounded behind." More certain was the fact of cooperation and good will between top and second in command. Just as Taylor showed high approval of Wool, the brigadier returned in kind. He could not close his report of the battle, he said, without making official his gratitude for the general's confidence in him and the extreme consideration that marked all his acts. For an officer who less than a year before had ranked his chief, he was generous far beyond the jealous and petty W. J. Worth of Monterey. Eyewitness accounts of Taylor and Wool falling into each other's arms after Buena Vista had at least a happy symbolic truth. American combat could stand more of it.

If Taylor said everything soldiers had put in his mouth, he was a long-winded general at Buena Vista. But the stories fit the army's picture of its hero: the craggy-faced old warrior, always up front, a marked target on a white horse, seeing every enemy move (except the last), setting up counters, and always driving the Mexicans from the field at the end. Captain Mansfield thought Taylor fought his battle without a mistake, though he "was made *ragged* by the balls passing through his clothes." Overstatement on both counts. When the general saw he had taken his left too much for granted, he weakened his center to hold it. A quicker Mexican strike at the plateau could have lost the day. As for those ragged clothes, Aide Charles Kingsbury allowed him only two holes—one in a cuff and one in the front of his coat.

The objections still left Mansfield close to right. Taylor had kept his men near enough at hand to throw them in when and where he needed them. To control his fight, once he reached the field, he stayed up front himself, up far enough to rate his ragged clothes, or "clothes torn and riddled with bullets," as Lieutenant Carleton had it. Hero legends feed on a basis of fact, and Old Rough and Ready supplied it. Carleton and the others went on from there. Kingsbury, for instance: "Throughout the action General Taylor was where the shots fell hottest and thickest. . . . Great quickness of perception, fertility of resource, and a cool unerring judgment were not to be baffled."[3]

---

[3] When Kingsbury's story, signed "Buena Vista," appeared in *Niles' National Register* on March 30, Taylor called it accurate on the battle, though too high in praise of Taylor. Reynolds was em-

Reynolds had already made his bow to his chief. To Sam French, Taylor at Buena Vista showed what one plain, common-sense, duty-conscious man could do. "Success, ordinarily, is the measure of the greatness of a soldier" and of a man who said "I will fight the enemy wherever I find him."

News of the battle was breaking along the Rio Grande, no thanks to ambitious G. W. Kendall of the *Picayune*. Not one of his men within a hundred miles, he admitted. After all, the war had moved southeast with Scott . . . Or had it? From off the Brazos, Captain Robert Anderson said "General Taylor has whipped their great man." Farther down the Gulf, Commodore David Conner fired a naval salute in honor of the battle and its leader.

One more voice rose out from camp in front of Vera Cruz. "My great regret now is that I was separated from General Taylor. His brilliant achievement at Buena Vista exceeding any feat ever yet performed by our arms, or which ever will be, I should have gloried to have shared in, and regret exceedingly fate should have decided otherwise."

Lieutenant George Gordon Meade was homesick for the old Army of Occupation and for Old Zach himself.

---

barrassed for the same reason and asked his family not to mention that Kingsbury was a friend. The article did favor the professionals, artillery in particular, which led the editor to hint that its author might well be in artillery (Kingsbury was a lieutenant of ordnance). Combat correspondents were often accused of warping truth to help their friends or break down enemies. Objections to E. Kirby Smith's glorification of Charles May after Resaca, mentioned in an earlier chapter, are typical. Fortunately both Taylor and Reynolds at Buena Vista had lived up to their press notices, or near enough to escape Army criticism.

CHAPTER VIII

MAN ON HORSEBACK?

The winter weeks of 1847, before Taylor fought his battle at Buena Vista, saw a harried man in the White House. Colonel Don Alejandro José Atocha had come and gone without results for Polk. To Buchanan and Benton the Mexican had willingly talked boundaries and money. His government, he said, was open to discussing the Rio Grande as a possible line between the two countries so long as the land running north to the Nueces River remained neutral. California? Well, President Santa Anna would listen to bids, say fifteen or twenty million dollars. But of all the New Mexico territory lying east he was regretfully "uninformed."

Too little offered; too much asked—especially for California, which Mexico had already lost to conquest. Polk would have to keep on fighting his none too popular war. Meanwhile a commissioner somewhere near the front, with full powers to negotiate, might hold Santa Anna's interest. Then, if only Taylor and Scott were up to their end of it. Neither general was, of course, as Benton insisted again on January 23. Although turned down as a lieutenant general, the senator was still available. "I will go as a major general or a lieutenant colonel, or in any other rank, provided I can have command of the army, and if I have such a command I will close the War before July."

Command was only part of what Benton wanted. He told the President he had no desire to go to Mexico simply to wear a plume and a bunch of feathers in his hat. He should also be granted authority to conclude a peace. When the cabinet balked at Benton's reach for power, Polk decided not to push. Now for a while he could fret about other things. "I have never in my life been so much oppressed with constant and most responsible duties as at present." For example, he had 400 military appointments to make, yet how could he hope to know one tenth of the applicants? They were needed to staff the ten new regiments Congress had finally voted—this Congress full of Whigs more taken by President-making than with the business of the country. The Whigs and their newspapers, braying about his treatment of Taylor: the "unceasing and malignant attacks upon the old Hero, by the carpet-knights and back-stairs chivalry at Washington."

Near the end of February the President was even bluer. Scott had made all that fuss about Colonel Harney's being assigned to him, and now he was parading his campaign preparations for the whole of Mexico and every foreign ship in the Gulf to see. At the same time the practically mutinous Taylor, by marching down to Agua Nueva, was inviting trouble from Santa Anna. Polk began thinking wistfully of Benton again. How could the senator supersede Taylor and Scott? Benton could replace the wounded Butler, now on leave in New Orleans, but the move still would leave three senior commanders: Scott, Taylor, and Patterson.

Naturally, as Polk saw it, undercutting Scott and Taylor was no vile scheme. What served the Democratic party best also served the country best. Benton was a good Democrat. Besides, all the military protocol and fighting wars by the book annoyed the President. A proper commander could act fast if he was only willing to throw out the tidy rules, stop asking for the last crate and barrel of rations, the last box of shells, and the last pound of horseshoe nails. Such a general would "destroy Santa Anna in a short time."

Benton was the man, an old soldier, and yet more than a soldier. He stood above the petty professionals with their textbook mentalities and never-ending demands. Why a thousand wagons to be used in a country ideal for packmules? Why a thousand horses from Ohio for Taylor's dragoons? Why not Mexican horses for Mexican climate and Mexican terrain? The trouble with old Army officers was that their long habit of enjoying their ease left most of them no energy for taking care of the public interest. "I am much vexed at the extravagance and the stupidity," Polk summed up.

On March 3, Senator Thomas Hart Benton declined the President's offer of a commission as major general. Next day the Democratic *National Union* lamented his loss to the service, and said the war in Mexico might have used his abilities. But against cabinet opposition Benton could see no gain in serving. Now if the President was going to win his war, he would have to do it with Scott and Taylor. He still had it to win, and in the field. Negotiations with Santa Anna had come to nothing. The Mexican government would talk peace only if and when the Americans withdrew from the country.

Taylor, of course, had already fought Buena Vista, but word of it still was almost a month away, even for New Orleans. The March 3 *Delta* could only report Santa Anna moving on Saltillo in great strength. Fears for Zach's supply line tremored all the way up to the Rio. Rumors encouraged Mexican guerrilla bands. They frightened the garrison at Matamoros into throwing up breastworks around the main plaza. At home faithful Whig papers like the Philadelphia *North American* and the Albany *Statesman* knew where to fix the blame. A jealous Democratic President had cruelly robbed Taylor of troops and exposed him to defeat.

The *Picayune* was hoping for peace. Atocha had landed in Vera Cruz from the United States. His presence promised something in the way of terms—words instead of bullets. The rumors continued to say otherwise: one of Taylor's supply trains caught between Cerralvo and Camargo; the general's army falling back on Monterey; the army whipped before it even began its retreat; the general himself killed. At Camargo, Colonel Sam Curtis was calling on the states for 50,000 volunteers. Worse than old Gaines, *Niles' Register* snorted.

From down in Tampico correspondent Kendall was assuring his paper that Taylor had not been in a fight, though he had retired to Saltillo and Monterey. Then on March 11 the "*Pic*" carried news from a major captured in the January ambush below Agua Nueva. The Mexican army was marching north, he said. He had talked with Santa Anna, who was riding in a large clumsy carriage behind eight mules. Surgeon Jarvis, in New Orleans on leave, discounted a Mexican advance. When he left Monterey near the end of February no rumor of a threat had been heard in the area.

The country in turn discounted Jarvis. So did President Polk. It was exactly what he had feared, he wrote in his diary on March 22. Taylor was in trouble. The ten new regiments must be put together as fast as recruited and rushed to the front. He had Secretary Marcy warn Scott that Taylor's exposed position at Agua Nueva could lead to disaster. A brief, numbing thought caught up with Polk here. Possibly he had let Scott take too many men from Taylor. "Gen'l Scott seems to have assumed the command with the single idea in his head of taking Vera Cruz, & with this view has probably reduced Gen'l Taylor's forces to too small a number. . . . Surely Gen'l Scott upon hearing of their critical situation will rush to their relief." Still, "If Gen'l Taylor has met with any disaster, it is certain that it has proceeded from his own want of military prudence and skill."

Another week piled up more rumors. A Mexican force had cut Taylor's line to the Rio Grande. Great amounts of supplies were in enemy hands. Scott would almost surely have to bail the old general out, due of course to Taylor's violation of orders: "from the beginning he has constantly blundered into difficulties." If he had fought out of them, it was only at a high cost in lives.

The President's refrain had the sound of rationalization. His own dream—his grasp for new country in the southwest—was costing lives. It was a big dream, big in its meaning for the United States. But too many people, both in and out of Congress, refused to share it with him. They begrudged him a war to see it through. Ohio Whig Tom Corwin in the Senate, for instance: "Why waste thousands of lives and millions of money . . . ?" Congress had stalled on the new troops needed to fight the war, had refused to appoint the kind of leader who could win it, and damned the President because it dragged out under the two incompetents he was forced to rely on.

2

For most of the country April opened with word that only fools would believe at first. Those 60 blooded horses of the express, along with the Magnetic Telegraph, had speeded the

245

news up the east coast. Outnumbered three to four times by Santa Anna, Zach Taylor's little army had whipped the Mexicans and sent them straggling south in a disorganized mob. The weight lifted at home. Fears dissolved. Old Rough and Ready had done it again! Hats in the air! Parades. Illuminations. Toasts to the glorious victory and old Hero Taylor.

The Baltimore *Patriot* carried the story on March 31, and gave it a proper party slant:

> The news from the seat of war by this evening's southern mail is truly glorious—not unmixed, however with a mournful tinge, on account of the loss of many brave and gallant officers and men of the small and glorious force led on to victory by that wonderful man and successful soldier, ZACHARY TAYLOR!
>
> What an escape for Mr. Polk's administration. How much it ought to feel indebted to Gen. Taylor for his victory! After leaving him without proper supplies—after setting his bloodhounds in Congress and bloodhounds of the press upon him—after interfering with his command and giving orders direct to one of his subordinate generals—after detaching nearly one-half of his command, and that the flower of it, after superseding him, by sending General Scott to take command of his army,—the patriot, the glorious old and ever "Rough and Ready" with but 5000 troops, mostly volunteers, meets Santa Anna with some 20,000 disciplined Mexican regulars, and wins an unexampled victory!

The White House omitted the toasts for Taylor. The battle was suddenly an embarrassing fact which no Whig paper would let Polk forget. Obviously, his rash general should never have fought the battle. "Having done so, he is indebted, not to his own good generalship, but to the indominatable bravery of the men & officers under his command for its success. . . .

246

Gen'l Taylor is a hard fighter, but has none of the other qualities of a great general." Proof? In May of 1846 he separated his army from its supplies to bring on Palo Alto and Resaca de la Palma. He moved on to Monterey with inadequate force, leaving over two thirds of his army behind with batteries and trains. This ineptness led to the hard three-day battle of September, with its heavy losses. And now Buena Vista. Far greater cost for stubbornly holding a position against orders.

Ten days later Scott took Vera Cruz. "This is joyful news," the President said.

Politically it was safer now to praise Scott. After Buena Vista, anything the general-in-chief might accomplish would come too late for a man already dumped by his party. Taylor was the man to fear. Throughout April the country was all Zach, or seemed to be. The "Young Indians" in the Congressional House, with their Taylor-for-President clubs, were on top. The group showed mostly southern coloration and was led by Alexander H. Stephens of Georgia, though Abraham Lincoln shaded it lightly toward the north. In the Senate, old friend John J. Crittenden pushed the general's interests.

Rough and Ready clubs boomed everywhere, even in Dan Webster's own borough of anti-war Boston. Columns and columns of copy on the feats of Buena Vista gave way to columns and columns on Taylor as the man to lead the nation. The Savannah *Republican*, the Vicksburg *Whig*; in Nashville the *Whig*, the *Atlas*, the *Union*; the Philadelphia *North American*, Albany *Statesman*, New York *Courier*—all these and other papers beat the bandwagon drums. The Charleston *Mercury*, snug in the country of John C. Calhoun, was showing interest in Zach. Rumors had the Squire himself ready to retire in the general's favor. In fact, why so much northern support for Taylor? "Are they not aware that he is a Southern man, a slaveholder, a cotton planter?" The *Mercury* sounded jealous of Taylor's northern sponsors.

The general's presidential prospects looked good up and down the Atlantic seaboard. His greatest strength, of course, lay in the South, but Pennsylvania and New Jersey were solid for him; also New York state except the belt running westward to the Great Lakes. A Kentuckian visiting Baltimore in April was sure Old Zach could be elected "by spontaneous combustion." The Sangamo *Journal* in Illinois declared for him. He was picking up strength in Indiana and Iowa. He killed the last hopes of John McLean in Ohio. The Whigs had won with old warrior Harrison in 1840, so why not old warrior Taylor in 1848? Huzzas for the general frightened the friendly New York *Courier* into pleading for restraint. Don't expose Taylor too soon; wait till the time is ripe.

Here and there pockets of resistance fought back. What did the Philadelphia *North American* (on April 14) mean calling Taylor "heart and soul a Whig"? When or where, the Richmond *Enquirer* of the 28th wanted to know, had the general ever expressed a political opinion? On the same day the Cleveland *Plain Dealer* asked how Whigs could justify their support of a slaveholder. A week later the *Delta* in New Orleans charged party hacks with riding the coattails of a national hero. In their foolish zeal they were heaving hard-won doctrines out of the window—the protective tariff, the bank, and distribution of public land. A holdout in Trenton, New Jersey, denounced Taylor as "a bloody mushroom of the battlefield."

The administration still was in sore need of new heroes to counter Old Zach. Neither Colonel Kearny nor Captain Frémont could ignite public fancy in faraway California, in a territory now fallen to the United States almost by default. Colonel Alexander W. Doniphan made a more dramatic splash. In the fall of 1846 he had dropped south from Santa

Fe, beat off a Mexican force near El Paso, occupied the city on December 27, then moved down toward Chihuahua with 924 men and six guns. On February 28, 1847, he routed 2500 enemy troops in the battle of Sacramento River, just north of the city. Six hundred Mexicans killed and wounded to nine for the Americans. More impressive than the victory was Doniphan's 300-mile forced march through desert and mountain country to reach his objective. But then what, except to make plans for joining Taylor in an area of the country already out of the war?

Even battles won by colonels now bothered Polk. "The truth is our troops, regulars and volunteers, will obtain victories whenever they meet the enemy. This [they] would do if they were without officers to command them higher in rank than lieutenants." To the small satisfaction over Doniphan's feats, the President could add his real distress over new bickering in California. Vague orders to Kearny, Frémont, and Commodore Robert F. Stockton left them brawling with each other for authority in the conquered territory. Polk sided with Kearny, but the messy infighting clouded his pleasure at seeing California subdued.

Actually Polk had no one he could safely cheer except Scott, even if the cheers stuck in his throat. So, through Marcy, he expressed his high gratification for the skill, endurance, and courage of the men and leader who took Vera Cruz. They both made a special point of adding that "while millions of our fellow citizens joyously exult at this splendid achievement, it is pleasing to reflect that so few of us have occasion to mourn."

Let the reckless victor of Buena Vista ponder that.

Vera Cruz had been easy for Scott. On March 9, with General Worth in the first surf boat, 4500 of Taylor's old veterans stormed the beach. There was no resistance. They sat down with the rest of the army to wait out Scott's bombardment of the city. Why not attack? some of the regulars asked. Under Old Zach they had taken the stronger Monterey in three days. But Scott estimated the cost of a frontal assault at 2000 men. He also knew the effect of losses on an administration unsure of support for its war. March 27 gave him Vera Cruz for only 67 casualties. Lieutenant Grant wholly approved the generalship of his new chief, though he laughed at the stuffy prose in Scott's orders.

Official thanks for Vera Cruz did nothing to soften the general-in-chief toward Washington. His case against the administration was a bitter one. Polk and Marcy had pushed him out of the capital before he was ready. Political opportunism—the country wanted action. Later behind his back, they had tried to make Benton a lieutenant general. Failing that, they pushed him for a senior major general. They had held up the ships for Scott's move down the Gulf, which cost him a three-months' delay. Only half his surf boats and half his ordnance arrived in time. By forcing him to accept Colonel Harney they denied him power to pick his own officers. In their panic over Taylor's exposure before the battle of Buena Vista, they had diverted new troops promised for the Gulf.

Scott's prose was up to Scott's hurt: "I will not trust myself to add a soldier's comment upon these attempts, but I thank God that He did not allow them, or subsequent injuries, to break down, entirely, the spirit and abilities (such as they are) with which he had endowed me." This led to verse:

> " 'True as the dial to the sun
> Although it not be shined upon,' "—

he would never relax in his effort to serve the country.

Certainly Scott could not afford to relax on the Gulf, now with the sickness, the *vomito* in the air. He headed his 8500 men inland on April 8. Some 70 miles back in the hills Santa Anna was waiting in a defile called Cerro Gordo. The Mexican president had commandeered a new army of close to 8000 and held a strong position. But too many battles on the old front in northern Mexico had broken morale. Vera Cruz added only one more proof of "gringo" power. Before Scott attacked at Cerro Gordo, his engineers—Captains Robert E. Lee, George B. McClellan, Joseph E. Johnston, and Lieutenant P. G. T. Beauregard—found a flanking trail around Santa Anna's left. This time it was Twiggs who got the call from Scott. April 17 and 18 shrank the Mexican army by some 3000 taken prisoner and over 1000 killed and wounded. Forty-three guns and 3500 small arms went over to Scott, along with a pay wagon containing $16,000 and one of Santa Anna's spare wooden legs. Proud Illinois volunteers guarded this last prize all the way back to the states.

The cost of Cerro Gordo to the Americans considerably topped that of Vera Cruz. Marcy was careful to note the greater mourning to be endured by the people at home. But again he passed on his President's admiration for the almost total rout of a large army, "an achievement seldom equalled in the records of military operations." The Secretary of War did not send on another Polk reaction. The President was sure now that American troops could win battles without any officers at all.

At last Kendall of the *Picayune* and his fellow correspondents seemed to have guessed right. The war was with Scott and would go on from there. Polk's other Whig general had picked up where Zachary Taylor left off.

3

Back in Monterey, Captain Giddings had sat out Taylor's last battle with the 1st Ohio and 1st Kentucky. On March 3 he started north for Camargo in an escort of 250 men and two guns. Thomas L. Crittenden, son of the general's senator friend, was carrying battle dispatches to Washington. An empty wagon train rattled along with the column. At the town of Marín, cavalry under General Urrea jumped the convoy, stampeded the teams, and butchered 15 of the unarmed drivers. The Mexicans also killed two soldiers and captured 40 wagons.

News of the attack brought Taylor up to Monterey with May's dragoons, two volunteer regiments of infantry, and the Bragg battery. Short work soon drove Urrea beyond the Sierra Madre. It was the last action against enemy regulars anywhere on Taylor's old front. A final sputter of guerrilla strikes stirred some mounted Texans into a fury of killings that Giddings called "one of the darkest pages in the history of the campaign." Their behavior jarred even tough Sam Chamberlain. Only the savagery of the guerrillas themselves could match it, he said.

Taylor blamed the Mexicans. In a proclamation to the states of Tamaulipas, Nuevo León, and Coahuila, he reminded the people of his long struggle "to cause the war to bear lightly on them." Why should his kindness be answered by the killing of American soldiers? It had to stop. When General Ignacio de Mora Villamil protested the Texan atrocities, Taylor admitted his failure to control entirely all acts of his own men in rear, though he tried always to punish the delinquents. Then he added an indictment of his own: "Mexican troops have given the world the example of killing wounded men on the field of battle." Old Zach could not forget the lancers in the gorges of Buena Vista.

On March 28, from his old camp at Walnut Springs, Taylor wrote the War Department that his front and his line of communications were secure. West Pointer Oliver Otis Howard, looking in on the site years later, spun an idyl: General Taylor's heart warming as he surveys the springs, the clear running stream, and the hills and mountains framing the city of Monterey to the south; sitting now in his simple wall tent, overhung by branches to cool the canvas. An orderly brings him bundles of letters, official and private. The old gentleman pulls his stool up to the improvised table and breaks first the seals of government envelopes. After a few moments of quiet meditation, he reaches for his pen and begins to write.

Howard seemed to imply a benign and contented general lolling in rustic comfort. Where once "came the rattle of musketry and the roar of cannon; now it is the hum of happy voices, with a beautiful and quiet landscape." In short, a commander who had only to sit around in euphoric glow and write thank-you's to congratulations on his recent victory.

Actually the Taylor who picked up his pen at Walnut Springs had slipped back into his dour mood of the months before Buena Vista. Of the battle itself, he wrote his brother Joseph on March 27 that the cost in lives had robbed him of any pleasure in winning. His losses hurt the general in two ways. They bore heavy on the conscience of a naturally compassionate man. Taylor hated killing. They also got under a thin skin, sensitive to charges of too much sacrifice to assure his victories. Still smarting over the cost of Monterey, he now had to bear the longer lists of Buena Vista. If Scott had only left him his regulars, he wrote his son-in-law on the 20th, the cost would have been small. The families and friends of men who fell should force the President to remove Marcy and send Scott back to Washington, "but it is possible things may be so artfully managed as to bring popular opinion to bear on me for not killing Santa Anna and the whole of his army."

The old plot was steaming against him—Polk, Marcy & Co. "But I have disappointed their expectations if not defeated their nefarious schemes." He was satisfied that he had saved the honor of the country by meeting Santa Anna where he did instead of remaining at Monterey on Scott's orders. To do so would have given all of northern Mexico back to the enemy. Thus Old Zach reasoned, always from the premise that he was fighting Washington as well as Mexico—yes, and Scott too. The general-in-chief would stop at nothing to gain his ends, Taylor informed his brother on March 25.

The hero of Buena Vista certainly had picked up his pen. Along with the private letters went his reports to a Washington that he felt was ignoring him. As of April 4 no word yet from Marcy on the battle dispatch. ". . . if he still persists in such a contemptable, pitiful & ungentlemanly a course for the purpose of insulting or outraging me, which is quite likely what he will do, but which is a matter of no importance, as the people will compel him to lay before the country in some one of the public journals said despatch, no matter how unwilling he may be to do so."

By now the general was repeating himself, in letters to his brother, to his son-in-law, and even to Wool at Saltillo— "The honl. Secretary of war seems determined not to correspond with me. . . ." The phrases piled up: the administration setting its friends to barking and snapping at his heels; plotting to keep him from acquiring additional reputation; and damning him for not capturing the whole Mexican army, including its general. Again Zach hoped the public would force Marcy and Scott to explain their robbing him of troops, the act which cost so many lives at Buena Vista.

Taylor still felt the weight of the last battle's casualties. So might the good people at home who continued to honor him with political favor. By now he had the news of Vera Cruz, with emphasis in the Democratic press on its small cost. Reports of another kind troubled Taylor too. Everywhere, and especially in the west, published letters were harping on the bad conduct of some of his volunteers. His own report of Buena Vista had added more fire in Indiana. "Two regiments of that state," Taylor lamented, "were all by the ears, including their General Lane, who I think an excellent man."

Was Taylor "a man on horseback," exposed and raw without his sword? He certainly was exposed and raw from attacks in papers supporting Polk, but as of May 9 he had not swung into a saddle, Washington bound. Of the presidency, he insisted to his brother, "I must say I have no wish for that high office, not considering myself qualified for it. . . ." Mr. Crittenden, he added, had said he must not decline if called. As to this, if a majority of the good people thought it proper to elect him, he could not say that he would refuse. Anyhow the election was a long way off, and so many changes might take place as to induce the people to prefer someone else. Five days later the old general repeated the same thoughts in a letter to his Delaware friend, Nathaniel Young.

Taylor was not ready to mount—not yet.

All the writing took up so much time when Zach had duties to carry out. "I can hardly find time to write a sintence [sic] from morning to night without interruption from some one, so much as to frequently almost come to the determination to give up except to my family all private correspondence; for I frequently am at a loss to know, where I left off, or where to commence a sentence." Taylor's prose was proving his case.

Still, the work went on. April 14 saw the 1st Kentucky starting homeward before its time expired. This was the bad-acting regiment the general had banished to the rear in November of '46. Taylor's next letter went off to Scott's headquarters on the 16th. Regardless of the general-in-chief's expectations, it read, he would not move south without a nucleus of two to three thousand regulars.

Taylor knew he would never see them, although he made the gesture of hoping. With 13 volunteer regiments about to leave, he had as replacements a regiment each of volunteers from Massachusetts, Virginia, North Carolina, and Mississippi. Sam Chamberlain set down the last two as mean troops. Taylor split the New Englanders on his supply line between Monterey and Cerralvo. The rest he sent to Wool at Saltillo. About the public stores in that city he could only advise his worried second-in-command to hold them under careful guard until something in the way of plans developed from Washington, if they ever did.

By May 9, Old Zach had at least, and at last, a reply to his Buena Vista dispatch. It included, he wrote his brother, "a highly complimentary order which I make no doubt was done with great reluctance." Taylor was right. On the 6th Polk had come around even to defending Patterson as his choice for chief command if anything happened to Scott. Robert Patterson, the Philadelphia merchant with an Army commission he had picked up at the age of sixteen. Until Polk sent him south to serve under Taylor in 1846, Patterson had never commanded more than a militia company or seen anything like a battle.

To what end, Taylor's forty years of active service—War of 1812, Black Hawk War, Florida War, and his victories over the Mexicans? Buena Vista, for example, bulked small in the mind of a President who now was touting Doniphan's little fight in front of Chihuahua as "one of the most decisive and brilliant achievements of the war."

Zach's record simply did not balance out against the credentials of almost any deserving Democrat who had ever buckled on a sword. A President bent on sabotaging his own war could hardly show more contempt for professional soldiery. And yet in his stubborn way Polk was pushing hard to win. He had fretted over Congressional delay in passing his new regiments bill, and now as fast as they assembled he urged them southward, and most of them for Scott.

The general-in-chief needed men. In May he had to send seven old volunteer regiments back to the coast: expired enlistments. About 4000 citizen soldiers refused to fight through to the Halls of the Montezumas. Scott put them on the road early to spare them from the *vomito*. Rightfully he could inform his government: "I beg to say, that I am myself too careful of human life, the lives of *all* the troops of this army, regulars as well as volunteers, to risk garrisons along the road during that season." Also, it could hardly displease Scott if his concern for soldier lives suggested to the administration a comparison with Taylor's losses in February.

In spite of the departing veterans, victory on the new front looked so sure that Polk had sent Nicholas P. Trist to join Scott as the commissioner to treat for peace. Scott first learned of it when Trist sent sealed dispatches from Vera Cruz to be passed through lines to the City of Mexico. The general refused. "I see that the Secretary of War proposes to degrade me, by requiring that I, the commander of this army, shall defer to you, the chief clerk of the Dept. of State, the question of continuing or discontinuing hostilities."

That for Trist. Then from Jalapa on the 20th to the War Department in purest Scott: "Mr. Trist arrived here on the 14th instant. He has not done me the honor to call on me.

Possibly he has thought the compliments of a first visit was due him." The general had heard, he added, that Trist was answering his complaint of May 7. "It is not probable that I shall find leisure to read his reply, much less to give a rejoinder."

Like Old Zach, Scott fought back, and with all his fuss and feathers showing.

4

General Taylor probably was better off writing in his tent at Walnut Springs. Problems always loomed bigger nearest the fighting, but in northern Mexico it seemed to be over. Polk had refused Taylor his 2000 regulars, logically enough by May. The old volunteers, his own and Wool's, were on the way out. A letter to the Adjutant General on the 9th noted the departure of the Kentucky regiments and the 1st Mississippi.

Private A. F. Ehinger noted the leave-taking too. The Kentuckians carried with them the bodies of Colonel McKee and Lieutenant Colonel Henry Clay. "We had a peculiar feeling when we stood in line to bid them farewell. Men who had endured the dangers of the campaign with us were leaving and we will never see them again." A volunteer from one state lamenting the departure of men from another . . . if Ehinger was anywhere near typical, something more than battles had been won below the Rio Grande.

Colonel Jeff Davis, on crutches, saw his Mississippians off. Of a regiment that entered the war with 926 men, only 376 now moved north to civilian life. Some sickness and disease, but mostly Monterey and Buena Vista had accounted for the rest.

Giddings pulled out with the 1st Ohio, "over a road numerously dotted with the skeletons of men and animals," past

258

"roofless and ruined ranchos and many a dark and smoldering heap of ashes." What he saw filled the captain with reflection: "They that plow iniquity and sow wickedness shall reap the same." A regiment in his own army had some reaping to endure. New volunteers had been turning out on parade to present arms for the old troops marching away. But not for the 2nd Indiana, which had funked out at Buena Vista. Lieutenant Benham saw the Hoosiers file past "in the sadness and silence of their own grieved hearts, while men of all new battalions remained in their tents. This is perhaps among the most sorrowful memories of the war."

Engelmann of the 2nd Illinois had been hit in the first fighting at Buena Vista. Cloth embedded with a bullet in his right arm kept the wound from healing, and he was held at Saltillo. A disability discharge would see him home free; otherwise passage might run as high as $500. In letters home the lieutenant mixed his worries over transportation with descriptions of valley crops. Barley, wheat, sugar cane, and sweet potatoes looked good; apples poor; peaches, quinces, apricots not in fruit; plenty of grapes, vegetables—especially fine cauliflower. The young lawyer was keeping an alert eye to the end of his stay. Also he had changed his mind about his colonel. Bissell was a real fighter.

One regular officer got away early, after spending 40 days on a cot. The surgeons could not find the ball in the leg of Lieutenant French. Finally he probed for it himself, found it, and insisted on having it cut out. Later he jounced north in an ambulance, complaining about an escort of only two men and remembering warmly a gift of flowers brought him by a little girl from an old Mexican woman who had seen him in pain.

Sam Chamberlain enjoyed the spring around Agua Nueva. The footloose dragoon found his duty light and pleasant. Occasional patrols, foraging for corn, or scouting for guerrillas filled in most of the time. And by his say, women took care of the rest.

By the end of May, Lieutenant Reynolds seemed to be the only regular left besides Taylor who had a busy pen. The young artilleryman kept his opinions within the Reynolds family, but he was full of them:

On the war—Let the celebrations continue from Maine to Louisiana, he wrote on the 23rd. For himself, he had no wish to add more cause for them. "I would like to see the war end now."

On Taylor and politics—The general was a Whig except on the bank question, and he was both more honest and honorable than any other man being talked of for the presidency.

On the volunteers—They had "seen the Elephant, snout and all" and had no stomach for meeting his highness again. Who could blame them? "If anyone is to be blamed, it must fall upon the Govt. which has adopted this kind of troops."

On brevets—The system was humbug, and judging by some of the breveted, he saw more distinction in being passed over; that is, unless standards of selection improved.[1]

Colonel Doniphan's Missouri volunteers moved in during the last week of May. They stayed just long enough before their time was up for Taylor to report close to 5000 men available to march south. But taking San Luis Potosí would be useful, he thought, only as a base for operating farther down, toward the Mexican capital. For that he had to have at least 2000 more troops.

Taylor was making his last real offer to carry on the campaign. After that, news from Scott told him how and where

[1] Reynolds' two brevets for his services in the war were still to come; one dated back to the battle of Monterey, the second to Buena Vista.

the war would end. He had seen it earlier, of course, in word from Cerro Gordo. Closing a letter to his brother on the 9th, the good soldier in Zach took over from the embryo politician: great battle—Mexicans defeated with heavy loss—their army dispersed—all their artillery taken or destroyed. Here was the old Taylor, one professional admiring the skill of another. He was remembering again that his business and Scott's business was fighting. Whoever won the battles helped win the war.

The summer added more victories for Scott—Contreras and Cherubusco, August 20; Molino del Rey, September 8; Chapultepec on the 12th. The enemy capital now lay open. For the Mexicans the war was almost over. For Zach Taylor's little army—old and new—it had been over since February 23. In November the general moved his headquarters to Matamoros, and on the 26th he boarded ship for New Orleans. The Crescent City gathered him in with bands, fireworks, illuminations, parades, artillery salutes, a banquet, and a second sword from the state of Louisiana.

Now only John F. Reynolds was left to fill in the record down on the last battlefield. He was sick of the country and everything it contained. He was tired of the eccentricities of Captain Sherman. "There is no probability of our ever seeing any more active service on this line, and to remain here another summer will kill me."

Reynolds no doubt was speaking for the other West Pointers as well, those in the two field batteries and the squadron of dragoons. Officers and men, they were the only veterans remaining of the army Old Zach had led out of Corpus Christi in March of 1846.

But while they fretted out their anticlimax in a written-off sector of the war, they could count some gains. Thanks to those who manned the guns, no future Secretary of War would ever easily auction off an artillery horse or shelve a 6-pounder. And no future politician would try to make his mark by singling out West Point for oblivion. The young men from the United States Military Academy had settled that. The country might still put dollars ahead of an adequate military force in peacetime, but speeches about standing armies as a threat to America's liberties would end. The officers and the regulars under them had settled that, too. They had settled it by sticking to their job and doing it well. They left policy-making where it belonged, in civilian hands.

Add one more gain, though cautiously. Volunteers, if fought alongside regulars, might yet be counted effective. Just possibly, under proper circumstances, "*this kind* of troops" would do.

In two years of campaigning Taylor and the West Pointers had combined to good advantage. Camp routine sometimes found the general lax in discipline. In battles he was not always sure in military theory. At company and field level the men from the Point supplied both. Taylor, in turn, supplied the over-all essentials of experience and leadership. To Napoleon the personality of the general was indispensable: "He is the head, he is the all of the army." If Old Zach did not measure up to this standard in full, he did give his army an identity. And with the army he helped further a President's dream. After his own four victories, most of his veterans had gone on to Scott and would do most to take the City of Mexico and end the war. Polk would soon be adding New Mexico and Upper California north of the Rio Grande to extend his country solid to the Pacific Coast.

Good. But in Agua Nueva, Saltillo, and Monterey the war was over. It was over, and the men from the Point wanted out!—out of Mexico.

They had done their job. And in all innocence, because it was no part of an army's job, they also had helped elect the Twelfth President of the United States.

262

Appendix I

The Historical Record on Taylor's Campaigns

Zach Taylor's Little Army is the first book on the Mexican War that begins and ends with the full story of Taylor's campaigns. Writing on any part of the war today becomes largely a matter of focus and interpretation. There is no important new material to exploit. The essential sources covering the Mexican War have been available for some years either in print or on microfilm. In fact their accessibility has been taken for granted by Otis A. Singletary in his book, *The Mexican War*, University of Chicago, 1960. Neither author nor publisher felt the need for the documentation of text commonly expected in historical studies, especially those issuing from university presses.

Research on Taylor and his army begins with the *Executive Documents*, Senate and House, for the two sessions of the 29th Congress and the first session of the 30th. Here for the years 1845 to 1848 are the presidential messages; Congressional speeches and bills; reports of cabinet members, including those of the Secretary of War and his subordinates in engineering, ordnance, the quartermaster's, the surgeon general's, and other departments; official reports and correspondence of the army commanders and their subordinates sometimes down to the rank of lieutenant. Our Mexican War President added richly to the administration's viewpoint on all the activity going on by keeping a daily record, *The Diary of James Knox Polk*, Milo M. Quaife, ed., Chicago, 1910.

For Taylor's private correspondence a writer has, in addition to the Library of Congress papers, *The Letters of Zachary Taylor from the Battlefields of the Mexican War*, William H. Samson, ed., Rochester, New York, 1908. A writer can know what people were thinking, or at least reading, by scouting the contemporary press of both parties in key cities of the various sections in the country. He will find the most detailed if not always reliable news of the army by reading New Orleans papers. Much of it was reprinted in *Niles' National Register* of Baltimore, edited by Jeremiah Hughes, who was rare in his day for keeping his party views (Whig) under reasonable restraint.

Next come the firsthand accounts of Taylor's campaigns, written by those who took part or saw some part or all of them. Given the small size of the army and its brief service in the field, the number of collections, journals, narratives, reminiscences, and memoirs is impressive. Here are the most important of those in book form:

Carleton, James H., *The Battle of Buena Vista*, New York, 1848.

Chamberlain, Samuel E., *My Confession; Recollections of a Rogue*, New York, 1956.

264

Croffut, W. A. (ed.), *Fifty Years in Camp and Field: Diary of Major General Ethan Allen Hitchcock*, New York, 1909.

Doubleday, Rhoda Van B. Tanner (ed.), *Journals of the Late Brevet Major Philip Norbourne Barbour . . . .*, New York, 1936.

French, Samuel G., *Two Wars*, Nashville, 1901.

Giddings, Luther, *Sketches of the Campaign in Northern Mexico*, New York, 1853.

Grant, Ulysses S., *Personal Memoirs of U. S. Grant*, 2 vols., New York, 1885.

Henry, William S., *Campaign Sketches of the War with Mexico*, New York, 1847.

Kenly, John R., *Memoirs of a Maryland Volunteer*, Philadelphia, 1873.

McCall, George H., *Letters From the Frontier*, Philadelphia, 1868.

Meade, (Capt.) George G. (ed.), *The Life and Letters of General George Gordon Meade*, 2 vols., New York, 1913.

Ripley, Roswell S., *The War with Mexico*, 2 vols., New York, 1849.

Sedgwick, John, *The Correspondence of General John Sedgwick*, 2 vols., Boston, 1902.

Smith, E. Kirby, *To Mexico with Scott; Letters of Ephraim Kirby Smith to His Wife*, Boston, 1917.

Thorpe, Thomas B., *Our Army at Monterey*, Philadelphia, 1848.

Wilcox, Cadmus M., *History of the Mexican War*, New York, 1892.

Other officers under Taylor wrote pieces which appeared at the time of the fighting or later in newspapers, magazines, and journals. Electus Backus, Charles P. Kingsbury, George Deas, and Henry Benham were contributors. The diary of

Adolph Englemann, the medical notes of Surgeon John B. Porter, and excerpts from the diary of another surgeon, N. S. Jarvis, were edited by others. War correspondent George W. Kendall did a series of magazine articles on Taylor's campaigns. Neither these writers nor the ones in the list above exhaust the roll of eyewitness accounts, but they do form the bulk of the contemporary record on the fighting in northern Mexico.[1]

With two exceptions Taylor's military reputation came off well at the hands of his author subordinates. Of the two dissenters, Hitchcock and Ripley, the first left Taylor before the battles and the second fought only at Monterey. Hitchcock, of course, had nothing good to say about anybody in the army except himself. Ripley's dim view of Taylor roused Isaac I. Stevens, who fought under Scott, into writing his *Campaigns of the Rio Grande and of Mexico*, New York, 1851. The considerable portion of the book which discussed Taylor's activities took the form largely of rebuttal.

A third member of the army who sometimes criticized his chief was George Meade. But far more often he could express only approval, especially after he had moved on to General Scott. Few higher tributes to any military leader exist than the letter Meade wrote to his wife after hearing of Old Zach's victory at Buena Vista.

Taylor found his strongest support in Grant, Henry, Carleton, Giddings, Kenly, Barbour, French, Wilcox, and Reynolds. For them it seemed that the general could do nothing wrong.

---

[1] I would certainly add the unpublished letters of General John F. Reynolds, Fackenthal Library, Franklin and Marshall College, Lancaster, Pennsylvania. Their special value lies in the fact that Reynolds was one of only two officers who served with Taylor in Mexico from beginning to end and whose account of that period is available. Samuel French was the other (see preceding list).

The same held for two nonmilitary contemporaries: Edward D. Mansfield, *The Mexican War*, New York, 1848; and Charles J. Peterson, *Military Heroes of the War with Mexico*, Philadelphia, 1850.

So it went through the rest of the nineteenth century. America's only recognized military historian of the period, General Emory Upton, *The Military Policy of the United States*, Washington, D.C., 1904, regarded Taylor's achievements as notable. Another general was embarrassing in his worship of Zach—Oliver O. Howard, *General Taylor*, New York, 1892. A two-volume history by George L. Rives, *The United States and Mexico 1821–1848*, New York, 1913, continued the overall favorable treatment of Taylor. The general's military reputation seemed secure.

Then it happened!—Justin H. Smith's *The War with Mexico* (2 vols.), New York, 1919. The Dartmouth professor listed some Taylor virtues: strong character, makeup of a hero, solid common sense, not a little shrewdness and ambition, a thorough knowledge of men, a military eye, a cool and resourceful if ponderous intelligence. But in the main, Smith seemed to be persuaded by the general's several detractors. He found Taylor rough, ungrammatical, unkempt—even dirty, ignorant, lacking in mental discipline, obstinate, mulish; and contemptuous of knowledge itself. In command Taylor was slow, unskillful, imprudent, insubordinate, lacking in penetration and foresight, and poorly grounded professionally. He was incapable of discipline; reluctant to accept responsibility. Brave, yes. At Buena Vista, for example, Taylor was "a fountain of courage and energy." But he was a poor general.

Smith's scholarship was awesome. He had completely digested all that was known on the Mexican War, had uncovered an impressive store of new material, and he wrote uncommonly well. Smith became *the* authority on the war, and his judgments of Taylor naturally influenced others. The historian, Nathaniel W. Stephenson, *Texas and the War with Mexico*, New York, 1921, repeated many of Smith's objections to the general. So did Major William A. Ganoe, *History of the United States Army*, New York, 1924. According to Ganoe, Taylor neither improved his time to learn about the country he was in nor to train his troops. He could chat pleasantly with the lowest private one minute and ignorantly sacrifice his life the next. He gave few directions in battle; he took few precautions. "His untutored mind would not admit of skill or prevision." He spent too much time sitting around and trusting to chance. Even at Buena Vista, "Though his [Taylor's] brave attitude gave confidence, he uttered few directions, which were poor." All three writers—Smith, Stephenson, and Ganoe—agree that the general owed almost his whole success to the brilliant West Pointers who fought under him.

Two military biographies of Taylor, one by Holman Hamilton, *Zachary Taylor: Soldier of the Republic*, Indianapolis, 1941; the other by Brainerd Dyer, *Zachary Taylor*, Baton Rouge, 1946, resisted the trend to downgrade the general. Both men freely discussed his faults, but in sum their judgments were favorable. Dyer, for instance, felt that Taylor had conducted his campaigns with a high degree of success. Always inferior in numbers, he nevertheless won four battles, and drove the Mexicans back nearly 500 miles in a year. Taylor showed unusual common sense and practical shrewdness, as well as unquestioned physical and moral courage.

But 1946 also marked the publication of Bernard DeVoto's *The Year of Decision* (New York). DeVoto reached the peak of the Taylor-no-general school. The earlier uncomplimentary adjectives applied to Old Zach he simply reduced to the single word "stupid." This airy contempt carried Justin Smith's "revisionism" of Taylor to the extreme. Revisionism, that is, as a historian's term for reappraisal, for a new look at personages and events after the laying of old ghosts, the discovery of new information, and with the detachment and objectivity that come with time.

After *The Year of Decision*, Taylor's military reputation could only rise. Alfred H. Bill's *Rehearsal for Conflict*, New York, 1946; Robert S. Henry's *Story of the Mexican War*, New York, 1950; and Lloyd Lewis's *Captain Sam Grant*, Boston, 1950, bring the balance back closer to that of Hamilton and Dyer. More recently a book appeared which is widely used in university courses in American history: *The Military Heritage of America*, R. Ernest and Trevor N. Dupuy, New York, 1956. These two army historians have pretty well rehabilitated General Taylor. In a 24-line footnote on page 146 they express doubts of Ganoe's opinions as being unduly influenced by Justin Smith; they cite Emory Upton's high praise of the general, along with the more qualified but still substantial support of Oliver L. Spaulding, *The United States Army in War and Peace*, New York, 1937. They conclude with these lines on Taylor:

He had a splendid army, with which he won important victories against considerable odds. Later when, because of circumstances beyond his control, he had a relatively poor army, he won a splendid victory against greater odds. He alone bore the responsibility, and if he was intelligent enough to make full use of the capabilities of brilliant subordinates, all the more credit is due to his leadership ability.

If this summing up continues to hold, General Taylor's good standing among American military leaders is safe once more.

Acknowledgments

John Porter Bloom, now teaching at Texas Western College, El Paso, wrote his Ph.D. thesis at Emory University, Georgia, 1956. Unpublished, it is titled "With the American Army into Mexico 1846–1848." It contains the results of some prodigious digging—letters, diaries, journals—in whole and in scraps; broadsides, posters, etc., relating to the American soldiers in Mexico during the war. While the content is largely peripheral to the war itself, much of it is new and full of interest and color. I am in Mr. Bloom's debt for several borrowed quotations and another half-dozen or more bits of information or description.

Another unpublished doctoral thesis I found useful is Joseph G. Rayback's "The Free Soil Revolt," Western Reserve University, Cleveland, Ohio, 1939. Dr. Rayback (now a historian of American labor) seems to have read every newspaper in the country bearing on the political campaign that led to Taylor's election as President in 1848. In order to include some of this campaign activity, which was not directly related to my interest in Taylor, I summarized certain of Rayback's findings and quoted or paraphrased several of his passages taken from the press. The only fault I find with "The Free Soil Revolt" is its readability. Parts of Chapter 3 would have met my needs, but before putting the thesis down, I had gone through all of it. My thanks to Joe Rayback.

Thanks also to Penn State graduate student Patricia Gordon, who helped decode Taylor letters in microfilm and who labored cheerfully through what looks to be seven miles of film of the Adjutant General's handwritten compilation of enlistments in the United States Army, from 1840 to 1846, National Archives, Washington, D.C.

Of the Pattee Library staff, Penn State, Mrs. Margaret Spangler and Mrs. Libbie J. Shannon gave me every kind of willing assistance. I thank them both. Two members of the History Department who offered helpful advice and suggestions are Drs. Philip S. Klein and Warren H. Hassler, Jr.

Finally, my thanks to two readers of the manuscript: my wife, Eleanor Nichols, former graduate student in American history at Penn State; and S. Leonard Rubinstein, Associate Professor of English at Penn State and novelist. They helped far more than I can make these words imply. My wife, in addition to aiding my research (especially the work on old newspapers in the Library of Congress Annex), and reading manuscript, typed the copy for this book. In fact, she deserves a by-line.

Appendix II

A list of West Point graduates who served under Taylor at one time or another during his Mexican campaigns and later rose to be officers with rank of general (brigadier, major, or lieutenant general) during the Civil War. Some inconsistencies appear in the rolls, especially for many of the officers who spent only several weeks under Taylor's general command, usually in the rear, and then shipped south to serve under Scott. A large number of officers, of course, served under both commanders. *U* after a name stands for *Union; C* for *Confederate.*

Alvord, Benjamin (U)
Anderson, Richard H. (C)
Armistead, Lewis C. (C)
Augur, Christopher C. (U)
Bee, Bernard E. (C)
Benham, Henry W. (U)
Bragg, Braxton (C)

Brooks, William T. H. (U)
Bryan, Goode (C)
Buchanan, Robert C. (U)
Buell, Don Carlos (U)
Buford, Abraham (C)
Casey, Silas (U)
Chilton, Robert H. (C)

Couch, Darius N. (U)
Crosman, George H. (U)
Davis, Jefferson (C)
Dawson, Samuel C. (C)
Donaldson, James L. (C)
Doubleday, Abner (U)
Early, Jubal (C)
Eaton, Amos B. (U)
Elzey, Arnold (C)
Franklin, William B. (U)
French, Samuel G. (C)
Gardner, Franklin (C)
Garnett, Robert S. (C)
Gatlin, Richard C. (C)
Getty, George W. (U)
Grant, Ulysses S. (U)
Hamilton, Schuyler (U)
Hardee, William J. (C)
Hatch, John P. (U)
Hayes, William (U)
Hays, Alexander (U)
Heintzelman, Samuel P. (U)
Hill, Daniel H. (C)
Hitchcock, Ethan A. (U)
Holmes, Theophilus (C)
Hooker, Joseph (U)
Johnson, Bushrod R. (C)
Johnston, Albert S. (C)
Jordon, Thomas (C)
Judah, Henry M. (U)
Kilburn, Charles L. (U)
Kingsbury, Charles P. (U)
Lee, Fitzhugh (C)

Longstreet, James P. (C)
Lovell, Mansfield (C)
Mackall, William M. (C)
Maclay, Robert P. (C)
Magruder, John B. (C)
McCall, George A. (U)
McCown, J. P. (C)
McDowell, Irvin W. (U)
McLaws, Lafayette (C)
Mansfield, Joseph K. T. (U)
Marcy, Randolph B. (U)
Marshall, Humphrey (C)
Martin, James G. (C)
Meade, George G. (U)
Montgomery, William R. (U)
Myers, Abraham C. (U)
Nichols, William A. (U)
Paul, Gabriel R. (U)
Peck, John J. (U)
Pemberton, J. C. (C)
Pleasonton, Alfred (U)
Pope, John (U)
Potter, Joseph H. (U)
Rains, Gabriel J. (C)
Ramsay, George D. (U)
Reynolds, John F. (U)
Richardson, Israel B. (U)
Ricketts, James B. (U)
Ripley, Roswell S. (C)
Ruggles, Daniel (C)
Sacket, Delos B. (U)
Sedgwick, John (U)

Sherman, Thomas W. (U)
Smith, Charles F. (U)
Smith, William S. (U)
Steele, William (C)
Stevenson, Carter L. (C)
Sykes, George (U)
Thomas, George H. (U)

Thomas, Lorenzo (U)
Tilghman, Lloyd (C)
Van Dorn, Earl (C)
Wallen, Henry D. (U)
Wilcox, Cadmus M. (C)
Williams, Seth (U)
Wood, Thomas J. (U)

INDEX

D5